GERMANY
BY BIKE
20 TOURS GEARED FOR DISCOVERY

GERMANY
BY BIKE
20 TOURS GEARED FOR DISCOVERY

Nadine Slavinski

THE
MOUNTAINEERS

To my Mom, who's the best—
and thanks to Markus for Ruff, Biba, and everything else

 Published by
The Mountaineers
1011 SW Klickitat Way
Seattle, Washington 98134

Published simultaneously in Canada by Douglas & McIntyre, Ltd., 1615
 Venables Street, Vancouver, B.C. V5L 2H1

Published simultaneously in Great Britain by Cordee, 3a DeMontfort Street,
 Leicester, England, LE1 7HD

8 7 6 5 4
5 4 3 2 1

Manufactured in the United States of America

Edited by Heath Silberfeld
Maps by Jerry Painter
All photographs by the author except as noted
Cover design by Watson Graphics
Book layout and typesetting by The Mountaineers Books
Cover photograph: Ramsau church © Ric Ergenbright/AllStock; inset by Karen
 and Terry Whitehill
Frontispiece: A quiet Sunday morning in medieval Hirschhorn

Library of Congress Cataloging in Publication Data
Slavinski, Nadine.
 Germany by bike : 20 tours geared for discovery / Nadine Slavinski.
        p.   cm.
 Includes index.
 ISBN 0-89886-387-2
 1. Bicycle touring--Germany--Guidebooks. 2. Germany--Guidebooks.
GV1046.G3G47   1994
796.6'4'0943--dc20   93-47676
                                                          CIP

CONTENTS

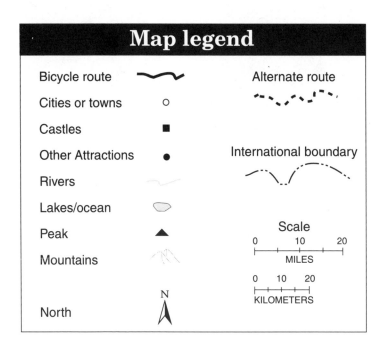

Bicycles complement classic art in a niche at Schloss Nordkirchen.

PREFACE

Thousands of tourists visit Germany and other countries in Europe each year—but how many truly explore the land? How many strike out to find sleepy corners as well as world-famous highlights? How many tour Germany by bike?

Bicycle touring is quickly becoming one of the most popular forms of recreation and travel in the Americas and Europe. Cycling has many advantages over conventional means of travel, the primary being its unique combination of up-close insight and long-distance range. These factors, plus the great flexibility of cycling, allow for a unique journey of discovery.

Why limit yourself to Germany? Because the possibilities there are limitless. Two of Europe's top cycling areas, the Danube and Mosel valleys, are found within Germany's borders, together with countless less known, undisturbed destinations in points west and east. Germany presents a split image in more than one way. On one hand, it is modern and cosmopolitan, with businesspeople, BMWs, and Autobahns. Cyclists, however, explore the other side of Germany, that of quiet pockets of nature and farmlands where little seems to have changed in centuries. This Germany charms the cyclist with friendly people, beautiful scenery, and such wonderfully surprising sights as castles and hidden village squares.

I first began exploring Europe on a grand scale, cycling a marathon tour across the continent. Once I undertook an extensive tour of Germany, however, I discovered the advantages of a one-country view. Instead of sudden contrasts and international adaptations, I could observe gradual changes within one culture. I worked to improve one language to good conversational level instead of constantly relearning basic terms in different languages, never moving far beyond left/right, yes/no. Hassles such as border crossings and money exchange were eliminated, replaced by familiarity with a single system.

A cyclist does not see any more in a 1,000-kilometer traverse of several countries than over the same distance within one land. As for cultural contrast, there is plenty within Germany alone—just compare farm life of the northern lowlands with highland Bavaria. Germany's different regions all maintain their own dialects, customs, and character. Once I slowed my pace and sharpened my focus, I realized how often my long-range view had missed the hidden delights that make a journey memorable.

Germany by Bike contains both general information and detailed tour outlines for bicycle tourists of all levels of experience and conditioning. Part I includes introductory information on Germany and cycling in general. In Part II, twenty researched tours provide

Sheep crowd a bicycle lane along a country route near Vogelsberg.

day-by-day route directions, sightseeing suggestions, and accommodations options. The tours cover Germany's best cycling destinations, including five in former East Germany. Individual tours are generally short and detailed, focusing on a single region; many tours connect to form longer routes. Finally, suggestions for further travel aid cyclists ready to strike out on their own.

To facilitate communication and orientation on your trip, German place names are used throughout this guide after an initial introduction of their English equivalents (i.e., Munich/München, Nuremberg/Nürnberg, Lake Constance/Bodensee). Similarly, common German terms (*Radwanderweg:* bicycle path) are often used without further explanation after one translation. Using basic terms right from the start will give you a great boost during your first days in Germany.

PART I

GENERAL INFORMATION

WHY BIKE? WHY GERMANY?
WHY GERMANY BY BIKE?

Friends and relatives still scratch their heads whenever I prepare for yet another European cycling tour. Now why, they wonder, does she insist on overloading her bicycle and schlepping it across an ocean? Why must she pedal from one forgotten little town to another? Why can't she just get a Eurailpass like everyone else? What could possibly be the attraction?

I've stopped trying to explain to them. Bicycle touring is not for everyone. Its allure will only be understood by those willing to try for themselves. What is there to understand? The feeling of a crisp breeze on a lakeside bicycle lane. The perfect silence of a medieval town in early morning. The weary satisfaction of a long day's ride. The elation of self-sufficiency. The ability and flexibility to turn in any direction and explore at whim.

Bicycle touring isn't for everyone? A weekend ride through Germany's Mosel Valley suggests otherwise. There, the typical cycling crowd includes young, active people traveling solo or in groups. Not-so-young, active people also tour the valley. Entire families pedal by, small children in trailers or bicycle seats, the next youngest pedaling alongside with training wheels still attached to their bikes. Retired couples spin steadily along, panniers strapped on trusty three-speeds. Teen groups rush by, more intent on passing each other or gossiping than pedaling a straight line. Some cyclists are out for a weekend jaunt, others are covering a transcontinental tour. Some are fully equipped with high-tech equipment and accessories, while others make do with strapped-on duffle bags and recycled mineral-water bottles.

Anyone, it seems, can bicycle tour.

Age or experience do not make a cyclist. Attitude does. Bicycle touring is for the independent, those who take pride in traveling by their own means. Cycling appeals to those wanting to break from the standard tourist pattern, to get out and see for themselves. Cyclists need a sense of adventure, the willingness to forsake some conveniences for the pride of a tour completed under their own power. As an independent, flexible means of travel, bicycle touring allows you to choose your own pace, route, and style. Cycling can be as easy or challenging as you wish—road-blazing fast or stop-and-smell-the-roses slow—based around campgrounds or hotels, historic sights, or beer halls.

Bicycle touring brings travelers into close contact with the land and people around them, particularly in Europe, where cycling is popular as both recreation and a practical means of transportation. As a cyclist, you will be both a tourist and a tourist attraction. Your two wheels will start conversations and promote friendships with people who know what it feels like to pedal, too. My bicycle initiated talks with locals and fellow bikers daily, ranging from brief cyclists' exchanges to lengthy conversations. A friendly old woman watching me devour lunch on a Nürnberg bench asked about my loaded bicycle; the subject eventually turned to local history and current events. My bike also attracted the attention of a cycling Kiel resident, and soon we were gabbing away as he detoured to show me the best bicycle path out of the city. In hostels I typically maintained longer, in-depth conversations with cycling roommates than with those traveling by car or train—several even invited me

Enjoying a sunny afternoon in an outdoor Biergarten *at Bamberg*

Bicycle touring with the whole family in Mecklenburg

to visit their homes later. In all these cases, a bicycle instantly allowed closer contact with my host country.

Germany is one of Europe's best bicycle-touring destinations for these reasons, and more. Nowhere in Europe is bicycle touring as popular as in Germany. In Italy or France, for example, most cyclists you meet are racers or housewives on their way to market. In Germany you are just as likely to find a fellow bicycle tourist—either exploring an unfamiliar corner of his country, as you are, or a local one. One "typical housewife" I pedaled with one morning described recent touring adventures in Canada and Alaska. Germans' love of

Nymphs grace a palace fountain at Linderhof.

bicycle touring both at home and abroad has made their country a true cyclist's delight. Natural attractions are supplemented by excellent cyclists' services, including well-marked touring routes, bicycle lanes, guidebooks, and detailed maps. These conveniences minimize the challenges of touring and maximize enjoyment of two-wheeled exploration.

Moreover, Germany offers many opportunities off your bicycle as well as on. A bicycle-friendly train network helps cyclists reach distant points quickly and easily, be it the popular Danube tour or the quiet Altmühl Valley. Well-organized tourist services smooth out potential wrinkles in travel plans. I have enjoyed bicycle touring in many different countries, but nowhere are so many incidental concerns relieved as in Germany. Instead of praying over my bicycle before handing it to a burly railroad employee or fretting over services, I can relax and concentrate on what I came to do: explore and enjoy Germany.

Some may read this and still not understand why. Bicycle touring is not for everyone ... but it may be for you.

Tempted?

SAFETY FIRST!

You are considering an exciting form of travel in a foreign country, eager to read about the many possibilities for biking in Germany. You picture a pleasant countryside tour of medieval towns, castles, and beer halls.... Hold that thought!

It is important to immediately establish a precedent of safety before pedaling madly off into the sunset. Cycling has some inherent risks, which are magnified when one sets off to spend several hours each day touring foreign ground. However, these risks can be significantly reduced with common sense and some basic precautions.

A helmet, reliable and familiar equipment, good planning, and alertness make cycling safe and enjoyable. Wear bright colors and use hand signals while cycling. The following pages provide information on many aspects of touring that help detail what to expect and how to go about your trip. Always put safety first!

Now, with that in mind, picture yourself on a bicycle tour in Germany, unwinding from a day of castles, wooded hills, and half-timbered houses in a lakeside beer garden....

PLANNING YOUR BICYCLE TOUR

The key to a smooth start and an enjoyable journey is good preparation. While it is not necessary to plan every detail of your trip beforehand, neither is it advisable to set off completely plan-

Traditional farmhouses of the Mecklenburg region

less and uninformed. One of the great advantages—and joys—of bicycle travel is flexibility: the independence and means to tailor a trip to your wishes or to any unexpected situation that may arise. Try to strike a comfortable balance between overly rigid structure and utter aimlessness, taking into account your goals, limitations, and what you feel most comfortable doing. Germany's compact nature makes changes in plan easy to manage, with short distances between sights, many accommodations, and easy train/bike connections.

INFORMATION SOURCES. This book offers general information on biking in Germany as well as many detailed tours that include town descriptions, practical information, historical notes, and the occasional attempt at comic relief. For more detailed information on other specialized topics, turn to the following sources.

Predictably, the German National Tourist Office (122 East 42nd Street, 52nd Floor, New York, NY 10168–0072) is efficient and helpful. Specify your interests (cycling, camping, a specific region of the country), and the office will send more information than you ever wanted, plus a good planning map.

Depending on your interests, choose a good general guidebook that includes sight information, history, and notes on travelers' facilities. *Let's Go: Germany* (Harvard Student Publications) offers lively, thorough descriptions and country information geared to-

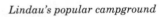

Lindau's popular campground

Cyclists rule Münster's streets.

ward budget travelers (albeit train-oriented travelers). *Michelin's Green Guide: Germany*, while suffocatingly dry in style, is exhaustive, concise, compact, and provides a basic introduction to the history, architecture, art, food, wine, and so forth of the country. The Michelin guides, with many town and city maps, prove especially useful when entering new towns or when tourist offices are closed. Accommodations options are listed in the separate *Red Guide* (see also Food, Lodging, and Supplies). The *Fodor's* series aims at middle- to upper-budget travelers, with extensive sections on culture, regional customs, and so on.

PAPERWORK AND MONEY. Passport application may stretch out into a lengthy process; don't put this important item off until the last minute. U.S. and Canadian citizens need only a passport to enter Germany for up to three months. Longer stays require a visa; check for restrictions with the German Consulate General (460 Park Avenue, New York, NY 10022). British citizens are exempt from the three-month limit. Cooperation between countries of the European Community makes for quick border crossings within western Europe. Some tours in Part II cross briefly into France, Austria, Switzerland, and Denmark at points; simply flash your *Paß* (passport) and be on your merry way. Most border guards will show more interest in your bicycle than your documents, and often wave cyclists straight through.

Germany's currency is the *Deutsche Mark*, abbreviated DM (for example, DM 25). Be careful when exchanging money in German banks since commission fees vary widely. To avoid a nasty surprise

Networks of bicycle lanes allow for safe and enjoyable cycling.

when exchanging travelers checks, ask if commission is charged on the total amount or per check. Travelers checks are safer to carry than cash since they can be replaced if lost or stolen. Choose a well-known check to facilitate exchanges and refunds. Some banks will only accept certain travelers checks. On weekends and holidays, offices in larger train stations often offer currency exchange at less favorable rates.

Major credit cards are accepted in many German restaurants and shops, but rarely in small establishments. Credit cards are most useful as emergency money sources in case you've underestimated expenses. Credit cards may be used at many bank cash machines, but be sure to know your PIN number. Over-the-counter cash advances are also possible in many banks.

When traveling and dealing with an unfamiliar currency, it is easy to lose track of expenses. In order to keep to a budget, record expenses daily. This will help you see exactly where your money goes and will prove especially eye-opening when adding up small, incidental expenses that quickly take unexpected bites out of a budget. A budget cyclist shopping at grocery stores and staying in campgrounds (and allowing for the occasional treat!) can aim for expenses of $15 a day or so (less with free camping and fewer treats).

In Germany, students under 27 years of age are entitled to many discounts, so it pays to travel with an International Student Identity Card. If you are under 27 but not a student, an International Youth Identity Card entitles you to many of the same benefits. The cards are most useful in reducing museum entrance fees. Both cards are available through student-council offices and some travel agencies. College and university identity cards from other countries are usually not accepted, but travel agents in Germany will take these as proof of student status for issuing official cards.

TRAVELER SERVICES. Cyclists planning lengthy trips can use several useful services. Holders of American Express travelers checks are automatically entitled to member privileges. American Express offices in large cities (Frankfurt, München) hold client mail for up to four weeks, a handy service for those on the road for long stretches. Mail should be addressed to you, care of the American Express office and marked "Letter Service." Your name should be capitalized and expected pick-up date noted. Mail can be forwarded to you at a different address at extra cost. Similarly, post offices also hold *Poste Restante* mail.

Euraide, an all-English-speaking travel office based in the United States with offices in Germany and across Europe, offers many convenient (if pricey) services. Its München office provides in-country contact (see Tour No. 4). If you absolutely must stay in touch with your family or business while abroad but want to maintain travel flexibility, Euraide is a great help. Through its message relay service, messages and mail from home or traveling friends can be picked up, forwarded, or read to you over the phone. You can also leave messages to be passed on to your business, friends, or family when they call. In this way the office serves as a reliable home base for travelers. For more information on this and other services, contact the U.S. home office: Euraide, P.O. Box 2375, Naperville, Illinois 60567; phone: (708) 420-2342.

EQUIPMENT

The style of touring you choose defines what equipment you pack. Campers and budget cyclists will carry a full load, while cyclists basing their tour around private rooms or hostels will carry less gear. Every cyclist has his or her own equipment preferences and quirks; some insist on carrying the absolute minimum, while others like to have their extras, additional weight or not. I was once weight-crazy, discarding every excess scrap, but nowadays I value certain comforts above their strict weight. After all, your bicycle frame will support the weight, not your back; a little extra will not make a big difference in speed or maneuverability. On the other hand, don't go overboard with extra gear. One pair of cyclists I saw pulled a trailer fully loaded with folding chairs and collapsible barbecue! Consider the following guidelines and make your own judgement on what gear is essential to you.

HELMETS. Wear a helmet at all times! While most bicycle falls result only in a few scrapes, it is not worth taking chances with a more serious accident. New, lightweight helmets are comfortable and well ventilated, not at all irritating to wear. Be aware, however, that styrofoam helmets are not completely effective without the covering nets that support them—do not remove these nets!

YOUR BICYCLE. As your primary means of transportation, a good, reliable bicycle is vital to your tour. Ideally, use a touring bicycle. Touring bikes are specifically designed to be sturdy yet comfortable over long periods of use, allowing a smooth trip with minimum maintenance and repair. Racks support panniers and accessories while padded seats and handlebars increase the comfort of your ride. Toe clips increase pedaling efficiency, but if you are unaccustomed to riding with them, keep the straps loose at first and practice withdrawing your feet quickly. A granny gear and good gear range make optimal use of your energy, easing passage over hills. Naturally, top models are high priced; shop around and try several models before making a big investment.

On the other hand, there is no need to sink hundreds of dollars into a new bicycle if you already have wheels. Many Germans tour on trusty old three-speeds. A touring bicycle is always most appropriate, making cycling easier and more comfortable, but older or non-touring bikes work just fine for the casual tourist.

The popularity of mountain bikes has boomed in both America and Europe. Remember, however, that these bikes are designed for off-road use; heavy components and frame composition make them inappropriate for bicycle touring. Although some tours include stretches of dirt track, a regular road bike remains a lighter, better choice. The only exception is in the former East Germany, where bicycle routes often cover extremely rough terrain, such as cobblestones or sand.

No matter what bicycle you choose, do your best to convert it for touring by adding good road tires and exchanging components if necessary. Above all, give your bike a good tune-up and inspection before setting off. Even the best touring bike will require replacement parts and adjustment over time.

Most carriers accept boxed bicycles as one of two allowed pieces of baggage. Bicycle shops usually have extra boxes on hand; get the largest one available to minimize disassembly (usually requiring only pedal and wheel removal and turning the handlebar). Airlines also supply boxes at the airport, but I have courted disaster in the past by relying on their broken promises. Box your bicycle ahead of time and arrive at the airport with extra packaging tape in case our friends at security choose your box for inspection. You can pad your bicycle with panniers and camping gear, but do not throw any small, loose items in since boxes are often punctured in transit. While minor readjustments are often required after shipping, serious damage is rare.

The only way to avoid shipping a bicycle overseas is either to buy or rent a bicycle abroad. However, bicycle prices in Germany are outrageously high. Renting is a good option for travelers planning to mix limited cycling with other forms of transportation. Shops

Schoolchildren flock around a loaded touring bicycle in Flessenow.

rent bicycles in many popular tourist destinations. Many *Bundesbahn* (German train company) stations also rent bicycles (ranging from clunky three-speeds to new mountain bikes) that can be returned at another *Bundesbahn* location; ask at any station for *Fahrrad am Bahnhof* information.

PANNIERS. To carry your gear comfortably while pedaling, invest in a good set of panniers. Cyclists planning long tours may need a full set of front and rear panniers. Regular rear panniers, together with low-riding front bags, create the most stable combination, including plenty of space for all your gear. Stability is far greater than with rear bags alone, and a little extra space is useful for pre-weekend shopping trips when two days of food must be crammed in—somewhere! Age and experience demonstrate that name-brand bags are more durable than generic models, and worth the extra initial cost. Good panniers attach quickly and easily to your racks, with several compartments for easy access.

A front handlebar bag with map window is a must for all bicycle tourists. A good, large bag will keep camera, snacks, wallet, and sunscreen on hand. Map cases allow instant viewing of your route without your having to rummage through bags at every confusing intersection.

ACCESSORIES. My accessory collection has expanded with each trip I take, providing useful and fun gadgets with which to amuse myself while on the road. For years I held out against buying a cyclometer for fear that an exact measurement of my speed and mileage would drive me crazy, especially on long mountain climbs. Finally, I gave in. Now I know my record lows (8 km/hr into a strong coastal head wind), but also my record highs (a breezy 62 km/hr). In addition to being nifty gadgets, cyclometers are also useful in route finding, as you can measure distances closely and know when to expect turns.

Every European cyclist attaches a bell to his or her bike, another practical accessory. A bell allows cyclists to give pedestrians a friendly warning ding instead of resorting to rude or silly comments (like shouting "Ding! Ding!").

A good tire pump and water bottles also attach directly to your bicycle frame. Standard European tire valves (Presta) differ from American (Schrader), so make sure your pump fits your valves. Reversible pumps allow you to switch between the two sizes.

Fenders keep both bicycle and rider drier and cleaner by blocking road spray on wet days. Cycling after dark is generally not safe, but a light provides an extra measure of safety in case the need arises. For example, you might need to cycle to your lodgings in the dark, or you might want to go to dinner, a movie, or a beer garden after dark. In such cases, a light will provide an extra sense of security.

Witch bikers lead the way through Harz forests.

Fill out your collection with a rear-view mirror. This indispensable accessory eliminates the need to turn your head (and veer unsteadily) to check if that roar from behind signifies a cement truck or a *Trabant* (East German cars that symbolize every inadequacy of the former DDR).

TOOLS. Many cyclists differ in their opinion of which tools to carry. Some insist on carrying nothing less than an entire workshop, while others rely on the bare minimum. You can get by as a minimalist, carrying only spare tube, patch kit, Allen wrenches, and pocket-sized repair book. Well-maintained bicycles cause few problems, and when the unexpected does arise, a bicycle repair shop is never too far away, even if it's in the next town or large city. For example, the worst breakdown I had occurred in a small town of the Harz Mountains, where my freewheel went completely *kaputt*. The town had no repair shop, but my problem was solved with a bus trip to a large town nearby. In all I wasted a few hours and a few Marks, well worth the otherwise incident-free months of pedaling I enjoyed without carrying heavy tools.

Non-minimalists might want to add spoke wrench and spare cables to the list, but not much more. Remember to bring all tools required for reassembly after shipping your bike. It's wise, too, to carry several spare spokes taped securely to your bicycle frame. Even if you never break a spoke, they make handy shish kebab skewers when the opportunity arises!

Mail-order companies sell tools and accessories at prices well below the average bicycle shop. Check at a library or in bicycling magazines to obtain names and addresses for such companies.

CAMPING GEAR. The extra burden campers carry will quickly pay off in savings and convenience. A sleeping bag, pad, and tent can crowd a rear rack but provide reliable, familiar shelter wherever you go. A brightly colored sleeping-bag stuff sack can provide another safety measure by increasing your visibility on the road. New materials have greatly decreased the weight and bulk of camping gear, but choose good, durable equipment carefully. It is not worth sacrificing your health and comfort for a few dollars saved on inferior equipment. Well-designed tents incorporate a separate fly sheet for extra protection. A candle lantern can be wonderful for nighttime reading and writing or a little extra dinner atmosphere.

CLOTHING. Clothing choice is another point of personal preference. Two or three sets of clothing (biking and day shorts, three shirts) washed often help to keep gear to a minimum. Typically, I bicycle from morning to afternoon, showering and changing upon arrival at the next accommodations and washing the day's clothes then. Light pants, one long-sleeved shirt, a sweater, and a bathing suit round out the basics. When touring at times other than during the peak of summer, running or cycling tights and polypropylene tights and shirts are indispensable additions. In April and November you can stay quite cozy with the addition of a hat, gloves, scarf, and waterproof rain gear.

Padded bike shorts will keep even the naturally padded derrière much happier during a tour. Cyclists aghast at the thought of Lycra will find padded shorts of looser materials and styles widely available. Padded biking gloves help protect your hands; spend enough time on the road and the knitted patterns will give you bizarre tan patterns (the easily distinguished biker's mark). As a cyclist exposed to the elements, you may encounter bad weather even in summer. Good waterproof gear makes a big difference in the event of longer wet spells. In summer, you can get by with only a rain jacket, adding rain pants to your gear in early spring or late fall. Bright cycling gear adds a measure of protection, particularly in bad weather: don't be shy about packing a colorful wardrobe.

The tours in this book include short cycling days and plenty of non-cycling time for sightseeing or relaxing. Therefore, comfortable sneakers are most appropriate, useful for time both on the bike and off. Cycling shoes are stiff, maximizing pedaling efficiency but uncomfortable for walking, therefore not a good choice for casual cyclists. For extra footwear, consider sandals; a pair can squeeze in among camping gear on your rear rack, providing comfort and a good airing out.

OTHER GEAR. Once the basics are packed, resist the temptation to throw in handfuls of miscellaneous gear. Select extras carefully for their utility and compactness. Essentials include a first-aid kit, Swiss army knife, and flashlight (headlamps are particularly handy), and perhaps a quick-drying towel, some reading material, and a journal. A compass will prove handy at unmarked country

A peaceful break in Ilsenburg

intersections. Strap camping gear down with bungee cords or webbing; your rear rack is likely to become the laundry/sandals/fruit/recycling department, with extra items secured atop your tent and sleeping bag.

For time off the bike, bring a shoulder strap for your front handlebar bag or, better yet, invest in a super-lightweight daypack that folds into its own front pocket. Such daypacks fit in easily with your gear and allow comfortable handling of small items during walks and hikes. Bring a camera and film to record your trip, but take care to protect them from bumpy rides and the elements.

A camper's stove and cookset pay for their bulk by saving your budget, and they make it possible to prepare warm meals to your taste. Cyclists, whether camping or not, can prepare morning coffee and evening meals with a small, lightweight stove. Different models run on different fuels, most of which are widely available in Germany. Bleuet camp stoves are most convenient, using small Camping Gaz cartridges that are sold in many campgrounds and stores around the country (as well as the rest of Europe and America). Whatever stove you choose, cook only in a well-ventilated area—never cook inside a tent, even with the doors open.

SECURITY

Although crime rates in Europe have risen slowly, the average European city is still much safer than its American counterpart. As a cyclist, most of your time will be spent in the countryside, where a sense of community and "old-fashioned" values prevail. Simple precautions will greatly decrease the chances of random theft or crime.

Keep all valuables in your front handlebar bag and take it with you wherever you go. A good money belt or discreetly stored wallet tucks money and papers away securely. Do not flash money or expensive items around in public places, and always keep alert for potential thieves. At times you must leave your bicycle and gear behind at a campground while you sightsee or shop. Pick a sensible location and use a good lock. Never leave your bicycle unlocked, even if only for a moment.

When camping, strike up conversation or simply wave to your neighbors so they will know who belongs with what tent—and who does not. Try leaving your dirtiest, most fragrant items near the tent door to discourage weak-hearted robbers, tucking more valuable items farther back. Carry money and important documents at all times. In hostels, tuck your wallet into the sleep sheet. Using these basic precautions, it's unlikely that you'll experience any problem.

FOOD, LODGING, AND SUPPLIES

The primary difference in the gear you carry (and therefore its weight) depends upon the type of accommodations and biking style you choose, which in turn depends on budget. Every type of biker will find facilities appropriate to his or her style of touring in Germany.

ROOMS. In addition to hotels and small inns (pensions), you will find private rooms (*Zimmer*) for rent throughout Germany, in cities, towns, and the countryside. *Zimmer* are the favorite choice of most German cyclists, allowing flexible, light touring with comfortable lodgings to look forward to after a day of biking. Many rooms advertise directly along popular bicycle trails—just look for the *Zimmer frei* (room vacant) sign. Prices for doubles average about DM 45; quality ranges widely. *Zimmer* are even a viable option to budget travelers in groups of three or more who split the cost.

Although reservations are unnecessary in these informal lodgings, you may be in for an involved search during peak vacation periods along popular routes. Early arrival will gain you an edge. Local tourist offices in both small towns and cities distribute lists of rooms. For a small fee, many offices will arrange for a room, facilitating your search. After working hours, refer to information boards marked *Zimmernachweis*. These list rooms, display locator maps, and in some cases provide free telephone lines to call ahead for reservations.

It is also possible to make reservations far ahead of time, but your flexibility will be greatly restricted as a result. Many city tourist offices book rooms regionally, allowing you to reserve a few days ahead without sacrificing long-term flexibility. Guidebooks also provide information about rooms of all classes and regions. One of the most comprehensive available in Germany is *Gut und Preiswert Öbernachten: Bett und Bad bis 80 DM* (Bed and Breakfasts under DM 80) by Kartographischer Verlag Busche (Dortmund). The guide is written in German, but simple, repetitive terms make it easy to decipher.

YOUTH HOSTELS. Hosteling is a very convenient and inexpensive way to see Europe. Germany's hostels are particularly recommendable as clean and reliable. Hostels are often situated in converted castles or historic buildings, making them unique as well as practical. You need only an International Youth Hostel Association membership and a standard hostel sleep sheet (or rent one each night). In the United States obtain membership through American Youth Hostels (P.O. Box 37613, Washington, DC 20013–7613), a student-council office, or travel agent. If you do not have a membership you may also buy a guest card on the spot for an extra fee.

Don't be fooled—"youth" hostels are not limited to youths. German hostels (*Jugendherberge*) have no age limit, and many offer private and family rooms in addition to standard dormitory-style rooms. Bavarian hostels are the exception, open only to members under 27 years of age. German hostels do not have kitchen facilities, and all include the price of breakfast in the rate, which hikes prices up to DM 15 to 25 per night. If hosteling will be the basis of your lodging, invest in a good guidebook. The best, *Deutsches Jugendherbergsverzeichnis*, is available at most bookstores and at hostels. This guide lists all hostels, their facilities, closing dates,

Cobbled street and well in Burkheim

and directions to each. Though written in German, the few basic terms are easy to translate. The *International Youth Hostel Handbook*, a more geographically exhaustive guide, is available in the United States, Canada, and Britain but does not provide the same degree of detail. ADFC (Allgemeiner Deutscher Fahrrad Club) cycling maps indicate hostels with a red triangle.

In summer, hostels can be overwhelming, packed with Eurailers or school groups. In the off-season, however, most hostel guests are Germans. Many will talk about their country and home regions, biking possibilities, and the like. It's a great way to make friends and connections with your host country. The German schoolchildren you encounter in hostels can be patient language tutors, and you may be able to practice your German with them less self-consciously than you can with adults.

The moral of the story is this: Hosteling in Germany remains a good option. Remember, however, that others also plan to take advantage of the convenience and value of hostels, so at times you will find them full. Check ahead, especially during summer or school holidays. If you travel without reservations, ask each hostel to call the next to check on availability. Many hostels are closely spaced so that when one is closed or full, the next is usually within biking range.

CAMPING. Camping is by far the cheapest accommodations option. Cost aside, it is also the most reliable option. Campsites may not be as centrally located as hostels or rooms, but they usually lie within comfortable bicycle range even of city centers. There are two main reasons that camping is such a reliable option. First, if you camp, you will rarely be turned away from a full site (there is always space for one small cyclist with one small tent). Even if something goes wrong (for example, the campground is closed) you can be secure in knowing that you will always have shelter and warmth in the gear you carry. Second, your tent and sleeping bag, while not five-star comfort, provide a measure of familiarity and therefore security in a foreign world of constant variables. This can be especially comforting when traveling alone. Rain or shine, long day or short, successful sightseeing venture or not, you can always curl up in your familiar little nest at the end of the day. These factors can make the extra baggage worthwhile.

Many Europeans also prefer camping, and as a result, plenty of campsites dot Germany, including huge camper-van-pop-up-paraphernalia homesteads. Again, for extra security, strike up a conversation with your neighbors so they know who you are—and who should not be poking about your tent or bicycle. It is highly unlikely you will experience any problem with theft or harassment, even when traveling alone.

All campgrounds offer central toilet/shower blocks (hot showers often available for an additional charge), and many also offer extras such as kitchens or laundry machines. Campgrounds charge fees per person and per tent, making it cheaper to travel with more people (rates vary: DM 5 to 10 per person, DM 5 to 7 per tent). Upon registration you are often required to leave identification at the office. To avoid surrendering your passport, pay immediately or offer another official-looking ID. Most campgrounds in Germany are open from April to October, corresponding to optimal cycling seasons.

FREE CAMPING. Some cyclists give up the facilities of organized campsites and save money by camping for free in fields or woods. This is generally a safe and acceptable practice in Germany if you ask the landowner's permission or make a reasonable attempt to check local regulations first. Public land regulations vary widely. For example, free camping anywhere in Nordfriesland National Park (Tour No. 17) is strictly forbidden (*gesperrt, verboten*), while in the Altmühl Valley (Tour No. 3), free, tents-only sites complete with toilets and picnic tables are provided by the riverside. If you feel comfortable with free camping (which is especially important for solo women travelers to think about) consider alternating free nights with official sites to keep expenses low but maintain some sense of civilization. A collapsible water container will prove handy for carrying cooking/cleaning water to your site.

FOOD. Cyclists of all budgets will have no problem fueling up on nutritious and appetizing food in Germany, despite the country's culinary reputation. You will be able to both sample local specialties (noted within individual tour descriptions) and find familiar staples wherever you go. Small specialty shops, restaurants, and grocery stores line every route, ready to keep you plump and pedaling happily. Small family-run specialty shops offer amazing variety and character. Larger American-style grocery stores now dominate the market; though low on charm, they help the budget. The most spartan and unappealing of these chains almost always offer the lowest prices. You can stock up on staples at large stores and browse smaller bakeries and shops for fresh foods.

Germans are extremely health conscious in some ways. Naturally grown vegetables and whole grains are common items. Fats, on the other hand, do not seem to be a big concern. You will find few fat-free dairy products (only low-fat: *fettarme*) or meat dishes.

Tastes and habits vary with the individual, but try the following favorites. Yogurt with *Müsli*, available in all flavors and degrees of crunchiness, forms a typical German breakfast and gives cyclists a good start on the day. If preparing your own meals, look for *Spätzle*, a spaghetti-like specialty of the Schwaben region, for a

Island campsite on the Altmühl River

tasty dinner base (although nothing beats homemade *Käsespätzle*, a cheese-topped dish, in a family-run pub). Apples and oranges in 2-kilogram sacks go quickly, providing refreshing snacks throughout the day. As emergency backup, carry something light and nonperishable, like dehydrated soup. Whatever your preferences, remember to keep a good nutritious balance in your diet to fuel your body for daily cycling.

During vacation, it is easy to lose track of the days and hours, but it's important to remember that shopping hours are relatively restricted in Germany. Generally, stores are open Monday through Friday from 9:00 A.M. to 6:00 P.M. (with an afternoon closure for one or two hours) and until 1:00 P.M. on Saturdays. The largest stores do not close for lunch and stay open late on the first Saturday of each month. Be sure to stock up early Saturday for weekend supplies. On Thursday nights, many stores remain open until 8:00 P.M. Cafes, restaurants, and beer gardens thrive on weekend business. Beware of those sneaky holidays that shut shops unexpectedly, including May 1, May 20, August 15, and October 3.

DRINKING. Typically, German bicycling guidebooks include information on all the essentials: shops, routes, accommodations, repair shops, and beer gardens. Many cyclists happily tour Germany by linking beer gardens instead of historic sights. And who can blame them, in a country that takes its beverage production (and consumption) so seriously? How seriously, you ask? Just ask the folks studying at München's beer academy.

Admittedly, I am no expert on beer or wine, so I must leave the research up to you. Hundreds of German breweries produce thousands of beers, some specific to season or certain festivals. In addition to big labels, small family-run breweries operate in towns across the land, offering more temptations. Germans also like to be creative with their beer—there is even a cyclist's drink, the *Radler*, a mix of soda and beer. The combination is not as bad as it sounds, but be warned that the drink is also known as *Alsterwasser*, named for the muddy waters of Hamburg's city lake. In Germany beer drinking is so much a part of the culture that you don't need an excuse to sample a *Radler* or a cool draft.

Several tours in this guide cover Germany's prime wine-producing regions, including the Rhine, Mosel, and Elbe valleys (Tour Nos. 7, 8, 10, and 13) as well as Franken and others (Tour No. 2). Large-scale producers as well as individuals open their cellars to *Weinprobe* or *Weinstube* (wine tasting), allowing passing cyclists to sample all types of wine. In some regions it is traditional for producers to simply lean a broom beside their doors to indicate that sampling is invited. A *Volksfest* provides another opportunity to sample local beers and wines, from well-known fairs like *Oktoberfest* and the *Cannstatter Volksfest*, to small-town celebrations of more manageable proportions.

RECYCLING. Hand in hand with consumption comes the topic of wastes and recycling. Germany ranks far ahead of most western countries in this respect, with an extensive recycling program. Look for the green dot on packaging, indicating a company's participation in a nationwide program aiming to reduce waste. For example, all unnecessary packaging (like cereal boxes) may be left at stores, encouraging companies to eliminate extra packaging. To both lighten your load and promote the program, look for recycling containers within stores.

Large, colored recycling bins found along streets or in parking lots collect *Papier/Altpapier* (blue bins for scrap- and newspaper), *Metalle/Dosen* (silver bins for aluminum and tin cans), *Glas* (glass, by color), and *Kunststoffe* (yellow bins for all plastics). Unfortunately door-to-door pickup services make public containers for plastics the most difficult to find (except in the former East Germany, where the yellow bins are more numerous). You can carry a mobile recycling department on your bicycle, such as a plastic bag strapped on the rear rack, ready for the first appropriate container. Yes, you are on vacation, and no, you need not go to extraordinary lengths to recycle that can, but as a good guest in a place where recycling is made so easy, you might as well do your part.

SUPPLIES. Many familiar products have their counterparts in Germany, including the full range of toiletries. Germans like things to be nice and neat and handy, and as a biker you can cash in on this tendency. Look for handy little soap bottles sold in many stores, such as the ones that have loops for hanging; they're particularly useful for shuttling to and from campground showers. Two-in-one soaps/shampoos (*Haut und Haar*) are also applicable to other uses, including laundry.

Campers using gas stoves will find refill fuel in many larger department stores or in sport shops. Karstadt and Kaufhof are two large department-store chains where you can always find Camping Gaz for a Bleuet stove, plus just about anything else you need (including book departments with cycling maps). These stores are found in every city and large town in Germany.

In the sports department look for unusual biking accessories. For kicks, get yourself a biking poncho, more a gadget than an article of clothing. The deluxe models come with transparent hood windows for peripheral vision, armholes, and hand loops for keeping the poncho draped tentlike over your body as you ride.

TIPS FOR TOURING

Bicycle touring is marvelously straightforward: Simply pack your gear and pedal. Simple does not mean haphazard, however. For safe, comfortable touring, it pays to develop certain practices and routines.

PACKING. The way you pack your gear is as important as what you bring. Haphazard packing will destabilize your bicycle and decrease efficiency. Thoughtful packing, on the other hand, makes for a smooth ride and convenient access to necessary gear.

First, be sure to pack your panniers evenly, heavy items low and toward the inside. First-aid kit, rain gear, and information sources should be kept readily accessible. With only a few days of practice, everything will slip quickly into place. After packing your panniers and loading up your bicycle, take a moment to check for loose straps and potential hazards.

Even the best panniers will not keep your gear dry, and simply lining each pannier with a plastic bag will not do, so wrap each piece of your clothing separately in double plastic bags. Put a loose sock or rag in each pannier to soak up water that accumulates between your plastic bundles. Protect everything every day since a rainstorm can sneak up even if morning skies are clear. Stores in

Germany sell plastic bags, but they don't provide free paper or plastic ones. For camping gear, use larger plastic garbage bags.

MAPS. While cycling Germany I learned the value of good, detailed maps. Cycling maps present all available options and help you stay on the route you choose. A cyclist's map suggests appropriate routes according to road surfaces, traffic levels, and points of interest. Long-distance bicycle routes are clearly marked, as are campgrounds, hostels, and repair shops. In Germany, cycling maps will show you exactly what to expect and will help you follow poorly marked trails and avoid busier roads.

Due to their detailed scale (1:200,000 or better), a full series of cycling maps covering all Germany includes over twenty maps, priced at DM 12 each. Michelin 1:400,000 road maps, in contrast, cover the country in only four sheets, a much less costly proposition for travelers planning lengthy tours. However, you are better off saving money elsewhere; a good cycling map is worth the price.

To some travelers, the bicycling section of a typical German bookstore can be an amazing experience. Several series of maps and many books focus on cycling opportunities in Germany and around the world. ADFC cycling maps, in my opinion, are the best available (27 maps of 1:150,000 scale). ADFC *Radtourenkarte* (bicycle touring maps) are clear and easy to follow, indicating primary and secondary cycling routes as well as many cyclists' points of interest. Most of the tours in Part II are covered by a single map of this series. ADFC maps are widely available in Germany but are difficult to obtain abroad. Use a general road map for pre-departure planning, and purchase ADFC maps upon arrival.

Special booklets, complete guides to popular touring areas, are also available. Each set includes maps and detailed touring information (accommodations, local services, and such). Pages fit neatly into handlebar map cases. Published by BVA or Esterbauer and Weinfurter (Wien), these *Radwanderführer* (bicycle-touring guides) cover the popular Danube Valley ride in three sections (see Additional Suggested Tours), as well as the Bodensee, the Mosel Valley, and Münsterland (Tour Nos. 6, 10, and 14).

In large towns or cities, ask for a street map at the tourist office. Many towns also post locator maps beside perimeter roads. Exchange information with other cyclists by passing your tourist map on to incoming cyclists when you leave a city, saving them the confusion of a blind entry—and minimizing waste.

ROUTE FINDING. Experienced cyclists develop a feel for route finding, picking bicycle-route signs out from leafy overgrowth and following their instincts through unknown territory. With the aid of a few starter points, novices can also find their way with little trouble. A good cycling map cuts your work in half, indicating sug-

A bicycle trail offers high Mosel views.

gested routes and landmarks. However, don't rely entirely on these tips. Consider all possibilities and make your own decisions.

Many long- and short-distance bicycle routes have been established in Germany; most are clearly marked with bicycle signs. These tours combine quiet trails with roadside bicycle lanes. In Münsterland, a castle symbol indicates the route; in the Altmühl Valley, the outline of a fossil leads cyclists along a meandering river. Look for bicycle symbols beneath road signs, on fences, on barns, or painted on trees. If you reach a confusing bicycle sign, pass it and turn around as if coming from the opposite direction to see if the sign makes sense from that angle. Bicycle *frei* signs (picture of a bicycle with *frei* printed beneath) are common sights and indicate that cyclists are free to pass. Roads closed to most traffic often say *Außer Fahrrader* (except bicycles), permitting cyclists to continue on.

If bicycle signs do not rush to your rescue, use obvious landmarks as navigational aids. Follow rivers or mountain ridges and use church towers as guides into town centers. Note railroad tracks and marked intersections as you pedal and think ahead to predict your next move. Cycling maps include many of these features, helping establish your position. Don't hesitate to ask locals for information. Remember, half the fun of going is getting there; don't be so intent on a predetermined goal that you pass up the chance at conversation or an unplanned, worthwhile detour.

The daily route directions in Part II tours are measured in kilometers. To convert the miles, simply multiply by 0.6 (or more accurately, 0.62). For example, 10 kilometers equal 6.2 miles.

The popularity of bicycling in Germany has established an excellent network of trails as well as the respect of people driving motor vehicles. Bicycle lanes parallel many roads and are usually marked with a circular, blue, bicycle sign. In towns and cities, bicycle lanes are often painted red, reminding drivers of your presence. You'll be pleasantly surprised to see cars yielding to your two wheels in many situations. Many drivers waiting to pull out from driveways will even back away if they are blocking the bicycle lane, a courtesy German cyclists expect. Pedal side roads and bicycle trails whenever possible, resorting to busier roads only if necessary. Never enter a road marked by blue signs with a white car—it will be an *Autobahn*, strictly off limits to bicyclists.

TOURING APPROACHES. Tours in Part II take various approaches to different regions. Some routes form loops, conveniently starting and ending in the same town, while others run point to point, covering longer stretches.

Beyond route structure, some tours also lend themselves to unusual approaches. For example, Island Hopping: Nordfriesland (Tour No. 17) uses ferries to hop between mainland and off-shore points. Cyclists covering that route can choose either the standard method of moving from one place to the next or use a home-base approach. In the latter case, cyclists establish themselves at a single mainland site and take day trips from that home base. This is a popular approach among German tourers.

The home-base approach is a particularly good option for family touring. Extra gear may be left at the campground or your room, and tired family members need not hold the group back because they can rest while the others bike. For the same reasons, this style makes an excellent choice for people traveling in a group of mixed interests. Cyclists can pedal their unloaded bicycles over sections of the route each day, while non-riders occupy themselves on the beach or in nearby towns. At the end of the day everyone can regroup at a familiar point and share their experiences. Cyclists may therefore share the company of non-biking friends without compromising their interests.

Of the tours described in Part II, the Island Hopping: Nordfriesland (Tour No. 17) and Bodensee (Tour No. 6) routes lend themselves most easily to this approach, although others may also be modified for the same purpose. Loop tours are especially easy to adapt. For example, you can pedal the Rhineland loop (Tour No. 8) while based nearby. Each day you can cycle one leg of the tour and return to your base by train, leaving your bicycle securely locked. The next morning you can return by train, pick up your bike, and resume the tour. This approach can prove practical while covering a new area. Whatever tour appeals to you, be creative in adapting it to suit your needs.

TRAINS AND OTHER TRANSPORTATION

Remember, your decision to bicycle tour does not limit you exclusively to life on two wheels. For practicality's sake—or simply a change of pace, take advantage of the many alternatives open to you in Germany.

TRAINS. I was once a stubborn cyclist, determined to draw only solid lines of bicycle travel on my maps, but the ease of train use in Germany has relaxed my stance. Now, I still connect shorter stretches by pedal power (one to two days, like the tour connections described), but link up more distant points by train.

Environmental awareness and the popularity of bicycle touring in Germany have created an extremely bicycle-friendly train system (the *Bundesbahn*). Train travel allows quick connections from city airports to touring areas, or between areas of primary interest. Even if time is not a limiting factor, train travel can bring you and your bike right to top touring areas without having to cycle for days over less interesting stretches. For example, the Water Castles of Münsterland tour (Tour No. 14), an isolated loop around the region's best sights, is best reached by train.

Particularly in or around urban centers, trains provide a good alternative to cycling. Networks of bicycle lanes exist but city biking is still no pleasure. Instead of a long, confusing entry into an unfamiliar city, hop on a train directly to the center—and right to the tourist office, usually located nearby. Within urban areas, bicycles are permitted on both the *S-bahn* (commuter trains to suburbs) and *U-bahn* (subway) at extra cost (half price or child's fare; no bikes during rush hours). Finally, trains are useful in cases of bad weather, difficult terrain, or in catching up to tight schedules after unexpected delays.

The bicycle-friendly *Bundesbahn* does have some tricky rules. First, it is always possible to ship your bike separately (DM 25, usually overnight service), but I always prefer handling my own bicycle. There are several types of trains—not every train accepts self-handled bikes. The fastest, "bullet" trains, never accept bicycles (*Inter-City Express/ICE* and *Inter-City/IC*). On all other trains, bicycles are permitted so long as a bicycle compartment or baggage car is available. Check for the bicycle symbol on departure schedules or at the train information office. You must purchase both a regular passenger ticket and a bicycle ticket (DM 9).

A cyclist's best friend is the *Inter-Regio* (*IR*), the next-fastest train type. Most *Inter-Regio* trains come complete with special bicycle compartments fitting up to eight self-handled bikes. To put your bike on an *IR*, however, you must make a bicycle reservation at least one day before departure (DM 3.50). Go to the information office and specify *Platzreservierung für Fahrrad* and be sure the ticket says *Mit Fahrrad*. Before I mastered the system I had several problems with incorrect reservations and misinformation, so be careful. The fine for traveling on an *IR* without reservation, on the other hand, is only DM 9, not the end of the world if you are in a hurry to move along. The popularity of bicycle travel and convenience of *Inter-Regio* trains means that bicycle compartments are fully reserved well in advance of major holidays and some weekends; check ahead when possible.

All other, slower trains (types *FD*, *D*, *E*, etc.) do not require bicycle reservations, but be sure to check that the train you want has a baggage car. Space and the conductor's mood permitting, one or two bicycles are often allowed on local runs not officially authorized for them.

To ask for train/bike information, start out with *Ich fahre mit einem Fahrrad nach Konstanz/München*, and so on, and wing it from there. Prices are high: Frankfurt to München costs DM 90 one way. Those making extensive use of the *Bundesbahn* should invest in a 50 percent discount *Bahncard*, which quickly pays off. Adult cards, available at train stations and travel agents, cost DM 220; youths under 23 and students under 27 pay DM 110. Officially, only German students are eligible for the DM 110 card, but this is often overlooked, particularly at small train stations and travel agencies.

BUSES. Buses do not normally accept bicycles, but in case of need it may be possible to take the open space intended for baby carriages on some buses. Airport connection buses will accept boxed bicycles.

FERRIES. Ferries offer many of the same advantages as train travel, with a fun, easygoing atmosphere to boot. Ferries not only travel longer distances along major rivers, they also offer shuttle services cross-river, taking the place of bridges. Boats carry passengers around lakes like the Bodensee (Lake Constance) or Chiemsee

Kayakers and a barge float a canal near Canow.

in Bavaria, and also provide international links (see Tour Nos. 18 and 19 for ferry tips to Scandinavia). Island Hopping (Tour No. 17) makes extensive use of ferry connections for a unique offshore ride. Not all ferry lines, however, accept bicycles. Again, check ahead.

WALKING. Cycling is an excellent, up-close means of experiencing new places, but at times an even closer perspective is appropriate. Put your bicycle aside for an evening walk or a day hike. Many tours in this book visit beautiful regions as well suited to hiking as biking. Add in a few days for a slower, closer view of the area on foot. No need to go charging over the river and through the woods— just take a break from your wheels and see what you can discover on your own two feet.

AIRPORTS. Cyclists flying into Germany need not be concerned about airport connections upon arrival. All of Germany's main international airports (Frankfurt, München, Berlin) are well serviced by both bus and train connections. If you are catching a bus shuttle, keep your bicycle boxed. Nearly all trains accept unpacked bicycles; check on restrictions at the airport.

Look for *DB* (*Deutsches Bundesbahn*) signs in the airport to locate the train company office, ticket counter, and information. Spur rail lines connect arrivals to the city's main train station. From there, local and long-distance trains will speed you on your way.

THE FORMER EAST GERMANY

When I collected information for my first European bicycle tour in early 1989, the East German tourist bureau answered my query in one short sentence: "Bicycling between cities in the DDR is not permitted." Period.

Things have changed rather quickly since then; today the former East is completely open and readily accessible to cyclists. On the other hand, progress is not as swift as many would wish. Therefore, while Eastern "window one for tickets, window two for payment, window three for pickup; all of the above closed" bureaucracy has been replaced by quick supermarket-style checkout and travel services, the East still remains a world apart.

When the wall came down, everyone rushed across the border in a mad dash for a piece of the action. Bicycle tourists, it seems, were right in with the pack. Detailed cycling maps are already available and a number of bicycle routes marked out. Cyclists were even ahead of the action: In places, bicycle signs are already posted, but oops! the road is still under construction.

Lesson number one: Never take anything for granted in the East. Changes and improvements mean detours, construction, hostels and campgrounds closed or relocated. Printed information quickly becomes obsolete, so double- and triple-check everything. Local tourist offices are your best source of information, though degrees of helpfulness and accuracy vary widely.

Bike shops are few and far between in the East, so be as self-sufficient with tools and spare parts as practicality permits. Private *Zimmer* (rooms) for rent are widely advertised in tourist areas. Eastern hostels often cater to families, with separate bungalows or private rooms in addition to the usual dorm-style bunks.

Lesson number two: Use defensive strategies—just in case. Yes, there are now many supermarkets about, but small towns have few conveniences. I always maintained a good food supply—just in case. Yes, the map indicates a campground ahead, but ask again—just in case. Using this strategy, you will rarely be disappointed or unpleasantly surprised.

Biking conditions vary greatly. Small back roads best suited for

Restoration work progresses rapidly in the East.

cycling are the last to be paved; a mountain bike would help smooth your ride over cobblestones, ruts, and sand. In places, bicycle lanes have been paved alongside new roads. However, most seem to be of the treacherous "is that a bike lane or did a gravel truck leak for 10 km?" variety. If not cautious, you may find yourself careening wildly about the back roads, desperately trying to balance along strips of asphalt dribble amidst mine-field-like cobblestone surfaces. The side edges of many roads are usually in the worst condition, leaving you in a tough position. You'll be forced to either jar painfully along the deteriorating edge or bike the smoother center strip of the road, taking your chances with cement trucks and warp-speed *Trabants* (affectionately known as *Trabis*). Defying all laws of physics—among others—*Trabis* attain warp speed at approximately 30 kilometers per hour.

Trabants are both the most dangerous and entertaining contraptions prowling Eastern roads. Drivers seem to be going along for the ride rather than actually in control. Often it is difficult to guess where these symmetrical cars are heading, but luckily, it is also impossible for a *Trabant* to sneak up silently from behind—you'll hear it coming a mile away.

Lesson number three: Appreciate the leg room on your bicycle.

In other words, the usual challenges of bicycle touring are compounded by extra elements in the East. View Eastern biking as an adventure rather than a vacation. *Trabis*, bad roads, and unpredictable services, however, are only examples of the East at its worst. At its best, the East rewards adventurous tourists with unspoiled scenery, tree-lined country roads, genuine people, and the excitement of exploring a newly opened land.

Thanks to the slower pace of post-war development in the East, large tracts of unspoiled, unpopulated land have been preserved, opening excellent opportunities for bicycle touring. Similarly, many historic sites were spared from "progress." Long overlooked delights like Quedlinburg are now reawakening, their medieval streets uninterrupted by modern intrusions. Cyclists exploring the East sacrifice the convenience of well-established routes for the charm of discoveries like these, off the beaten path.

Conversely, as more and more travelers venture east, rutted paths become easier to follow—to your advantage. The East still operates its own half of the railroad (the *Reichsbahn*) but all services, procedures, and tickets correspond to the West's *Bundesbahn* and the same rules for shipping bicycles apply (tickets valid on either half; *Bahncard* valid). The only delays you may encounter in dealing with the *Reichsbahn* are obtaining information (long lines, some staff unfamiliar with new rules or routes) and paying by credit card (back to "window one, window two, all of the above closed" procedure). When possible, try to take care of such business in the West, where it's most easily done in areas along the former border, such as Berlin or the Harz Mountains.

The descriptions of the five Eastern tours in this guide (Tour Nos. 12, 13, 15, 19, and 20) will help minimize many unpredictable and unknown factors. Tips on stores, accommodations, conditions, and general orientation will spare you much of the usual confusion. The tours encompass some of the best cycling opportunities in the East, though many other possibilities certainly exist. Those with a specific interest in areas not mentioned here should research carefully before setting off. Remember, anything is possible.

Finally, a word on attitude. Even as a person with extensive exposure to lifestyles and standards in Eastern Europe, I found my Western perspective difficult to shed at times. Direct comparisons are inappropriate and unfair: View the East on its own terms. Prepare for the worst and you will discover the best. Most important, remember that the people of the East are still struggling to reestablish their identities and roles in a difficult transition period. Think of yourself as a guest and act with due respect and an open mind.

LANGUAGE TIPS

German is a wonderful language, particularly for English ears. The close relationship of the two languages and the logical character of German gives beginners a great boost. Guess what *Haus* means? *Bier*? *Handschuhe* is my personal favorite—"hand shoes" (gloves). Think of parallel terms for English words: dog, for example, is *Hund*, as in hound. I spoke with one cyclist about traveling with a *Hund;* he joked with me and said that I should buy an *Anhänger*, or trailer (literally a "hanger-on-er"). Communication gap? What communication gap?

If you speak little or no German, *Kein Problem*. Many Germans speak English—so many speak English so well that it can be difficult to practice your German. A few basic German terms are listed below to get you started. Sign language will fill in the blanks. An important part of language comprehension is attitude. Don't look at a sign and think, "Forget it. I don't speak German." Instead, look and think, "Now let me see, what words do I recognize or remember?" You may surprise yourself with the results.

As a cyclist, you will enjoy an advantage over other travelers: Your bicycle will serve as the starting point for conversations with Germans, either cyclists themselves or simply curious locals. If your command of German is minimal (and your confidence even shakier), many Germans may simply switch into English; others will patiently coax you along, curious to hear your story. Mastery of the usual cyclists' exchange will take you the next step. You'll soon venture from the basic "hello/where to/where from/how far" greeting to more involved conversation: "beautiful scenery/friendly people/nice weather," and so on. When you learn a new word or phrase, try using it yourself.

German pronunciation can be a bit difficult for the English tongue, especially vowels like *ü*, *ö*, or *ä* (roughly equivalent to ue, oe, and ae sounds). When you see *ei* or *ie* combinations, pronounce the second vowel (Freiburg: "Fry-berg," Chiemsee: "Keem-zee"). Listen closely to German speakers and do your best to imitate them. There is no such thing as a silent *e* in German; hence *Brunhilde* ends with an "uh" sound. The *β* symbol is interchangeable with "ss," as in *Gross/Groß*.

The best dictionary for cyclists is *Langenscheidts Mini-Wörterbuch*, Volumes 51 and 52 (one English to German, the other German to English). Many bookstores carry these miniature yellow books, baby volumes (about a cubic inch in size but containing 9,000 entries) that slip easily into your handlebar bag, ready to be pulled out at the sight of a word like *Jugendherbergsverzeichnis*. In German, words are often tied together in long chains. Break them apart to decipher them: *Jugend*/youth; *Herberge*/hostel (inn); *Verzeichnis*/catalogue—youth hostel catalogue.

Memorize question words and numbers to begin. Common words and phrases often used by cyclists are listed below. Words like *Bahnhof, Dom, Marktplatz,* and *Rathaus* refer to common, important landmarks and are interjected throughout Part II tour texts, so take special note.

Altstadt—old town
Apotheke—pharmacy
Auf Wiedersehen—goodbye
Bahnhof/Hauptbahnhof—train station/main station
   (abbrevations: *Bhf/Hbf*)
Bank/Geldbank—bank
Berg—mountain
Bitte/Bitteschön—please
Brücke—bridge
Burg—castle
Campingplatz—campground
Danke/Dankeschön—thank you
Dom—cathedral
Fähre/Rundfähre—ferry
Fahrkarte—ticket
Fahrrad/Rad—bicycle
Freilichtmuseum—open-air museum

Gleis—track (in a train station)
Guten Tag / Abend—good day/evening
Imbiss—food stand
Innenstadt / Zentrum—city center
Ja / Nein—yes/no
Jugendherberge—youth hostel
Karte / Radtourenkarte—map/bicycle-touring map
Kirche—church
Kloster—monastery/convent
Links / Rechts—left/right
Marktplatz—market square
Münster—minster/cathedral
Nord / Süd—north/south
Ortsmitte / Stadtmitte—town/city center
Ost / West—east/west
Radwanderweg—bicycle path
Rathaus—town hall
Richtung—direction
Schloss—castle/palace
See—lake or sea
Strasse / Weg / Gasse / Allee—street/way/alley
Tal—valley (contracts with place name, as in Mosel Valley:
   Moseltal)
Tor—gate
Tschüss—*ciao*/bye
Verboten / Gesperrt—forbidden
Verkehrsamt—tourist information office
Wald—forest
Weinprobe / Weinstube—wine tasting/wine-tasting room
Zimmer—room (for rent)
Zug—train

Substitute appropriate words in these handy phrases:

Ich fahre mit Fahrrad nach Darmstadt / Sontheim.
   I am going by bicycle to....
Ich möchte einen Fahrkarte.
   I would like a ticket.
Haben Sie Eis?
   Do you have ice cream?
Wo ist der Bahnhof?
   Where is the train station?
Wieviel kostet das?
   How much does this cost?

Those of you on longer trips who are interested in improving your language ability may want to invest more in learning. Apart from instructional books and courses, try playing a trick on yourself: Take the focus off language by concentrating on an incidental interest. Choose something that will motivate you to plow through the unpleasant task of dictionary references. "I sell bananas, you sell bananas, he sells bananas"-type exercises will never motivate you the way something of interest to you will. Skim newspapers, follow sports, or find a magazine of particular interest to you. Slowly but surely, repeated terms and grammar will slide into your memory, ready to be adapted to other themes.

POP QUIZ ON CYCLING IN GERMANY

So you think you are ready to pack your bags and bid your friends *Auf Wiedersehen?* First, try a simple test of your level of preparation:

Category One: Important Elements of a German Old Town
1. Whenever entering a new town, a safe bet is to head for the:
    a. *Autobahn.*
    b. nearest bar.
    c. *Marktplatz.*
2. In a typical *Marktplatz*, we find the following:
    a. *Rathaus.*
    b. fountain.
    c. shady bench for picnicking.
    d. all of the above.
3. The building style frequently used in medieval architecture is:
    a. Doric.
    b. Ionic.
    c. Moronic.
    d. Half-timbered.

Category Two: Definitions
1. A *Rathaus* is:
    a. the place big mice go when they grow up.
    b. like the teamsters' union, but for rodents.
    c. the town hall.
2. A *Ratskeller* is:
    a. the place rats keep their best wines.
    b. a cellar infested with rodents.
    c. the traditional cellar/bar found in the town hall.

3. A *Schloss* is:
   a. a term German cyclists use to describe nasty wipeouts on slushy roads.
   b. like floss, but in German.
   c. a castle or palace.
4. A *Fahrrad* or *Rad* is:
   a. an expressive term used by hip young Germans.
   b. the Swahili word for beer.
   c. a bicycle.
5. *Bad* means:
   a. not good.
   b. tough or cool, as in "I'm Bad."
   c. bath or pool.
6. A *Biergarten* is:
   a. the place hippies grow their beer.
   b. like Kindergarten, but for baby beers.
   c. outdoor drinking areas and popular meeting places in Germany.

(Your score is 100 if you picked the last choice for each question. Congratulations!)

A NOTE ABOUT SAFETY

Safety is an important concern in all outdoor activities. No guidebook can alert you to every hazard or anticipate the limitations of every reader. Therefore, the descriptions of roads, routes, and natural features in this book are not representations that a particular place or excursion will be safe for your party. When you follow any of the routes described in this book, you assume responsibility for your own safety. Under normal conditions, such excursions require the usual attention to traffic, road conditions, weather, terrain, the capabilities of your party, and other factors. Keeping informed on current conditions and exercising common sense are the keys to a safe, enjoyable outing.

Political conditions may add to the risks of travel in Germany in ways that this book cannot predict. When you travel, you assume this risk, and should keep informed of political developments that may make safe travel difficult or impossible.

The Mountaineers

Circular Signs—Give Orders

White bar on red background. No entry for vehicles. (One-way traffic coming at you!)

Red ring around motorcycle and automobile. No motor vehicles. (OK for nonmotorized you!)

 Red ring around bicycle. No cycling. (Tunnel, freeway, busy road, or bike-eating dog ahead!)

 White bicycle on blue background. Pedal cyclists only. (Sometimes obligatory. Follow local custom.)

Rectangular Signs—Give Information

Black letter "i" on blue field. Tourist information. (Where am i?)

White bar with red tip on blue. No through road. (This sign can lie—check it out if you feel adventuresome.)

Triangular Signs—Give Warnings

Black bump in red border. Uneven road. (Look out for potholes!)

Black gate in red border. Railroad crossing with barrier. (Slow down for tracks or trains!)

 Black train in red border. Unguarded crossing. (Slow down for tracks and look for trains!)

 Parallel lines bending closer. Road narrows. (So long, shoulder!)

Black hill in red border. Steep downhill. (Yahoo!)

Black hill in red border. Steep uphill. (Could be a "pusher"!)

PART II

20 TOURS IN GERMANY

Painted shutters on Burg Vischering in Münsterland

TOUR NO. 1

THE NORTHERN ROMANTIC ROAD

Nördlingen to Rothenburg ob der Tauber

Distance: 167 kilometers (104 miles)
Estimated time: 3 to 4 days (3 biking days)
Terrain: Endless rolling hills, some
challenging sections
Map: ADFC #21
Connecting tour: Tour No. 2

Germany's Romantic Road (Romantische Strasse) links historic towns and castles of Bavaria in a single long-distance tourist route. Though this well-established route attracts busloads of tourists (a hint about its popularity: road signs are printed in both German and Japanese), cyclists use quiet side roads and bicycle trails to visit not only the most famous sights, but also to explore off the beaten path. This tour includes the best of the Romantic Road's northern section plus a few detours to nearby attractions. Tour No. 4 in Upper Bavaria covers a southern stretch of the Romantische Strasse.

Rothenburg ob der Tauber, with its half-timbered houses and crooked streets, is the most famous medieval town of the Romantic Road, as perfect in architectural preservation as in its lovely setting in the green Tauber Valley. Less visited towns offer a quieter opportunity to step back in time, including multitowered Dinkelsbühl and walled Nördlingen, where a town crier still calls out the time. Detouring west from the official route, the tour also visits Schwäbisch Hall and Langenburg, a village crowded on a ridge in the hills. Throughout the tour, wooded hillsides and sleepy villages provide a scenic backdrop for peaceful country cycling.

Nördlingen

Nördlingen, the starting point of this tour, is often overlooked in a country full of half-timbered medieval towns. However, the picture-perfect little town stands out as the only place in all Germany where medieval town walls remain in their entirety, and one can walk the complete circuit. Within the walls, a maze of cobblestone streets and tidy houses tempt visitors to explore further.

For excellent views over the old town, climb Daniel Tower of St. Georgskirche (DM 2). The climb rewards with a good impression of the Ries, a large meteor crater in which Nördlingen is situated. If you stay late in town to sample the local beer, Ankerbrau, listen for the call of the town crier, a centuries-old tradition.

Nördlingen lies along a secondary rail line, necessitating a few transfers from distant points. Incoming cyclists may also choose to pedal in, for example, from the Danube Valley at Donauwörth, or other points. The tourist office opposite the *Rathaus* in the center of town will help find rooms. The youth hostel lies outside Baldinger Tor, and there is a bike shop within the town walls on Deiningerstrasse, by Deininger Tor. The nearest campground is 6 km away in Utzmemmingen. Ride southwest out of Baldinger Tor to reach the site, or find a spot to free camp closer to town.

Nördlingen to Dinkelsbühl: 42 kilometers

Leave Nördlingen on **B25**, following signs for Dinkelsbühl and Rothenburg. Bike 5 km alongside this busy road, using the **bike path** to **Wallerstein**. You can stop to see the palace and trinity column in town, but the countryside ahead will quickly draw you away. Leaving B25 behind, follow signs to **Birkhausen** to access pleasant country roads, pedaling rolling hills on to **Maihingen**. Entering Maihingen, turn **right** at the T (peek at the castle on your left) and pick up signs to **Hochaltingen**, 5 km farther. Long, steady hills continue for much of the way.

Do not turn right into Hochaltingen—instead turn **left** for **Fremdingen** and Dinkelsbühl just before the town. You will **rejoin B25**, the official Romantische Strasse. The busy road makes for an uncomfortable 4-km ride until the left turn to **Rühlingstetten**, with another long climb to **Tannhausen**.

The official Romantic Road **bicycle route** is marked to the **right past Rühlingstetten** and follows unpaved paths to **Mönchsroth**. I preferred to remain on the pavement of quiet side roads to Tannhausen, Eck an Berg, and then on to Mönchsroth. Stay with signs for Dinkelsbühl and Ellwangen along the way.

In Mönchsroth signs to **Limes Turm** lead to a reconstructed Roman watchtower of the Limes, a first-century A.D. wall that protected Roman-held territories from unconquered northern tribes. A last **7 km** from Mönchsroth brings you to **Dinkelsbühl**.

Some medieval towns remain intact today thanks to local heroes, others due to their location or simple flukes of history. Dinkelsbühl owes its near perfect state of preservation to its children. During the Thirty Years' War, children carried flowers to the attacking army, melting the commander's heart and convincing him to spare the town. Or so the story goes. The Kinderzeche festival in July commemorates this event with a historic play and dances.

The Wörnitz River winds around the snug old town. Survey Dinkelsbühl's many towers and gates from the green park surrounding the town. Walking and photo opportunities abound along both the inner and outer edge of the town walls. Centuries-old houses line the streets, crooked with age but tidy as can be. An interesting courtyard hides behind the *Rathaus*, easily missed but worth seeking out.

Town maps posted by the *Rathaus* and town gates help orient visitors. There is a Norma supermarket by the *Marktplatz* in the center of town and a bike shop by the Rothenburger Tor. Check side streets or the outer town for rooms, or stop at the tourist office in the center of town. The huge fifteenth-century *Kornhaus* (granary) by Segringer Tor now serves as a hostel. To reach the campground, ride 2 km northeast to Gersbronn (direction Dürrwangen).

Modern sculptures on a stairway in Schwäbisch Hall

Dinkelsbühl to Schwäbisch Hall: 55 kilometers

The second biking day detours west from the Romantic Road to visit Schwäbisch Hall, crossing from Bavaria into Schwaben. As on the first day (and the one to follow), rolling terrain continues. The hills are not so bad, but there is just no end to them. However, pleasant scenery also characterizes this ride, through fields and woods, now and then rolling through another tidy, half-timbered town. A few unmapped and non-touristy castles and old towers (no information boards listing dates and facts) punctuate the ride. All the better for active imaginations, these small, unheralded places nicely counter better known sites.

Leave Dinkelsbühl through Segringer Tor and turn **right** for **Fichtenau** 1 km out of town, starting the day along quiet roads. In **Buckweiler**, turn **right** for **Wildenstein**. There, turn **right** again for Crailsheim, and **left** at the church to **Krettenbach**. Entering this small town, keep **left** for **Weipertshofen**, and watch for the **left** turn to **Rechenberg**. Another 3 km brings you to **Stimpfach**.

Turn **right** toward Crailsheim on busy **Road 290**, swinging **left** into tiny **Appensee** 1 km later. The first (and only) **left** turn in this village leads up a long, gradual hill to **Honhardt**. There, follow signs for **Crailsheim** (the town that seems to be everywhere), pass the church, and go left for **Obersontheim** (11 km). Ignore signs to Schwäbisch Hall, following instead signs to **Untersontheim**, **Oberfischach**, **Herlebach**, and **Einkorn**. With **two steep climbs**, the home stretch is a bit nasty. At the top of the **second hill keep left** to go downhill, ignoring the Einkorn sign. Finally, enjoy a well-deserved, sweeping downhill ride into the valley. If it is still early, you may wish to detour north from Untersontheim to **Vellberg**'s fifteenth-century fortifications before continuing toward Schwäbisch Hall.

Pass **Comburg**, an imposing Romanesque abbey, then **Hessental** as you near Schwäbisch Hall. The campground is signposted to the **left** in **Steinbach** (5 km from the center). To ride into town, pass the *Bahnhof* and follow information signs to the office below town. The hostel is above town on the Galgenberg.

Schwäbisch Hall is another wonderful medieval town, though unlike its Bavarian cousins Nördlingen and Dinkelsbühl, it is based on a vertical axis, up a steep hillside. Although crowded with tourists, Schwäbisch Hall retains its own character, playing variations on the usual recipe of *Marktplatz*, *Rathaus*, and half-timbered

Riverside view of Schwäbisch Hall

houses. These elements may be familiar, but their arrangement is unique—take for example the mixed style of the *Marktplatz*, with its Baroque town hall, wide steps of St. Michael's Church, and timbered buildings. Side-street exploration rewards with small discoveries—fountains, shops, and viewpoints.

Since wandering about with an ice cream seems to be the thing to do in Schwäbisch Hall, and since you'd hate to be culturally insensitive, get yourself a cone. Just one of the little sacrifices a traveler must make to humor her host country. Thus prepared, you can head to the riverside park below town to take in the best overall view of the historic town.

Schwäbisch Hall to Rothenburg ob der Tauber: 70 kilometers

Leave Schwäbisch Hall on **Road 19** toward **Würzburg** to begin a hilly day's ride. The road is busy but you will only have 5 km before turning to side roads in **Untermünkheim**. From there follow **signs** to Langenburg. An initially easy valley ride soon becomes more difficult, with 3 km **uphill** from **Braunsbach** to **Orlach**. Pass a giant model strawberry (how's that for a landmark?), then enjoy a sweeping glide down to **Bächlingen**. Beautiful views of Bächlingen's red roofs and Langenburg perched high above may even tempt you to interrupt the fun of the descent for a longer look or a photo.

Langenburg is a real treat. The one street town is a quietly kept, non-touristy treasure hidden in a curve of the hills that guidebooks and tour buses overlook. Langenburg may not boast the superlatives of other towns, but its modest scale only adds to the charm. There is a catch, of course: The town is perched atop a high, steep hill that will make you wish for a great-granny gear.

The main road up from Bächlingen bends sharply **right** near the end of town; at the bend, continue straight **up** (and up) the small white road more directly to Langenburg. The road is unpaved but the surface is suitable for biking even if the gradient isn't. You'll huff and you'll puff, and finally marvel at the views from the upper town. There are several cafes, a bakery, and a few restaurants in **Langenburg**. Make your way to the *Schloss* at one end of town. You can pay to enter the grounds or simply take in the panorama from the nearby terrace.

Rothenburg is clearly signed from Langenburg, another 32 km along quiet or moderately trafficked roads. The **hills continue** but killer climbs do not. Easterly winds can roar steadily on this section of the ride and may continue all the way to Nürnberg.

Finally, you will enter the **Tauber Valley** with early views of

Half-timbered houses crowd Rothenburg's streets.

Rothenburg's medieval towers jutting out above forests and red rooftops. Even from afar, it is clear that Rothenburg deserves its reputation as an outstanding historic town. Pass a double-tiered **bridge** (a fourteenth-century fortified viaduct) and pedal the **curving road up** to town, your final climb of the day. Bike through the first **gateway** to enter the **old town**. The main street straight ahead leads directly to the *Marktplatz* and tourist information (in the clock building opposite the square; entrance around the left side). There you can pick up maps (with outlined walking tours) and information in the language of your choice.

   Rothenburg ob der Tauber is everything it's cracked up to be—a large, unusually well-preserved medieval town with a lovely setting in the Tauber Valley. Throngs of tourists crowd the narrow streets, as Rothenburg's international reputation makes it the quintessential medieval German town to visit. This stereotypical town is so precisely picture-perfect that many foreign visitors pause at the town gates, looking for a ticket booth as if entering a theme park.

   All the same, you'll enjoy the decorative shop signs and centuries-old houses, both modest and grand. The most impressive houses line Herrngasse; fewer tourists venture to equally interesting side streets. Tourists regroup in the *Marktplatz* several times a day to see the *Glockenspiel* (clock show and chimes). Snoop around the back of the *Rathaus* to find the inner courtyard, and note the large fountain in the market square. The town fountains do not play a merely decorative role; in medieval times they provided water for extinguishing fires as well as for drinking.

The tourist-office map indicates a walking tour and includes a key to principal sights—churches, houses, town gates, and museums. Background information can be helpful in better appreciating the sights, but remember not to keep your nose buried in a guidebook; come up for air and take in the general impression, too. For a picnic in the park and a panorama of the green valley, go to the Burggarten on a promontory above the Tauber.

Rothenburg's youth hostel is in the old town, a sixteenth-century millhouse near the Spital gate. Rooms are widely advertised, although centrally located vacancies may be difficult to come by (doubles listed from DM 45 and up). Take your pick of the two campgrounds in Detwang 2 km north of town (east bank of the Tauber). The adjacent sites are practically identical in price and facilities. Before coasting downhill to the campsites, stop at a supermarket in town (Aldi is marked off Road B25 east of the town walls). Several hiking trails wind along the river near the campsites, the perfect place for an evening walk.

This Romantic Road tour ends in Rothenburg, but possibilities for further biking do not. First, you can round out the tour by continuing north along the Romantic Road to Würzburg (65 km away). You can also head east into pestering winds, riding to Nürnberg and the Franken tour (see Connection below). To literally round out the tour, circle south back to Dinkelsbühl via the signed Romantische Strasse Radweg (46 km). Pick up this bike route in Gebsattel, 4 km south of town. Rothenburg's train line is only a spur track, necessitating transfers to travel farther afield, but once on a bigger rail line you'll quickly be on your way.

Connection to Tour No. 2

Rothenburg to Nürnberg: 92 kilometers. From Rothenburg bike Schweinsdorfstrasse to (you guessed it) Schweinsdorf; there, follow signs to Hartershausen but turn right for Nordenberg. A steep climb out of town in the direction of Ansbach will bring you to signs for Burgbernheim, crossing a hilly divide between the Tauber Valley and the more open country east to Franken. In Burgbernheim center ask for the (unmarked) road to Marktbergel. Then follow signs for Langenzenn until Neuhof. For a nice lunch stop along the way, pull over to the cozy fountain square in Obernzenn.

In Neuhof turn right to Hirschneuses. Go left in town, then right for Kirchfarrnbach, and continue along to Seukendorf on the outskirts of Nürnberg. Cross B8 and ride through Fürth-Burgfarrnbach. To reach the bicycle trail along the Main–Donau Canal, turn left under the railroad bridge, then right immediately before the second bus stop. Follow the canal's west bank for 12 km south, counting bridges for orientation. Cross the canal on the bridge after the third train crossing.

Signs to *Centrum* take over from here, but take care: Pass the first *Centrum* turnoff for the *Autobahn* (blue car sign), then take the second, slower paced road also marked *Centrum*. Bike lanes throughout the main streets of Nürnberg facilitate the ride in. You should emerge on Frauentorgraben, part of the ring road encircling the old town. Signs indicate the *Bahnhof*, right, where tourist information can provide you with a map and tips on city sights. For more city information, see Tour No. 2.

TOUR NO. 2

FRANCONIAN DELIGHTS
A Loop Tour from Nürnberg

Distance: 222 kilometers (138 miles)
Estimated time: 4 to 5 days (3 to 4 biking days)
Terrain: Flat canalside biking, then difficult hills
Map: ADFC #18
Connecting tours: Tour Nos. 1 and 3

A short, circular tour surveys the best of the Franken region of northern Bavaria, from small towns tucked in the hills to important cultural and historic centers. Nürnberg (Nuremberg), the starting and ending point of the tour, offers a variety of interesting sights within and outside the old town walls, including a number of museums relating the city's important role throughout both German and world history. Following level terrain alongside the Main-Donau Canal, the tour heads north to historic Bamberg, a cathedral city at the edge of the hills.

Leaving the canal behind, the tour then enters the hilly region known as the Fränkische Schweiz (Franconian Alps) for more strenuous cycling. Bayreuth is one of Germany's leading centers of classical music, best known for its summertime opera festival held in the theater designed by Richard Wagner himself. Another challenging stretch over the hills allows a closer look at the sleepy heartland of Franken before returning to Nürnberg and concluding the ride.

In addition to visiting historic towns and enjoying beautiful scenery, cyclists following this tour also have the opportunity to sample regional specialties like Nürnberger Liebkuchen (gingerlike cookies) and typical Franken white wine served in unusually shaped *Boxbeutte* bottles. Beer lovers, on the other hand, should try Bamberg's unique *Rauchbier*, a smoked brew.

Nürnberg

Careful post-war reconstruction has restored much of the *Meistersingers*' (mastersingers) historic Nürnberg, a beautiful city of open squares and winding cobblestone streets. An important cultural and crafts center in medieval times, Nürnberg retained its

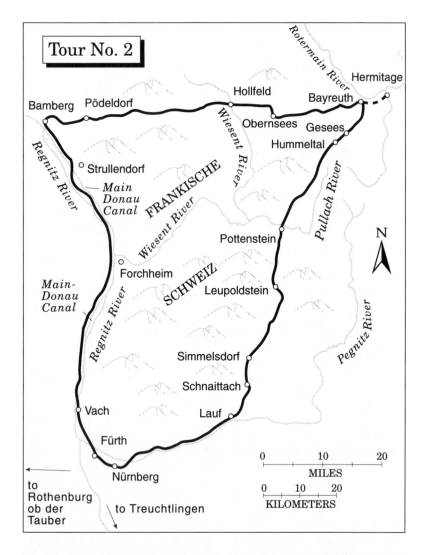

leading role through the centuries. Apart from its ancient traditions the city was more recently known as host to the Nazi party's
annual meetings, and later, site of the war trials. Reminders of all
periods of the city's varied history remain to this day.

Nürnberg's main sights cluster within the walls of the *Altstadt*.
The lively *Marktplatz* with its colorful *Schöner Brunnen* (fountain)
forms the heart of the old town, where food and craft stands sell
their wares. The house of Albrecht Dürer, the influential fifteenth-
century artist, is both an outstanding example of medieval archi-

tecture as well as an interesting destination, now housing the Dürer Museum. Outside, the flower decked square is one of Nürnberg's most pleasant corners.

Traditions of craftsmanship continue even to this day. Walk through the *Handwerkerhof* alley beside Königstor; it's a bit touristy, but the artisans' workshops demonstrate both processes and end products of typical Nürnberg craftwork. The mastersingers of Nürnberg, the subject of one of Wagner's operas, held their school in St. Marthakirche close by. Lorenzkirche contains several notable

Daily market in Nürnberg's historic Marktplatz

artworks, including the *Engelsgruss*. The *Tugendbrunnen* (fountain) outside is sure to set you giggling, as jets of water squirt out of interesting places on the female figures representing the virtues. After seeing the sights, head for a shaded riverside bench.

Nürnberg's information offices are located at the *Hauptbahnhof* (signposted immediately outside the town walls) and on the *Hauptmarktplatz* in the old town. They provide room listings for the city and its environs but help with bookings only by advance correspondence. The hostel in the old town's castle (*Burg*) offers princely

Street festival in Forchheim

views. Campers will get a close look at the former Nazi parade grounds on Große Strasse, near the campsite. To reach the quiet site, head for *Stadion* and follow camping signs 5 km southeast from the city center. Shop ahead before heading out; there is an Aldi on Königstrasse near Königstor.

Nürnberg to Bamberg: 71 kilometers

To begin the easy ride to Bamberg, leave Nürnberg by Fürther-strasse, commencing at a corner of the *Altstadt* by Spittlertor. **Bicycle lanes** lead most of the way to and through **Fürth**. Ride along **Road 8** toward **Würzburg** and **Zirndorf**. When you are almost past Fürth turn **right** for **Vach**.

In Vach follow signs to **Veitsbronn** to pass under the **Main-Donau** (Danube) **Canal**. This impressive canal is built like a highway, passing directly over roads, rivers, and any other obstacles in its path. Turn **right**, up to the canal's bank to reach the bicycle path **north** (unpaved but suitable for cycling). On weekends and holidays the trail becomes a highway of bicycles, with dozens of cyclists out to enjoy the plesant ride. At times, winds may blow strongly along the canal.

Near the lock **south of Frauenaurach**, swing **left** with the path, but then **turn** as if to cross over the canal. The canalside bike path continues along the west bank from there. Bike under a train **bridge**, then turn **left** to circle up to a small car **bridge** beside it. Cross to the opposite shore and regain the canal trail through the **parking lot** to continue your merry way **north**.

While trails line both banks of the canal in most places, keep along the **official route** as marked on the map and by *Aischtalweg* signs. The official path switches from one bank to the other but always takes the better paved trail. Watch for bridges and church steeples to track your progress and to know when to expect a changeover.

Bike under the pedestrian **bridge** to **Forchheim** and then **circle** up to it, crossing the **canal** for a detour through this pretty town (follow *Radweg zur Stadt* signs). With stores and an old town center, Forchheim makes a perfect lunch spot. Both the market square and *Rathaus* are well preserved, and a narrow stream gurgles through the pedestrian zone.

My map indicated both Eggolsheim and Buttenheim as historic points, but I was disappointed and therefore do not recommend the detour. Better to return to the **west bank** *Radweg* and continue straight on to Bamberg's sights. You will **cross** back to the east bank of the canal by **Strullendorf** and come to a **lock** on the outskirts of Bamberg 5 km later. To reach either of the two campgrounds in **Bug**, cross over the lock and head south, crossing the Regnitz River. The campsites are marked from the road (3 km from the lock, 6 km from Bamberg center). Along the way you will also pass a **recycling point** for all materials (including those elusive plastics containers).

Bicycle trails parallel both the **Regnitz River** and **Main-Donau Canal** into **Bamberg**. Tourist information is located around the corner from Maximiliansplatz (Hauptwachstrasse 16; room-finding service here). Two hostels in Bamberg also offer accommodations: one near the stadium (east of the *Bahnhof*), one on the west bank of the Regnitz between Bug and Bamberg.

Bamberg's many art and architectural treasures were collected over the centuries and largely escaped wartime damage. Clergy dominated the upper half of town, and burghers the lower valley; Bamberg's unusual *Rathaus* connected the often opposing interest groups by spanning the Regnitz River between. The building is decorated in a bizarre but entertaining mix of fresco, half-timbering, and rococo.

Bamberg's main attraction, the *Dom*, is another atypical building, with four towers and several interesting artworks inside (including the Bamberg Rider statue). Next door you can enter the pretty courtyard of the Old Residence (*Alte Hofhaltung*), the former imperial palace, for shade and a break. For a panoramic view of the entire city and the hills of Franken beyond, head up to the terrace of the Benedictine Monastery on Michaelsberg.

Bamberg, a good Franconian town, takes its drinking very seriously. I came into town at noon on a holiday and found every *Brauerei* open, if not a single bakery or store. Here's your chance to try Bamberg's smoked *Rauchbier* or local wine from a squat *Boxbeutte* bottle.

Bamberg to Bayreuth: 62 kilometers

The ride from Bamberg to Bayreuth leaves level canal biking behind, entering the rolling Fränkische Schweiz. Leave Bamberg on the **first eastward road** south of the *Bahnhof* (marked *Fernverkehr* and with bike signs to Pödeldorf). A separate **bicycle lane** to **Litzendorf** leads through leafy tracts beside the main road. After **Tiefenellern**, the hilly ride begins with a long series of switchbacks and constantly rolling terrain all the way to **Hollfeld**—and beyond. A picnic table above Hollfeld makes a good place for a break, taking in views over town and the surrounding hills.

In Hollfeld follow **B22** signs toward Bayreuth. After crossing the **Kainach River** for the second time, turn **right** on Friedrich-

Pezoldstrasse instead of leaving town on B22. The quiet and mostly unpaved side road leads to **Pilgerndorf** and **Schönfeld**, pocketed in a deep scoop of the hills. **Rejoin** B22 for 3 km, then turn **right** for **Obernsees** to access a less traveled road to Bayreuth. As traffic picks up near the small city you can join **separate bicycle trails**. The bike route marked *Stadtmitte* may leave you guessing in places but keeps to quiet lanes. Head for Maximilianstrasse, the fountain- and shop-lined pedestrian street in the center of town.

Bayreuth owes its international reputation almost entirely to Richard Wagner. Well, entirely. The annual *Festspiele* (late July to late August) attracts thousands of visitors intent on the same goal: to attend an opera performed in the hall designed by the composer himself. A tree-lined avenue north of the *Bahnhof* leads to Wagner's *Festspielhaus*, atop a hill. Unfortunately, tickets for the renowned festival are very difficult to obtain. Unless you've found tickets ahead of time (typically months or a year) or are willing to pay exorbitant amounts for scalped tickets, you may be better off avoiding Bayreuth during the festival, as the entire town becomes packed.

The central tourist office on Luitpoldplatz (near the Opera and Maximilianstrasse) distributes room listings and city information. Many locals rent out rooms, but vacancies may be few and far between, especially during the festival. The hostel is 2 km south of town: turn right off Road 85/2 after the gas station, then left on Universitätsstrasse. Bayreuth's only campground occupies a small field behind the hostel (no car access), opening only for July and August.

Wagner's home, Villa Wahnfried, is now a museum. Behind the house lies the composer's grave—as well as that of his faithful pooch, Russ. Patches of fresh, cool shade dot the *Schlossgarten*, farther back. Bayreuth strikes visitors as the perfect town, with a number of interesting sights and activities, but not more than can be easily toured in a short time, leaving one free of tourist obligations and ready for an ice cream on Maximilianstrasse or a walk in the shade of the palace park.

A 4-km excursion to Princess Wilhemina's Hermitage Castle makes a pleasant excursion from Bayreuth. Pretty parks dotted by fountains surround the eighteenth-century palace. To visit the site take Road B22 east out of Bayreuth, cross under the *Autobahn*, and turn left on Schlossallee.

Bayreuth to Pottenstein: 29 kilometers

This is only a short hop of a day, but a nasty one, with one long hill after another all the way to Pottenstein. Once you reach Pottenstein, however, you will have all afternoon to spend exploring or relaxing in a pretty valley. Hard-core cyclists can combine this day with the next, making a long day's run directly into Nürnberg.

Leave Bayreuth **south** from Wittelsbachring, following signs to Pottenstein on Ludwig-Thoma Strasse. Be careful not to get side-tracked as you pedal the parallel bike path, since the separate lane veers gently **right** while the road bends left.

Almost immediately, the first of a seemingly endless series of **hills** begins, a climb straight over the ridge behind **Saas**. In **Gesees** turn **right** for quiet roads to Hummeltal, ignoring Pottenstein signs straight ahead. You'll encounter little traffic along these back roads. In **Hummeltal** resume following signs to Pottenstein. Don't bother counting all the arrows indicating steep hills on the map, just keep pedaling away. Could be worse, could be raining, so keep in mind these words of comfort: This will be a short day!

After several long, difficult climbs, you will reach **Hohen-mirsberg** with good open views of upper Franken, and then enjoy a downhill ride to **Pottenstein**. Pottenstein is the ideal base from which to put hill cycling out of your mind and see the Fränkische Schweiz up close. The town lies in a deep valley, its castle perched on an isolated cliff above.

The twisting landscape makes orientation tricky even in this small town, so follow signs to tourist information and pick up a town map. There is a Norma market and many rooms for rent in Pottenstein, as well as a hostel. Riverside camping lies 2 km west of town off B470 (direction Forchheim), with a second site in Tüchersfeld. Having visited the cities where Franconian culture and products are concentrated, you can now explore one of the hilly corners where these elements originated. For a new perspective on Franken, visit one of the region's caves (like Teufelshöhle, just east of Pottenstein) or explore hiking trails through the twisting valley.

Pottenstein to Nürnberg: 60 kilometers

Although this day begins with another tough climb, by Betzenstein you will have mostly level or downhill terrain as you pedal to Nürnberg, rounding out this tour of Franken. Get started by following **signs** to **Leupoldstein** off B470 (direction Weiden). Ride through **Betzenstein**, then to **Simmelsdorf** and **Schnaittach**, surmounting one last difficult hill. The surrounding hills slowly shrink in size and the woods thin out as you near the edge of the Fränkische Schweiz. The run down to the Pegnitz Valley and Lauf consists mainly of downhill or flat terrain. Traffic gradually increases along this road, making the ride less quiet, but not uncomfortable.

Follow signs to Lauf and **B14** to leave the Franken hills. Leave busy B14 to cut **left** through the town gate and enter the medieval town center of **Lauf**, a convenient stopping point. Half-timbered houses surround an islandlike *Rathaus* in the center of the *Marktplatz*. At the end of the square turn **left**, crossing the **Pegnitz River** to see Lauf's shuttered castle. Past Lauf, a **bicycle lane** parallels busy Road 14 straight into Nürnberg; look for clearly posted **Fünf-Flüsse bike signs**. The bicycle route switches between sidewalk lanes and stretches separate from the road.

When you cross the city limit marked "Nürnberg" in **Erlenstegen** (a community on the city's edge), do not go under the underpass with B14. Instead, turn **left** with a **bicycle path** paralleling train tracks. Keep straight along this path, then follow Seemainsweg and the Pegnitz straight into the heart of **Nürnberg**. You will enter the old town gates near Wöhrder Wiesen *U-bahn* station. Simply continue along the river to reach Nürnberg center.

Back in Nürnberg you can catch up on sights you may have missed earlier or enjoy familiar places. Many opportunities for continued touring present themselves from this point. One good option is the Altmühl Valley tour to the south (Tour No. 3), which emerges on the Danube in a few days.

Cyclists curious to see the former East Germany may opt to turn north again to join the Thuringia tour (Tour No. 12) at Eisenach, two biking days away. Biking connections involve an easy canalside ride and riverside trails to Coburg (hostel, rooms, camping 10 km east of town) with its huge fortress, then more challenging terrain over the Thuringer Wald. If you are through biking or heading for more distant points, board a train at Nürnberg's *Hauptbahnhof* for your next destination.

Connection to Tour No. 3

Nürnberg to Treuchtlingen: 70 kilometers. A pleasant ride over unchallenging terrain connects you to Treuchtlingen and the Altmühltal bike route. Follow the Main-Donau Canal south from Nürnberg for 25 km. Pass the Leerstetten lock and 5 km later bike along the paved road paralleling the canalside trail. This road gradually drops down to pass under the canal, then on to Meckenlohe and Roth. Bike straight through and past Roth *Stadtmitte*. At the train tracks turn right on the marked Brombachsee bike route.

Follow the tracks to Georgensgmünd, then signs for a quiet road to Pleinfeld. In Pleinfeld cross the river as if to Road 2 but instead take the small road paralleling the river. By degrees this road comes closer to Road 2, ending at a rest area alongside the main road. At this point you must bike 2 km on the uncomfortably busy main road before the turnoff to Ellingen.

Ellingen, with its *Schloss* of the Teutonic knights, and walled Weissenburg are both interesting historic towns. For the final stretch, cross over railroad tracks near the *Bahnhof* in Weissenburg. Turn left to parallel the tracks, following the marked Treuchtlingen bike route along poorly surfaced trails. Keep on the west side of the tracks until Graben, then cross over and pedal into Treuchtlingen.

TOUR NO. 3

BAVARIAN BACKWATERS
The Altmühl Valley

Distance: 176 kilometers (109 miles)
Estimated time: 3 to 4 days (3 biking days)
Terrain: Easy riverside biking
Map: ADFC #22
Connecting tours: Tour Nos. 2, 4, and 5

Many excellent bicycle tours follow river valleys, combining the advantage of gentle waterside terrain with a scenic landscape. While thousands of cyclists tour the Loire, Danube, and Mosel valleys annually, smaller, quieter valleys are left to those in the know. The quiet green valley formed by the Altmühl River, a tributary of the Danube, is often overlooked by cyclists in search of better-known game. The Altmühltal may not boast as many castles or the manicured market squares of more famous tourist destinations, but that is all part of the valley's charm.

This is not just another pretty valley dotted by historic towns.

A clifftop monastery overlooks the twisting Altmühl Valley.

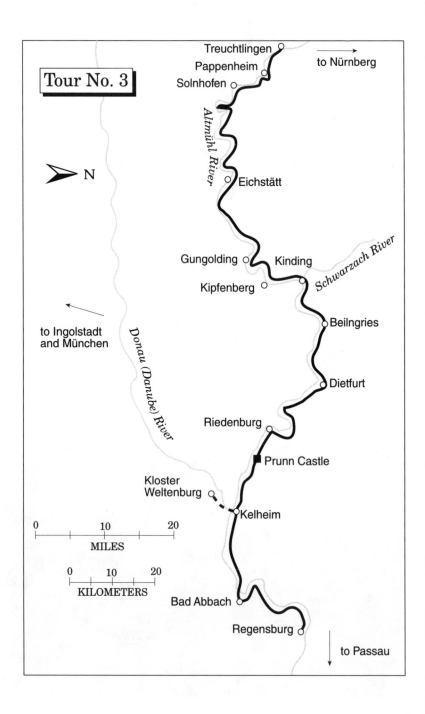

Covered by a Jurassic sea millions of years ago (proof that there was a premedieval Germany), the Altmühltal is known today for its rich fossil deposits. An Ammonite shell fossil, symbol of the *Naturpark*, marks a well-signed bicycle trail that winds through the nature preserve.

Word spreads quickly; recently this route has gained popularity among German cyclists, but trails remain uncrowded. Unfortunately, "progress," in the form of the Main–Donau Canal, has already invaded the valley at the halfway point of this tour. You will notice a marked difference between the river's gentle meanders on the first day and the sharp, intrusive lines of the canal on the second. Therefore the genuine Altmühl will not accompany you throughout the entire tour. Nevertheless, this Bavarian "backwater" remains one of the best biking destinations in Germany.

Treuchtlingen

The tour begins in Treuchtlingen, a convenient point of entry into the valley. Bike into town from Tour Nos. 1 or 2 in the north (see Tour No. 2: Connection to Tour No. 3), or overland from Donauwörth on the Danube to the south. Though not a large town, Treuchtlingen lies on a direct train line to Nürnberg, Würzburg, and München, quickly reached with the help of the *Bundesbahn*. In Treuchtlingen you will find an information office, rooms for rent, and a supermarket.

If arriving by train, turn right out of Treuchtlingen *Bahnhof* and ride down the hill. Immediately ahead, signs indicate the bicycle route (*Radwanderweg*) for Pappenheim and Solnhofen.

Campers get a head start by pedaling to the nearest site, 8 km away in Pappenheim (supermarket here also). The Altmühl bicycle route passes right by the campsite entrance. Pappenheim's campsite is my all-time favorite in Germany. Like many others in the valley, the campsite stretches along the river. Best of all, cyclists get their own little island in the Altmühl, connected only by a small footbridge that keeps caravans on the main shore. You may even get the island to yourself, complete with riverside steps and views of the church and castle above.

A *Naturpark*, the valley caters to cyclists, hikers, and paddlers. A system of riverside maps and signed shore rest points intended for canoeists and kayakers also aid bikers. Best of all, free campsites have been established for tents-only travelers, small grassy clearings directly along the river. These sites provide an excellent opportunity to free camp in clearly defined, easy-to-locate areas. You'll have to do without the amenities of commercial sites. No running water, but garbage cans, picnic table, and a toilet are provided at each. Look for these *Zeltmöglichkeit* (tent-only) sites at Inching, Gungolding, Kipfenberg, Kinding, Kottingwörth, Töging, and Dietfurt. Although this tour is based on commercial sites, riders comfortable with free camping can use the free sites where convenient to their progress. The Gungolding site in particular makes an appropriate stopping point, making the first day 60 km.

Rocky outcroppings and the occasional *Biergarten* punctuate the green valley, narrowing and widening at successive river bends, unmarred by busy roads or development. Cyclists looking for rooms will find *Zimmer* advertised throughout the valley.

Treuchtlingen to Beilngries: 82 kilometers

Altmühltal *Radwanderweg* signs are so consistently posted throughout the day that detailed directions are unnecessary. Simply follow the Ammonite symbol from one town to the next. Signs may indicate either the next town or more distant, important points. Ride to **Solnhofen**, **Hagenacker**, and **Dollnstein**. Most sections of the route are unpaved but perfectly suitable for biking.

One of the Altmühltal's most significant fossil finds, the *Urvogel*, also marks bicycle-route signs for a section of the route. *Urvogel* demonstrates a transition stage between reptile and bird. A small museum in Solnhofen displays many excellent fossil samples. Across the street (just before the *Bahnhof*), a store sells more ordinary examples, worth a stop in order to hold fossils in your hands and examine them closely.

After 38 km of idyllic valley cycling, you will reach **Eichstätt**, the most important town of the upper valley. You may be a bit shocked by the transition from solitary riverside meandering to the relative clamor of the town's prelunch rush—as well as by conspicuous evidence of the town's Italian rococo style.

There is plenty to see and do in Eichstätt. The tourist office merits a stop if only for entertaining reading. In the words of the official brochure, "Eichstätt is a delightful mosaic made up by a wide variety of interesting facilities, full of frolicsome gaiety, romantic, and yet bustling with lively activities." Visitors may "indulge in unrestrained pleasure." Whew!

The following statements from the brochure provide a sampler of the official top ten reasons to visit Eichstätt: "Numerous special and profane buildings which are well worth seeing. An interesting set of museums. Peaceful tranquility unaffected by mass tourist amusement." Among the profane and special structures in town are the impressive *Residenz*, with its square and Column of the Virgin, and the market square, its Willibald fountain honoring the city's

Medieval watchtowers guard Beilngries.

founder. More profane buildings cluster outside Eichstätt: the *Sommerresidenz* of the Prince-Bishops, Rebdorf monastery, St. Walburg Abbey, and Willibaldsburg Castle high across the river (Jurassic museum inside).

Shop for food in Eichstätt if you are planning a picnic or to free camp at Gungolding, as there are no stores near the site. Return to the riverbank to pick up the **bicycle trail** again. The free camp site lies just past Gungolding. From this point, Arnsberg's cliff monastery comes into view across the valley. Another 16 km of **sharp bends** will bring you past **Kipfenberg**'s castle and to a broad section of the valley, where the Schwarzach River merges with the Altmühl. **Cross under** the *Autobahn*, riding to **Kinding** and Beilngries.

You can **detour** to Greding, 8 km north in the Schwarzach Valley. The walled town is fairly interesting but a horrendous bicycle trail spoils the ride. The trail consists of rough gravel, following a valley roaring with *Autobahn* noise.

At the end of the day, campers have their pick of two campsites, one in quiet Kratzmühle, the other in Beilngries. The latter lies to the right of the bicycle trail. Again, tents get an island site, this time shared with caravans. Head for **Beilngries** center to shop and visit the old town, a modest little collection of medieval walls, short towers trying their best to look menacing. Walk the town perimeter, and view Hirschberg's *Schloss* looking down from high above.

Beilngries to Kelheim: 49 kilometers

From Beilngries **continue** along the valley, following **signs** for *Altmühltal/Tour de Baroque Radweg*. Unlike the first day, the bicycle route now links side roads instead of separate trails. At some points upon entering towns, the bicycle route ends, but signs will resume once you are past town.

By **Dietfurt** the valley widens and the Main–Donau Canal enters to smother the meandering river. So much for progress. The valley ride remains nice, but sharp canal edges cannot compare to the pretty, meandering Altmühl. Dietfurt's medieval center has been similarly overshadowed by modern additions.

From Dietfurt ride to **Mühlbach** and **Schweinkofen**. After 2 km **cross a lock** to **Deising** and the south side of the valley. Soon signs lead past **Haidhof** camping on the way to **Riedenburg**, the last campsite before Regensburg. Campers can choose this site, free camp near Kelheim, find a room, or bike on to Regensburg from Kelheim.

Riedenburg's old town lies on the west side of the valley, with a small *Marktplatz* and castle ruins above. Switch back to the **north bank** for the 4 km ride to **Prunn**. High above on a sheer cliff, Prunn

Sheer cliffs of the Donau gorge near Kloster Weltenburg

Castle is the valley's most impressive. In the castle's shadow, water-side picnic tables make a good place for a break.

From Prunn, choose from **two bicycle trails**. Paved routes numbered 5/14 parallel the road, while farther from car noise, the unpaved *Tour de Baroque* trail continues beside the canal. After another 12 km, you will enter **Kelheim**. Follow bicycle signs to the *Altstadt*, sandwiched between the canal to the north and the Donau to the south. A slim, single church tower serves as your guide to Kelheim's *Marktplatz* and tourist office. Take a curving pedestrian bridge over the canal and duck under the town gates to explore Kelheim's small town center. Signs advertise *Zimmer* around town. The hostel lies on the north bank of the canal in Ihrlerstein.

Kelheim marks the confluence of the Altmühl and Donau; this tour continues east along the *Donauradweg* (see Additional Suggested Tours) to historic Regensburg. Before moving on, however, look into boat excursions to Weltenburg Monastery. The highly recommended boat ride takes you south through a dramatic gorge of the Donau (DM 5 per person one way, DM 3 per bike). The monastery can also be reached overland, but only a boat trip provides views of the *Donaudurchbruch* (gorge). Kloster Weltenburg is famous for its Baroque architecture and masterful artisanry, but most people go to sample the monastery's home brew. Boats depart south of Kelheim center from *Schiffsanlegestelle* (moorages) on the Donau.

Kelheim to Regensburg: 45 kilometers

Resume the eastward ride along the **north bank** of the canal and then the Danube proper, now following *Donauradweg* signs. This long-distance route connects sections of road with trails, clearly marked at most intersections.

The ride begins along a wide but quiet road. Ten km from Kelheim, cross **under train tracks** and ride through **Poikam**. The campground west of town is not open to the public, but may accept cyclists in a pinch. At the ambiguous bicycle sign in town, go **left**, not straight toward the church. The *Radweg* will bring you across the Donau to **Bad Abbach** and all the way to Regensburg along the river's south/east bank.

Apparently the bike people and the road people forgot to consult in Bad Abbach: the *Donauradweg* points north onto the road, where a sign forbids bikes. Take your pick of the **sidewalk or forbidden road**. In either case you will soon turn onto an **unpaved track** along the river. Later **return** to the lightly traveled road (now permitting cyclists), and finally back along a riverside **bicycle lane** into **Regensburg**.

This bicycle trail leads directly past Regensburg's campground, a pleasant, wooded site full of hopping bunnies (4 km west of the center). Pass the site, then turn inland and right to reach the entrance. Ask directions to the cheap Netto supermarket nearby. To find a room or the hostel (on an island just north and east of the city center), continue along the riverside trail. For orientation on the way in, check the city map located next to a canal lock 2 km outside town.

A lively university city, Regensburg dates back to Roman times. Of the Roman fort, only the Porta Praetoria gate remains, but many artifacts are displayed in the *Stadtmuseum* on Dachauplatz. A Gothic *Dom* dominates the old town streets, lined with shops, cafes, and pedestrians. Regensburg has gone untouched by war since Napoleon's days, accounting for its excellent state of preservation. You can't miss the *Marktplatz* with its fountain, but be sure to search out smaller squares as well, like *Fischmarkt* nearer the Donau. Off *Marktplatz*, walk Hinter der Grieb, an alley lined with historic houses. In Regensburg, city residents complain of high annual rainfall—hence the city's name (*Regen* means rain).

From Regensburg several biking possibilities will tempt you to pedal onward. Most cyclists continue east to Passau and Austria with the *Donauradweg*. You can also double back over Kelheim to Ingolstadt and then turn south to München (see Connection to Tour No. 4, below). Hardy cyclists may leave crowds behind by turning into the hills to the north. Regensburg's tourist office sells guides to various long-distance bicycle routes in the area, including the *Donauradweg* and the *Fünf-Flüsse* tour, among others.

Connection to Tour No. 4

Regensburg to München: 189 kilometers. From Regensburg retrace your route along the Donau to Kelheim, and continue following the *Donauradweg* west to Ingolstadt. This ride is entirely level except for a 3-km climb over the hill to Kloster Weltenburg. Clever riders will take a boat from Kelheim to the monastery, enjoying views of the gorge and avoiding the climb.

The *Donauradweg*, while clearly signed in most places, meanders quite a bit. If you're impatient to reach your destination, keep a close eye on your map and take shortcuts over side roads whenever the trail wanders. The red bicycle route indicated on the ADFC map takes a more direct route than the *Donauradweg* but still keeps to quiet roads.

Ingolstadt, like Regensburg, is a Donau city with a long history. Much of the city wall remains, including the impressive Kreuztor. Make your way to Ingolstadt's castle and visit one of the historic churches, most notably the Maria de Victoria Kirche with its frescoes. Ingolstadt is 88 km from Regensburg and 101 km from München, therefore a convenient overnight point. There is a hostel near Kreuztor and the old town. The lakeside campground 4 km east of the city can be difficult to find if coming straight from the Donau's shore, but signs from the city center lead to the site.

From Ingolstadt turn south for the long run into München. Stay on Road 13, where traffic remains fairly light since the nearby *Autobahn* diverts most cars. Bicycle lanes parallel Road 13 from Ingolstadt center to Reichertshofen. There, take a side road to Starkertshofen and Freinhausen, where you can join Road 13 again. The rolling road leads to Pfaffenhofen, Hohenkammer, and finally Unterschleißheim on the outskirts of München.

In Unterschleißheim leave the road in favor of bicycle trails. For the easiest route into München, turn east on the bike trail to Garching, Ismaning, and Freimann to reach the Isar River. Then simply follow the riverside bicycle trail south to the city center or the campground beyond (see Tour No. 4). To speed entry into the city, take an *S-bahn* commuter train from Unterschleißheim directly to München *Hauptbahnhof* (bikes permitted on *S-bahn* except during rush hours).

TOUR NO. 4

CASTLE TOWERS, MOUNTAIN PEAKS

München, Upper Bavaria, and the Romantic Road

Distance: 368 kilometers (228 miles)
Estimated time: 7 to 8 days (6 biking days)
Terrain: Challenging mountain climbs
in middle section of tour
Map: ADFC #26
Connecting tours: Tour Nos. 3 and 5

This challenging tour of Upper Bavaria includes many of Germany's superlative sights, from the Zugspitze, the country's highest mountain, to Neuschwanstein, its most celebrated castle, and München, one of the most interesting cities. A combination of spectacular natural setting, friendly people, and unique sights makes this alpine area a favorite touring destination in Germany. Designed on the basis of several trips and the help of local friends, this route

Lake waters reflect mountain peaks in Upper Bavaria.

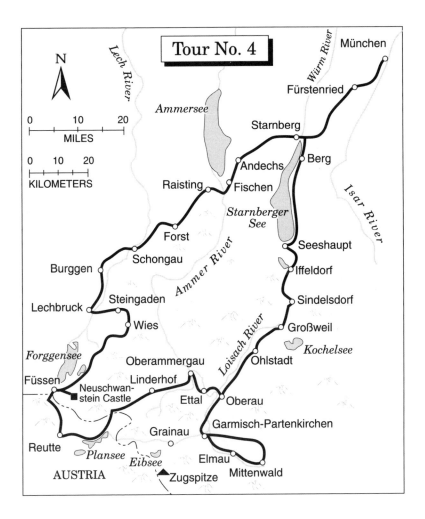

tours the best of Oberbayern (Upper Bavaria) in a week-long loop.

Historic München (Munich), home to BMW, *Oktoberfest*, and Germany's best soccer team, is the starting point of the trip, one of the liveliest and most enjoyable of German cities. From there, pedal south along lakeshores, a stunning panorama of mountains drawing you onward. Ride on to the resort of Garmisch-Partenkirchen, taking time off for hiking or biking day trips, then Oberammergau, site of the famous Passion Play, and finally the picture-perfect pilgrimage church of Wies. Two of Mad King Ludwig's fantasy castles also lie along this route, both the "Disney" castle (Neuschwanstein) and less-known Linderhof.

Like Tour No. 1, this tour includes a section of the Romantic Road near its terminus in Füssen. Although the middle section of this route involves challenging mountain climbs, the first two days take advantage of lakeshores and valleys for a nearly level ride. No matter what the terrain, new sights—and cool local beers—reward cyclists on this outstanding Bavarian tour.

Bayern (Bavaria)

Each of Germany's states has its own distinct character, history, and even dialect. Bayern, a separate kingdom until 1871, remains very independent-minded: Most residents consider themselves Bavarians first and Germans second. The stereotypical image of Germany is most obvious here in Bayern and especially München, from beer halls to oom-pah bands, right down to *Lederhosen*. Cyclists touring Bayern will notice these and more subtle differences. Language in particular varies widely. Though you will be surrounded by many tourists and English-speaking Germans in München, Bavarian mountain dialect may confuse you to the south. For starters, remember that the standard greeting in Bayern is *Grüss Gott*, not *Guten Tag*.

This tour begins and ends in München, capital of Bavaria.

München

Make your first stop in München the helpful Euraide office alongside Track 11 in the train station. The all-English-speaking office provides free city maps, train and tourist information, and room reservations both in the city and surrounding countryside (including Chiemsee area, handy for Tour No. 5). The office, open from May to mid-October, also receives mail and forwards messages (see Part I, Planning Your Bicycle Tour).

München's Thalkirchen campground lies directly along the Isar River's west bank, 8 km south of the city center. From your point of entry into München, head directly for the river and turn south on the east-bank bicycle trail, an excellent paved lane through the riverside park. On weekends, this becomes something of a kamikaze endeavor, as the trail turns into a bicycle *Autobahn*. Keep track of the bridges and reference points you pass under and by: (1) a railroad bridge; (2) a busy car bridge; (3) a pedestrian bridge over small but wide waterfalls; (4) a brick-colored auto bridge; (5) the zoo on the east bank; (6) another pedestrian bridge. Cross this last bridge over three arms of the river and turn left for the campground entrance.

The large campsite usually fills only during *Oktoberfest*. Services include a shop, laundry machines, and *Imbiss*. There is a cheaper supermarket near the Thalkirchen *U-bahn* stop. Crowds of young tourists will either entertain or drive you crazy during your stay. Though far from the city center, *U-bahn* connections and the nearby bicycle trail make the site a convenient place to stay.

München's hostels fill quickly. One is located only two blocks from the Thalkirchen *U-bahn* stop, near the campground, another farther south in a castle (Pullach), and a third near Schloss Nymphenburg. Remember, Bavarian hostels only accept members under 27 years of age.

There's plenty to keep you busy for days (weeks, years) in München, though the compact city center also lends itself to quicker tours for those on a tight schedule. The *Glockenspiel* at Neues Rathaus features jousting knights and dancing coopers, plus the bonus of crowd antics as tourists videotape the show. München is also one of the great museum cities of Germany (and Europe), with outstanding collections ranging from antiquities up to modern art and technology.

Follow the unsteady footsteps of enthusiastic travelers to the Hofbrauhaus, the oldest, most famous beer hall in München. For a good beer and *Bretzel* (pretzel) in a quieter setting, head for the outdoor beer garden in Englischer Garten. München's many churches are also (hic!) very interesting.

Farther from the city center, Olympiapark's cool green hillsides and quiet lakes make an excellent place to relax and picnic. If there happens to be a home game of the popular FC Bayern *Fußball* (soccer) team, forget about relaxing as the park swarms with riotous fans. Tickets for sporting events and concerts are sold in nearby Eisstadion or at the door on game days.

Of course, München is best known for *Oktoberfest*, running from the third Saturday in September to the first Sunday in October. The festival dates back to 1810; these days *Oktoberfest* consists of beer, rides and amusement booths, tourists, and more beer. Depending on your interests, therefore, either skip town or schedule extra time into your plans. Remember that accommodations are hard to come by at that time of year, and keep doubly alert about your bicycle and valuables. For extensive exploration without your bike, *U-bahn* day passes (DM 10) quickly pay off.

München to Seeshaupt: 54 kilometers (45 kilometers from Thalkirchen campground)

This first day makes an excellent introduction to the tour. Biking is easy and exciting with tremendous views of distant mountains slowly growing nearer and nearer. In another day you'll cycle right into the range, but meet no major climbs until leaving Garmisch-Partenkirchen on the third day.

Ride **southwest** out of München, aiming for **E6/A95** *Autobahn*. An excellent **bicycle path** (marked for Starnberg) parallels the highway on the **west side**, making for a loud but convenient and quick ride out of the city. (Cyclists wishing to skip this section of the ride may go directly to Starnberg by *S-bahn* commuter train and begin the tour from there; bicycles permitted except during rush hours; the S6 line runs directly from the main München station to Starnberg.)

Eventually the bicycle path joins a quiet road, still alongside the *Autobahn*. Once south 10 km from **Solln**, pedal through **Wangen** and 2 km later cross **under** the *Autobahn* with the **side road**. Descend on a bike lane into **Percha**, gaining your first views of the beautiful Starnberger See (lake).

In Percha you will come to an **intersection**. **Turn for Berg** on the road running **south** along the east shore (*Ostufer*) of the lake. Ride 3 km on a separate **bicycle lane** along the main road before veering **right** for peaceful lakeshores (square white bicycle sign: *Kreiswanderweg*).

However, as you head south along the road, take a moment to **detour** to the lakeshore on any dead-end street to the right. From the northern beach you will have breathtaking views of the long, blue lake pointing south. In the distance, the mountain ridge of Oberbayern suddenly rears up, snow-capped peaks white between a (hopefully) blue sky and water. The best vantage point is here in the north because the narrow lake runs due north-south, with trees often blocking the view during the ride to **Seeshaupt**. Hazy afternoons sometimes obscure the view, making morning the best time to catch this amazing sight.

Kreiswanderweg leads to a good dirt track through woods, past the small *Votivkapelle* in Berg, then along resident-cars-only lanes by the shore. You'll enjoy a lovely, woody ride on quiet roads all day. Pop out onto narrow strips of pebbly beach to take a closer look at the lake and mountains on occasion.

At one point near Berg the bicycle route turns away from the lakeshore but soon returns. In **Ambach** the waterside lanes end, bringing you back to the road for a short stretch. Pass by a campground south of Ambach in favor of the St. Heinrich campground or a third site, just east of Seeshaupt. The St. Heinrich site seems to have the longest shoreline, therefore offering a better chance at waterfront space with partial views both north up the lake and south to the mountains. Seeshaupt's site is tidier and closer to town but faces north, offering good views up the lake but not of the mountains.

Stop at the Rewe supermarket in **Seeshaupt**, where you will also find several cafes, restaurants, and a bicycle shop. Claim a lakeside bench by the ferry landing to enjoy the scenery's greens and blues and get excited for the mountains ahead.

Seeshaupt to Garmisch-Partenkirchen: 50 kilometers

Just east of the Seeshaupt campsite, take the **marked turnoff** on a quiet back road to Schechen. Ride through **Schechen** and **Sanimoor**, emerging at a Y intersection with a golf course ahead. Go **right** here (not left to Eurach), then **left** on the main road into **Iffeldorf**. Follow signs to **Antdorf**, circling around town for signs **south** to Garmisch-Partenkirchen. Two km later go left for Sindelsdorf.

Pass under the *Autobahn*, then turn **right** into **Sindelsdorf**. From the south edge of town follow **signs** to Großweil, paralleling the *Autobahn* on a quiet road. Although you will pedal right up to and into the mountains on this day, gaps between peaks allow a nearly flat ride.

In **Großweil** turn **right** for Schwaiganger, picking up **bicycle signs** for the remainder of the ride into Garmisch-Partenkirchen. Pedal behind the white **Schwaiganger** church, riding dirt and then paved trails to **Ohlstadt**. Follow the main road straight through Ohlstadt, but turn **left** on Heubergstrasse just before the railroad crossing for a **bicycle path** to **Buchenried** and **Eschenlohe**. In Eschenlohe pedal right up to a **bridge** over the Loisach, but **do not cross** the river. Again, bear **left** along paved paths **south** to **Oberau** and Garmisch-Partenkirchen. These trails are unpaved at first but good rideable surfaces for the most part. One short, gravelly section is better walked, but by Oberau the paths are well paved. Finally, follow a bicycle lane south along **Road 2** into the twin towns, passing **Burgrain** with its hostel on the way.

Camping lies 4 km east of the center; follow signs **right** for Garmisch and Fernpaß/Reutte/Grainau to bike **Road 23** to the site, passing a supermarket on the way. Avoid traffic with the help of a separate bicycle lane on the left. There are plenty of rooms in **Garmisch-Partenkirchen**. However, I am biased toward Grainau, a small town with a quieter setting directly under the Zugspitze. To reach the town, pass the campground and the first Obergrainau sign, then go left for Grainau. Go down Loisachstrasse 2 km and make a left turn toward Obergrainau to reach a street lined by decorated houses, all offering rooms.

In order to host the 1936 Olympics, two towns merged as Garmisch-Partenkirchen. They remain a top European winter sports center even today, hosting many world-class competitions. Off season, the towns draw hikers and vacationers. While the center hums with activity, quiet corners preserve their original character. Beautifully painted houses, typical of this alpine area, cluster around Garmisch's Alte Kirche. Look around the towns, then look out—and up—to the area's real attraction.

Dominating the valley, the Zugspitze is Germany's highest mountain. Choose from any of countless hiking and excursion possibilities in the area. A popular hike leads through the woods from Grainau to beautiful Eibsee, a lake mirroring the Zugspitze's peak in its clear waters. Less frequently trod paths explore other pockets of the valley. The tourist office and kiosks in town sell hiking maps, practical guides that double as souvenirs of the area.

The mountains may also be enjoyed with minimal effort, via a cog railway to the Zugspitze's very summit. A hefty fee (DM 50) buys you a fun ride and an amazing panorama: On a clear day, you can see the Dachstein Glacier in Austria, the Tyrolean Alps, and Bavarian lowlands to the north, including the Starnberger See. Board the train either in Garmisch *Zugspitzbahnhof* or in Grainau. For a challenging day trip, ride the Mittenwald loop described below.

Mittenwald Day Trip: 45 kilometers

Typical of the alpine region's decorated towns, Mittenwald makes an excellent day trip from Garmisch-Partenkirchen. On the advice of friends, I followed a roundabout route and loved the ride. Tourers wary of conditions described below may opt to make a back-and-forth trip along the usual way (Road 2) instead.

This trip is more of a hike/bike excursion than a cycling day trip, so be patient. It lets you enjoy the journey as much as the destination, provided you approach it with a good sense of humor and adventure. The route climbs the steep Partnachklamm Valley and follows dirt roads through the lower mountains, past alpine lakes and endless woods with spectacular views of neighboring peaks from a new angle. A few steep sections and poor roads force you to dismount at times; hence the hike/bike.

Begin the trip behind the Olympic ski **stadium** in Garmisch-Partenkirchen. Take a **dead-end road** to the foot of the Partnachklamm, following hiking signs to **Graseck**. So far, so good. But next, you will come to a long, incredibly **steep uphill** (paved); time to practice "hiking with bike."

When the pavement ends in **Vorder Graseck**, take the **left** branch of a smooth dirt trail up to **Hinter Graseck**. Once over the hill's crest, follow signs to **Elmau** (lower right trail). Now you can begin the biking portion of the trip along the Ferchen Valley, following a good **dirt track** through the woods. Pavement by Schloss Elmau provides only temporary relief as you must immediately take a **sharp right** turn into a parking area, picking up signs to Mittenwald. The dirt road continues past pretty **Ferchensee** and **Lautersee**, where pavement finally resumes. After a sweeping downhill run into **Mittenwald**, you are ready for a well-deserved lunch.

Mittenwald's fame stems from both its scenic alpine location and the many painted houses in town. Unfortunately, this reputation (and convenient location between Garmisch and Innsbruck) often clogs Mittenwald's streets with visitors. For a clearer perspective on the old town, poke around quieter side streets. Multicolored decorations encircle windows, while intricate scenes painted on house walls feature folk or Biblical figures. There are many bakeries and shops in Mittenwald, and cheaper grocery stores just outside the town center (in the direction of Garmisch).

Returning to Garmisch is less of an adventure. Leave Mittenwald center on the main road to Garmisch-Partenkirchen (**Road 2**), but turn **left** for **Klais** to gain a quieter road soon after. In Klais **do not cross** the train tracks. Instead, bear **left** to pick up bicycle signs to Garmisch-Partenkirchen. The bicycle trail is first **rough but then paved**, leading you on a quick and easy ride to Garmisch. The path ends shortly before town where you will rejoin the main road.

Garmisch-Partenkirchen to Füssen: 82 kilometers

This challenging day includes a sampler of this Bavarian tour's best, riding through beautiful mountain valleys to visit castles and historic towns. With plenty to see and do along the way, you can count on a long, full day. Campgrounds at Plansee (56 km) and Reutte (67 km) help shorten the ride but may be inconvenient as they are in Austria, meaning you might be obligated to change a small amount of money into the Austrian *Schilling* (although in border areas, the *Deutsche Mark* may also be accepted). Otherwise stock up in Garmisch and make the ride all the way into Füssen.

Retrace your route **north** from Garmisch on the bicycle trail **paralleling Road 2/23**. (If you miss the trailhead, follow the main road to Farchant and turn right on Bahnhofstrasse to pick up signs for the pleasant, paved trail to **Oberau**.)

In Oberau **cross** the **river**, **train tracks**, and **Road 2** to join **Road 23** to Ettal. The 6 km to **Ettal** are mostly uphill, but there you will enter a beautiful mountain valley and enjoy level riding for most of the morning. On the way, you may meet Ettal's gym teacher, who pedals this long hill every morning.

To reach little Ettal's main attraction, turn off the road and pass

Wood carvings animate a roadside near Ettal.

under an arch into the *Kloster* courtyard. The Benedictine abbey's church is beautifully painted from each small niche to the cupola high above. An informative pamphlet in English details both the abbey's history and artworks of the church.

From Ettal bike onward to Oberammergau, turning **off Road 23** for a bicycle path along the Ammer River. As you approach town, ignore the sign pointing right, under the road. Instead, continue **straight ahead** as if to Unterammergau, passing apartment buildings and a hill within the valley. Around the corner, the tower of Oberammergau's church serves as your guide into the town center.

Oberammergau is most famous for its Passion Play, staged by town residents once every ten years as thanks for being spared from a seventeenth-century plague (next play performance: the year 2000). Clever, these Oberammergau citizens: Put on a big play every ten years, and enjoy free tourist trade all the years in between! Passion Play aside, the town is worth a detour for its painted houses (one near the church depicts the first play performance) and shops, as Oberammergau is also a renowned woodcarving center.

Return to the Linden Valley by crossing to the Ammer River's **west bank** and riding a quiet road to **Graswang**. The flat road to Linderhof carries only infrequent traffic—the few tourists who make it out of München's Hofbrauhaus rarely make it this far. At the **sign** for Linderhof, turn off the road and bike past a toll gate (fee for motorized vehicles only) to the main entrance. The small Baroque palace and formal gardens contrast greatly with Neuschwanstein, King Ludwig II's most famous castle, in every aspect except its beautiful natural setting. A hefty DM 7 entrance fee is charged at the gate, but no one checks your ticket until the palace door, so you can see the grounds for free.

While the Austrian border is actually 7 km farther on, the German checkpoint stands just beyond Linderhof. I was surprised to find the road closed in early May and listened, mortified, as a guard described how I could push my bike over a long detour through the woods. Apparently the road sometimes closes due to danger—of what, I didn't quite catch—something to do with falling forces of nature (avalanche? flood? locusts?). In summer this is rarely a problem, he assured me. There may be an hour around noon when you may pass through, as I did (evidently siesta time for falling forces of nature).

The road to Austria begins on the level and then climbs in a few steep sections, but you will soon descend to the blue waters of

Picture-perfect Schloss Linderhof

Plansee. There are two campgrounds here, one on either end of the lake. The ride to **Reutte**, 11 km farther, includes a few more uphill sections, and again a downhill into town. The campground is signed from Reutte center. If you end your day here, consider visiting castle ruins south of town. Füssen, however, is only 15 km away at this point.

Follow **signs** to Deutschland and Füssen through Reutte. At the north edge of **Pflach** turn **right** for a quieter road north, signed to **Pinswang**. Regrettably this road climbs over the **Kniepaß**, but all those arrows on the map exaggerate the hill's difficulty. Soon you will be coasting by **Unterpinswang**. Then rejoin the **main road** to Füssen and **recross** the border into Germany. Even if the guards wave you through, take a moment here to see the waterfall beside the road.

It's just a quick 2 km to **Füssen**. Time to confront the last challenges of the day: food and lodging. Across the Lech River, Füssen is a compact, pleasant town complete with pedestrian zone, scores of tourist shops, and a central fountain. For cheap shopping, ask for the Lidl grocery store. As popular tourist destinations, Füssen and the surrounding towns offer many accommodations options, including a hostel west of town. There are plenty of rooms for rent throughout the area. A pleasant lakeside campsite lies 4 km away in Brunnen— marked from the main road north (Road 17 to Schongau).

Füssen to Lechbruck: 35 kilometers

This day is short for two reasons: first, to allow plenty of time at King Ludwig's nearby castles, and second, to shorten the next day's return to München. Those in a hurry can squeeze this day together with the one before or the following, but you will be pressed for time at the sights and face a long total distance.

Other monarchs earned titles like Grand and Great, but King Ludwig II of Bavaria (1845–1886) enjoys lasting fame as the Mad. His most fantastic creation, the fairy-tale Neuschwanstein castle, served as a model for Disney's Cinderella castle. The multitowered castle is an amazing sight in itself, the impression further enhanced by its spectacular mountain location. Follow the *Königschlösser* **bicycle trail** (*K*) from Füssen to reach the castlebound foot path. It's a hefty hike up, but the castle is a must-see, so go see. For best views of the castle and mountains, hike to the bridge spanning a gorge behind.

Ludwig II spend much of his youth in Hohenschwangau, the yellow, lakeside castle below. Having toured both Linderhof and Neuschwanstein, you have now seen two of Mad Ludwig's three castles; to visit the third, Herrenchiemsee, follow Tour No. 5 from Salzburg to München.

Mad King Ludwig's Neuschwanstein castle

The short ride to Lechbruck begins to close the loop to München by leading **north**, away from the mountains. Terrain gradually begins to flatten out, except during the hilly detour to Wieskirche. Leave the Füssen area along **Road 17**, riding the **parallel bicycle trail**. The trail diverges slightly from 17 but rejoins it in **Halblech**. There, you must pedal with traffic until **Unterreithen** and the **right** turn for **Wies**. Follow hiking signs and the *K* **bicycle route** across meadows (*Wies* means meadow) on paved or firm unpaved surfaces. Don't be fooled by those arrows on the map—there are several short, steep sections over the rolling terrain but no killer climbs.

The pretty, white Wieskirche sits in a deep green meadow and against a bright blue sky (in good weather), the perfect beacon for pilgrims. Nowadays most pilgrims are tourists, but for good reason, as the tiny frescoed church is indeed a beautiful sight. Even Dominikus Zimmermann, designer and painter of the church, was reluctant to leave the site of his masterpiece, and lived the rest of his life nearby. The Wieskirche ranks high among the most tasteful rococo you'll see, so I highly recommend this detour.

Afterward, cruise down to **Steingaden** and follow signs to **Lechbruck**. The campground above the lake is just north of town, with views of the mountains. For rooms, check in Steingaden or head right for Schongau.

Lechbruck to München: 102 kilometers

The last day of this tour brings you back to lakes and flatter terrain near München. From Lechbruck bicycle **north** along a quiet road to **Burggen**. Ignore all those frightening arrows on the map—you can expect a few short, steep climbs but nothing more. In Burggen first follow **signs** to Schongau. By a small corner chapel, turn **right** on Engenwiesstrasse for a quiet shortcut. Turn **right** when the road emerges onto busy **Road 472** into Schongau. To enter the old market town that lies along the former Roman road from Italy to Augsburg, turn **right** for *Stadtmitte*.

Bike straight through **Schongau** on the single main road. Just before the opposite gate, turn **left** on Lechtorstrasse to exit. Go down a **steep hill** (marked "no bikes," best to walk down) and **join the road** below. **Cross** the river and follow **bicycle lanes** along the main road toward Peiting. The lane ends for a short stretch but soon resumes on the opposite side of the road.

The **road splits** 2 km past Schongau center. Take the quiet **left** branch to **Herzogsägmühle** and **Birkland**. Here, unfortunately, those arrows on the map indicating uphill are true—prepare for a **long, slow climb**. Continue on the rolling road **right**, to **Forst**, passing tidy one-barn "towns" along the way. In **St. Leonhard**, go left for **Zellsee**, an enjoyable downhill ride.

At the T go **left** for **Wessobrunn**, then take the first **right** marked only by a *K* bicycle sign. Where the pavement ends bear **right**. Bump along a wide, rideable dirt road to Raisting, rejoining pavement after **Unterstillern**. In **Raisting** go **right** at the church and ride toward **Pähl**. After 5 km turn **left** for Fischen, skirting the Ammersee. To avoid traffic, pedal a paved **tractor trail** alongside this busy road. In **Fischen** turn **right** for Erling and Andechs, bracing for a 4-km **uphill** ride with views over the Ammersee. Once in **Erling**, however, you will reach easier terrain. Stop at the Spar market for picnic supplies before riding 1 km to **Andechs**, the "beer monastery." The name speaks for itself.

Buses bring many tourists to sample the monks' home brew. The heavenly odor wafts around the church tower and cobblestone alleys of the monastery. Many Germans swear that beer is just the thing for a hot afternoon of cycling—if you want to test the theory, here's the spot. There is more than just beer at Andechs: J. B., Dominikus Zimmermann's big brother, painted the frescoes of the monastery's *Klosterkirche*, accounting for similarities with the Wieskirche.

Back in Erling follow **signs to Starnberg**. A **bicycle lane** parallels the busy road over rolling terrain, ending at **Söcking**, where you must join the traffic. Watch out for kamikaze traffic on the way down to this ritzy suburb. Expensive boutiques and traffic line **Starnberg**'s downtown area. To reach the quieter lakeside promenade, follow signs to *Bahnhof* (pass under the tracks to the right of the station). There you can relax and take in the lake and mountain view, surveying the area you toured in the past days.

In Starnberg you have practically closed the loop of the tour, which began nearby, at the north end of the lake. A good alternative to backtracking the monotonous 25 km back into München is to simply hop on an *S-bahn* at Starnberg *Bahnhof* for a quick and easy return to the city center, making a total of 77 km ridden today by bike. (If you are headed back to the campground in Thalkirchen, on the other hand, biking remains a good option because the *S-bahn* does not stop near that area. Ride the main road, with a bicycle lane in sections, through Starnberg toward München and the *Autobahn*, then exit for Perching and retrace your original route via Wangen and Fürstenried.)

Back in München, grab a beer, do a victory lap of the old town, see sights you missed before, grab another beer, and head back out on the road. Taking easterly winds into account, you can take a train to Salzburg and ride Tour No. 5 back to München, putting off your final goodbye to the Bavarian capital. With legs toughened by the past tour, you can consider biking west over the Allgäu region to reach Tour No. 6 and the Bodensee (Lake Constance). Constant ups and downs characterize that challenging ride along part of the German Alpine Road. As a major rail hub, München's *Hauptbahnhof* offers frequent connections to points near and far.

TOUR NO. 5

BAVARIAN HIGHWATERS
Salzburg to München

Distance: 263 kilometers (163 miles)
Estimated time: 6 to 7 days (4 biking days)
Terrain: From easy level sections to long mountain climbs
Maps: ADFC #26 and #27
Connecting tour: Tour No. 4

Bavarian Highwaters focuses on two of Europe's most enjoyable cities and the high alpine lakes between. Challenging mountain cycling characterizes the first half of the tour, with more gentle terrain in the Bavarian lowlands. From Mozart's Salzburg, just over the border in Austria, the tour rides up—and up—to the first alpine lake, picture-perfect Königsee. The lake and nearby Berchtesgaden

Typical Bavarian farmhouses line the route near Taubensee.

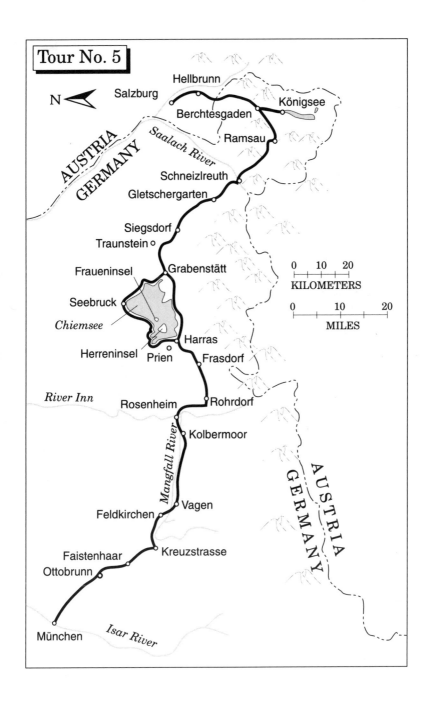

Tour No. 5

N

Salzburg
Hellbrunn
Königsee
Berchtesgaden
Ramsau
AUSTRIA
GERMANY
Saalach River
Schneizlreuth
Gletschergarten
Siegsdorf
Traunstein
Fraueninsel
Grabenstätt
Seebruck
Chiemsee
Herreninsel Prien
Harras
Frasdorf
River Inn
Rosenheim
Rohrdorf
Mangfall River
Kolbermoor
AUSTRIA
GERMANY
Feldkirchen
Vagen
Faistenhaar
Kreuzstrasse
Ottobrunn
München
Isar River

0 10 20
KILOMETERS

0 10 20
MILES

draw crowds curious to see Hitler's Eagle Nest retreat (Kehlstein, perched high above). Descending to Chiemsee, a popular recreation area, cyclists can visit Mad King Ludwig's third castle on an island in Bavaria's largest lake. Finally, pedal into München, your tour of Germany's alpine corner complete.

Steady easterly winds recommend against making this tour in the reverse direction. Of course, it is also possible to begin the tour in München and ride toward Salzburg, with many exciting biking options from that point. However, those pestering winds may fight your progress; check on conditions before setting off.

Salzburg

Inter-Regio trains with bicycle compartments run frequently between München and Salzburg, the best way to reach the tour's starting point from Germany. At the Salzburg *Bahnhof* do not go downstairs before stopping for tourist information on Track 10. A helpful office there distributes city maps and offers a room-finding service. Take the elevator to ground level and you are ready to hit Salzburg.

Turn left out of the station to pick up signs to Salzburg center. The nearest campground is 4 km away off Road B1 (direction Linz). B1 begins at the main auto bridge in the center of town (Staatsbrücke; follow Linzer Gasse onto B1). Ride northeast on B1, cross train tracks, and take the first right onto Parscherstrasse. There are also several hostels in Salzburg, the most central on Josef-Preis Allee just outside the old town. To change money, head for a bank in the city center. Austria's currency is the *Schilling*, and store hours are similar to the German schedule.

Sitting smugly in the protective shade of the hilltop fortress, Salzburg's old town serves up just what visitors expect—lively street scenes with horse-drawn carriages and corner musicians, cozy side streets and grand squares. Although the city is absolutely crushed with tourists, Salzburg's undeniable charm overcomes all intrusions. Slip into tourist denial mode ("I do not see these tour groups, they are not interrupting my view, I am biker....") and enjoy a wonderful old town.

Inevitably, a visit to Salzburg comes down to a treasure hunt for Mozart and *The Sound of Music*. The composer's birthplace is one of many historic houses on a shaded street; his residence now houses a museum. Appropriately, street musicians keep Mozartplatz, in the center of town, echoing with strains of Wolfie's music. Wherever you go in town, you'll be struck by familiar-looking places where Fräulein Maria and the kids once romped—*Domplatz*, horse pond, bridges over the Salzach—humming "doe, a deer," the whole time.

But Salzburg does not consist entirely of history and reruns. Today South American folk bands also liven the streets, and unexpected sights hide in nooks and crannies of the old town. Across the river, pretty Mirabell Palace with its gardens makes a good getaway, as does Schloss Hellbrunn to the south. Hike up to the fortress for views over the city's domes and rooftops to mountain peaks all around.

Salzburg to Berchtesgaden and Königsee: 32 kilometers

A short first day's ride brings you back to Germany and to Königsee. The road up is slightly graded the entire way, but you will encounter no truly difficult alpine climbs. Yet.

Leave Salzburg **south** on **Road 150** (305 in Germany). Signs from the old town point toward Berchtesgaden and the *Autobahn*. The road near Salzburg is very busy, but traffic lightens once you pass **Hellbrunn** and cross the *Autobahn* turnoff, leaving you a quiet ride all the way. The only difficult part of the ride is the last **short climb** into Berchtesgaden center (*Ortsmitte*).

Berchtesgaden is a small mountain town, very appealing in its combination of architecture and natural setting. See the *Schloss-*

Fountains and frescoes color the streets of Berchtesgaden.

Traditional decorations adorn a building at Berchtesgaden.

Mountain panorama at Königsee

platz, walk the small pedestrian area, or stop at a cafe. When ready for Königsee, follow **Road 20 south** for 5 km. The short biking distance from Salzburg leaves plenty of time for a boat ride, hike, or long picnic.

A large entrance sign says "Königsee Parkplatz," an unfortunate irony. At times it really seems that this stunning lakeside has turned into one giant parking lot. I was initially disappointed at the commercialization of the site. A narrow Disney-like tourist gauntlet leads to the waterfront where you can get a boat ride (DM 15 to 20), the only way to see the lake. Despite the herdlike atmosphere of the docks, the ride is worthwhile, with stops at tiny Königsee towns like St. Bartholoma with its pretty lakeside church. Once out on the water in a quiet electric boat, however, you will feel your hopes somewhat restored.

A bend obscures views of the lake's full length, but a quick 15-minute hike to Mirawinkel (left from the docks) will gain you the full panorama of sheer mountain walls dropping into the lake if you are not taking a boat ride. By hiking the quieter path and putting off my visit until late in the day, I got a much better (though still tarnished) impression of the lake.

The other top excursion (literally) is of course Kehlstein, Hitler's mountain retreat, which can be seen perched high above the Königsee (just look where all the pay binoculars are pointing). If you leaf through historical brochures sold at kiosks you will see the tremendous effort that went into building the mountain road, which (fool-)

hardy cyclists may pedal up. Others can take a bus for a spectacular mountain panorama including the lake and *Parkplatz* below.

If you are looking for a room, tourist offices in Berchtesgaden and Königsee *Parkplatz* can help. There are rooms close to the lake, but you may enjoy Berchtesgaden more, particularly in the evening when most tourists have departed. The nearest hostel is in Strub.

Picnickers and campers should shop ahead in Berchtesgaden (Kaiser's in the pedestrian area, Tengelmann at the bottom of the hill, or Edeka on the road to Königsee). There are two campgrounds within walking distance of the lake, both marked off Road 20. The first is cheaper but closer to the road (tents get a cozy corner facing the river) and also offers rooms. The second site is slightly nearer the lake, offering a full restaurant and other perks.

Königsee to Harras (Chiemsee): 76 kilometers

From Berchtesgaden, begin the day directly on **Road 305** from town. (If you are camping near Königsee begin your day by following the direct road to Schönau. Then follow signs to Ramsau to join **Road 305** farther west.)

Road 305 begins quietly, as most morning traffic (tourism) heads the opposite direction, up to the mountains. By the time you reach the lower mountains and Road 306, however, traffic will have increased uncomfortably. A few stretches of bicycle lane will offer some relief but for the most part you must ride the busy road. As typical of mountain regions, a scarcity of side roads offer few practical alternatives.

The challenges of this day's ride immediately present themselves, beginning with a **long gradual uphill** to **Ramsau**, a continuation of the climb from Salzburg. Follow Road 305 toward Traunstein most of the day. From Ramsau this road climbs a long, difficult series of **switchbacks** until **Taubensee**. Eventually you will be rewarded by a long, thrilling **descent** down the next valley—only to reach the next **long uphill**, past **Schneizlreuth**. For a short break, pull over at **Gletschergarten** before **Weißbach**. A quick walk brings you to a "glacier garden" where the effects of glacial erosion are clearly visible. By **Inzell** you will be on **Road 306** and in the foothills, with only a last few rolling hills to surmount.

Just after **Siegsdorf** you will finally turn off 306 to gain quiet country roads. Pass Siegsdorf, **cross under** the *Autobahn*, and 3 km later turn **left** over a one-lane bridge with signs for Haslach. In **Haslach** first turn right for **Traunstein**, then **left** for **Bergen** to curve behind the **church**. There, take the first **right** for Einham. Whew! Back to farmlands and quiet roads!

A last **steep climb** brings you to **Einham** and panoramic views of the Chiemsee ahead. At the **yield sign** in Einham go **left** and at the end of town, bear **left** for Neuling. **Descend** a hill and go straight at the stop sign, following signs to **Hiensdorf** and **Wörglham**. Bike straight into **Marwang**, pass the post office, and emerge on a **bicycle lane** along the main road. Ride to **Grabenstätt** and head for the *Autobahn*. Just before the highway turn **right** onto a **bicycle path** indicated by blue Chiemsee signs.

Follow Chiemsee or *Uferweg* (shore way) signs around the **south shore** of the lake. This is not the most scenic section of the lake trail, as it closely follows the *Autobahn*. If you are completely pooped by this point, stop at Baumgarten campground and ride the quieter north-shore trail the next day to reach Harras and the islands. Otherwise, go ahead along the south shore. In **Felden** you will cross under the *Autobahn* (toward the water) and swing around the lake's southwest corner with the **Chiemsee Trail.** A short distance later you will pedal right up to the lakeside campground in **Harras**.

Prien, one of the lake's bigger towns, lies only 4 km north of Harras. Follow the roadside **bicycle trail** right to the docks and *Ortsmitte* for supermarkets and rooms to rent. At Chiemsee there are plenty of opportunities to either relax or get out and see more (see tips below).

Chiemsee Day Trip: 55 kilometers

Chiemsee, the "Bavarian Sea," is a popular recreation and holiday area. The top tourist attraction of the lake is Herrenchiemsee, Mad Ludwig II's palace on the island of Herreninsel. Boats leave Prien frequently for both Herreninsel and Fraueninsel, site of a picturesque monastery (15 to 30 minutes one way; fare DM 8 to one island, DM 10 to both). The woods of Herreninsel hide a Versailles-like palace complete with fountains, gardens, and a Hall of Mirrors (entrance fee DM 6). In building Herrenchiemsee, Mad Ludwig emptied the Bavarian treasury. Not long after, the young king was deposed and found drowned under mysterious circumstances in the Starnberger See, a sad but appropriately unusual end.

Ideally, put aside a full day for relaxation and exploration of these islands and the Chiemsee's shores. For a complete tour, follow the marked **bicycle trail** on paved and unpaved tracks around the lake. With a high alpine ridge to the south as a background, any point along the beautiful lake makes a perfect bathing or picnic spot. Many establishments rent windsurfers, a very popular sport at Chiemsee. **Ferries** link Prien, Gstadt, Seebruck, Chieming, and Feldwies; bicycles are accepted at extra fee, though cycling on Herreninsel is not permitted.

Harras to München: 100 kilometers

This long day completes the tour between Salzburg and München. However, because all the tour's principal sights are now past, you can also opt for a **direct train** from Prien to München as an alternative to this long day.

From Harras campground, turn **left** along the road (not the *Uferweg*) and follow **signs** to Frasdorf, **climbing away** from the lake basin **over a long, steep ridge**. By Frasdorf you will regain level ground for much of the way. In **Frasdorf**, pick up **bicycle signs** for Rohrdorf and Rosenheim to follow an excellent trail (dirt for only one section along a stream and then train tracks). In **Rohrdorf** cross **under** the *Autobahn* for Rosenheim, riding the bicycle lane and then the road's shoulder. Pass **Thansau** and turn **left** at the bicycle sign to Rosenheim. The path follows the bank of the River Inn, then crosses a **bridge** near Rosenheim.

An old market town, **Rosenheim** remains a busy commercial center with a confusing tangle of roads. It is best to take the longer, clearer way around than attempt a shortcut. From the Inn's west bank, turn **north** for Wasserburg on the bicycle path, crossing under train tracks. At the nearby **auto bridge**, turn **left** into the town center, heading for Kolbermoor and Bad Aibling. As you near Kolbermoor, look for a **left** turnoff toward the *Autobahn*. **Cross** the Mangfall River, then ride west through **Schwaig**, **Mitterhart**, and **Pullach** along the river's **south shore**. This is an uncomfortably busy road with no shoulder, but once in Pullach the route returns to quiet roads.

At the stop sign head **straight** through Pullach, then follow signs to Brückmuhl until **Waith**. In Waith, keep **left** for **Vagen** and ride pleasant country roads right to **Feldkirchen**. Feldkirchen is a good stopping point, with a supermarket and bench-lined park beside the church. After this point, the route parallels busy roads toward München for a stretch, but **bicycle lanes** keep you away from the traffic. Pass the turnoff for Aschbach, then turn **left** for **Holzkirchen** and another quiet but hilly stretch through the woods.

At Kreuzstraße turn **right** for München, a road surprisingly free of traffic. As traffic funnels in closer to the city center, good bicycle lanes begin. (You can also avoid this road as long as possible by detouring slightly from Faistenhaar to Hofolding, north to Brunnthal, Kirchstockbach, and Ottobrunn, and rejoining the main road with bicycle lanes there.) Wide woods and fields south of München make it difficult to believe that a city hides beyond, but city streets will soon take over.

If heading for München center, simply follow *Stadtmitte* signs.

The road takes a few curves but is always well marked. Remember not to take a blue-signed *Autobahn* into the center (some are also marked *Stadtmitte*). Stay on the other roads, which all have bicycle lanes.

To reach Thalkirchen's campground or hostel, turn left on Mittlerer Ring before reaching the city center. You can't miss this large ring road (with bicycle lanes) or the posted campground signs (or *Zoo*, in the same direction). If at any point you get sidetracked, simply bike to the Isar and follow bridges to the campsite.

If you are visiting München for the first time, see Tour No. 4 for city tips. Tour No. 4, another Bavarian tour, leaves from München, or you can strike out on your own to visit Augsburg, 70 km west. From München, you may also take trains to Lake Constance (Bodensee) for Tour No. 6. Tough cyclists may opt to pedal there, adding yet another beautiful lake to their list of sights—plus the scenery of the Allgäu region in between. München's international airport and *Hauptbahnhof* will speed you on your way to more distant points.

TOUR NO. 6

A THREE-COUNTRY TREAT
Along the Shores of Lake Constance

Distance: 260 kilometers (161 miles)
Estimated time: 4 to 5 days (4 biking days)
Terrain: Easy lakeshore biking
Map: ADFC #25 or *Bodensee Radwanderführer*

Bicycling Europe is an excellent alternative to the stereotypical "if it's Tuesday it must be Belgium" mentality of many bus or train tours. Cycling allows up-close, reasonably paced exploration and the opportunity to see and experience new places. With this tour of the Bodensee (Lake Constance), cyclists can enjoy the best of both worlds. Three countries meet at the shores of the largest lake in the German-speaking world, allowing the excitement of a multicountry tour while maintaining the close perspective of cycling.

Gentle lakeside terrain together with a well-marked bicycle route through Germany, Austria, and Switzerland combine in a unique, enjoyable tour. Castles, medieval towns, and prehistoric sights punctuate a typical day's ride. Switzerland's Alps form a spectacular backdrop to the sail-dotted waters of the Bodensee, while flags of pleasure craft remind travelers of the lake's international character. An excellent cycling guide to the popular area, *Bodensee Radwanderführer* by Esterbauer and Weinfurter (Wien), makes touring even easier. The complete map booklet (1:100,000) includes information on sights, accommodations, repair shops, and suggested cycling routes.

Ferries link many points around the lake, allowing cyclists to shorten parts of the ride by hopping on a boat. Ferries also allow a home-base touring approach with the advantage of unloaded biking and a comfortable, familiar place to return to each day by boat (see Part I, Tips for Touring). Many Germans use this system for comfortable touring. Home-basing is a particularly good option for families and mixed-interest groups: Cyclists can pedal sections of the lake each day, while others can concentrate on historic towns, windsurf, or lie on the beach. At the end of the day everyone can regroup and share their experiences. In this way, each person can indulge in personal interests and still enjoy the company of friends.

Lion and lighthouse guard Lindau's harbor.

Konstanz

This tour and both Oberbayern (Upper Bavaria) tours (Tour Nos. 4 and 5) have much in common, with all visiting lakes that have spectacular snow-capped mountain backdrops. Since Lake Constance is a single region made up of three countries, not divided by them, it is most interesting to complete the entire lake circuit, not simply the northern, German shore. And then you'll be able to take pride in touring the entire Bodensee.

Konstanz (anglicized as Constance) lies directly at the terminus of the main Rhine train route, with quick *Inter-Regio* connections to and from Frankfurt and Stuttgart. Train connections from München in the east, however, require three changes. Lindau, on the other hand, lies on a direct line to München but is indirect from the Rhine line. If you are only covering the German part of the tour it is logistically easiest to start in Konstanz, arriving from a bicycle tour in the Rhine Valley area, then pedaling to Lindau and hopping on a train or bicycle to München for a Bavarian tour (or vice versa). Otherwise, avoid multiple train transfers by taking a ferry to the most direct train station.

The Konstanz tourist office with room-finding service and an information board lies 50 meters outside the *Bahnhof*. On holidays, room and hostel vacancies may be difficult to find. Shop in Konstanz before heading to the nearest campground, 4 km away near the Meersburg Ferry landing. Ride north from Konstanz, cross a bridge, and follow camping signs past all varieties of sports parks to reach the campsite.

Thanks to its proximity to neutral Switzerland, Konstanz escaped wartime damage. See the beautiful *Rathaus* and *Münster* in town, then head out to *Stadtgarten* for fine views of the lake. For a head start on the tour, bike to Mainau (8 km from Konstanz). Another campground lies just past the island in a more woodsy, quiet setting than the first.

Konstanz to Meersburg: 57 kilometers

The first half of this day's ride is the only difficult part of this tour, crossing a hilly area between the lake's two western arms. Ferries directly to Meersburg from Konstanz or Mainau offer the option of shortcutting the Überlinger See.

Otherwise follow **bicycle signs** from Konstanz and the campground to Mainau, the garden island. You will soon become familiar with the Bodensee Radweg logo, a bicycle with the rear wheel colored in blue. These signs lead directly to the bicycle parking lot at the **bridge** to **Mainau**, your first hint at the popularity of this bicycle tour. Princes of Baden turned their island retreat into a lush garden, today a favorite destination for Bodensee visitors. Many local and exotic species decorate Mainau, carefully tended year-round. You will have to fork out a hefty entrance fee to see the gardens, however (DM 13, students DM 6).

From Mainau, bicycle signs continue to lead around Überlinger See. At points the route joins the main road, with turnoffs onto quieter lanes signposted. Successive bicycle signs point the way to Bodman (do not ride into the center), **Sipplingen**, and **Überlingen**. You must ride a busy road from **Dettingen** to **Liggeringen**, then a quieter road to **Bodman**. The lake's English name stems from the town of Konstanz, but the German name, Bodensee, is said to derive from this small town. You will be **back along the main road** toward Ludwigshafen, then on **bicycle paths** parallel to or directly along the **shoreline**.

Besides good examples of the usual historic buildings (*Rathaus* and *Münster*), **Überlingen** also boasts a well-preserved moat and several guard towers, well worth a walk in good weather. Several more sights lie between Überlingen and Meersburg. Camping in nearby **Nußdorf** opens the option of putting them off until the next day. To finish in Meersburg, follow **bicycle signs** to **Nußdorf**, Birnau, Unteruhldingen, and Meersburg from Überlingen.

In **Birnau** you will pass below a rococo pilgrimage church surrounded by vineyards and commanding a tremendous view of the Swiss Alps across the lake. The church's beautiful interior and terrace make the detour up worthwhile. Don't miss the "Honey-Eater" statue inside. From Birnau, quiet lanes bring you to **Unteruhldingen**. There, follow signs to Freilichtmuseum Pfahlbauten to see reconstructed post-house settlements and artifacts of the Bodensee's earliest settlers (from 3000 B.C.). Even if you are not excited about archaeology (or the hefty entrance fee: DM 13, students DM 6), peek at the stilt houses from the neighboring beach.

Pass Meersburg's ferry landing and pedal into the pretty lower town. Two castles crown **Meersburg**, a well-preserved and perfectly tended old town. The Altes Schloss has the distinction of being Germany's oldest inhabited castle (parts date to the seventh century). Although it is tempting to simply enjoy the view from below, trek to the upper town for a closer look at the castles, *Marktplatz*, *Rathaus*, and ancient, twisting streets. An information office in the lower town helps find rooms. In late May I saw many *Zimmer belegt* (room occupied) signs instead of the usual *Zimmer frei*, so try to get an early start if you are looking for accommodations. The Bodensee bicycle trail runs past several campsites 4 km east (direction Hagnau). Hostels ring the lake, at Konstanz, Überlingen, Friedrichshafen, and Lindau.

Meersburg to Lindau: 48 kilometers

Another sight-filled day of easy cycling brings you to the Bodensee's most unique town, Lindau. The **bicycle path** parallels the main road from **Immenstaad** to **Friedrichshafen**, but after passing through the pedestrian zone of this large town you will have quieter biking closer to the lakeshore. Friedrichshafen stands out only because of Count Zeppelin, who invented and tested his flying machines here. Otherwise the harbor town offers little of interest to tourists.

Outside Friedrichshafen, the *Radweg* **crosses** a small **river** and runs **straight** ahead. Turn **right** after crossing the bridge to enjoy quieter cycling through lakeside nature preserves rather than continuing beside the main road. This path turns to dirt in sections, always fine for cycling.

A concentration of sights toward the end of the ride will slow your progress to Lindau. **Langenargen**, **Nonnenhorn**, and **Wasserburg** are all good stopping points, each with a pretty harbor area. In Wasserburg, Montfort Castle adds a new shape to the usual sky-

Wasserburg's lakeside promenade on a sunny summer day

Sailboats in Romanshorn's port

lines of church spires. Detour for good views in Bad Schachen. The
ritzy hotel's waterfront park faces Lindau, an island town. The two
bridges connecting Lindau to the shore look like mooring lines, as if
the island is only temporarily anchored in place, able to move about
the lake with the sailboats.

Insel Lindau signs lead directly onto the small island and into
the heart of the old town. **Lindau**'s decorated *Rathaus* is one of the
most colorful you'll see anywhere, while street performers, fountains, cafes, and more painted houses color Maximilianstrasse.
Contrast traditional designs to the 1939 house painting at the end
of the street, with figures depicted in a style reflective of the period.

A Bavarian lion and lighthouse guard the flag-lined harbor entrance, a scene enlivened by the colorful promenade. Or, in the
words of the tourist brochure: "In massive indomitability looms the
Old Lighthouse...." Holiday crowds squeeze into the scene as well,
since the popular German Alpine Road begins here in Lindau. Look
out from the harbor at the white-topped Alps and the Rhine's point
of entry into the lake.

The information office across from the *Bahnhof* helps with rooms. Lindau's hostel is on the mainland; lakeside camping is 4 km east near Zech (supermarket at the site). Signs indicate the campsite off the bicycle trail, bringing you to within 1 km of the Austrian border. The site offers excellent views of Lindau Island, especially at night.

Lindau to Konstanz: 80 kilometers

Yes, this is it, your big three-country day. Yee-ha! The ride back to Konstanz is entirely flat and easier than ever to follow—with the exception of one stretch between Gaißau and Rorschach in Austria. I like to celebrate international border crossings by ringing my bike bell—and on this day, it saw plenty of action. Cross the Austrian border and ride yellow-dotted bicycle lanes along the main road. After 2 km more turn **right** at a blue bicycle sign for Bregenz.

Pedal the promenade in **Bregenz**, keeping with red Bodensee bicycle signs. Follow *Uferweg* or *Seeufer* to **Hard** (a town, not an adjective), **Fußach**, and **Schweiz** (Switzerland). The route may be serpentine at points, but always clear. **Cross** the Neue Rhein and follow it inland with signs for **Rorschach**. This is the official Bodensee route, marked in yellow on the ADFC map. Another route closer to the lakeshore is also possible, but it is not as consistently marked.

Cyclists eager to add another country to the tour may opt to detour south at this point, riding 40 km to Liechtenstein. The tiny principality covers only a few square kilometers, its territory sweeping from the Rhine to dramatic mountain peaks above the valley.

Watch carefully for bicycle signs at all times, especially after **crossing** the train tracks in **Gaißau**. Your next move should be to cut **under** the *Autobahn*. From Rorschach, navigating all the way back to Konstanz is easy. In sections where the bicycle route joins regular roads, bicycle lanes are delineated by yellow dots, as in Austria. Here in Switzerland, the usual Bodensee Radweg signs are supplemented by square blue bicycle signs and solid red arrows indicating *Seeradweg* and each successive town: **Arbon**, **Romanshorn**, **Uttwil**, Kreuzlingen, and finally Konstanz. The two best places for a break are Arbon, with its pretty port backed by old town towers, and Romanshorn, with its colorful harbor scene. Ferries connect these and other towns with Konstanz. For weekend money exchange, head to the *Bahnhof* of any large town (Bregenz, Rorschach, Arbon, Romanshorn).

From the pleasant bicycle trail, now higher above the shoreline, you will have excellent views of the opposite shore (a landscape now familiar to you) for the last few kilometers toward **Kreuzlingen**.

The German border beyond Kreuzlingen is practically in **Konstanz**, where you can return to the lodgings of your choice. Although you have now circled the main body of the Bodensee, a last day trip around the Untersee will make your tour complete.

Untersee Day Trip: 75 kilometers

Now that you have already seen the Rhine's entry point into the Bodensee near Rorschach, pedal to its exit point at Stein an Rhein. The official Bodensee route will lead you around the Untersee on a combination of separate trails and sections of road.

From the **bridge** spanning the lake's narrow neck in Konstanz, follow a **bicycle path** west for **Gottlieben**. There, pick up the Bodensee route to circle the Untersee's **south shore** (Swiss territory) to **Stein an Rhein**. The lower lake narrows considerably, eventually funneling out at Stein as a river.

Stein an Rhein is a picturesque little town with beautifully painted houses, an excellent place for a break. At this point the Bodensee tour continues around the Untersee, but hardy cyclists may detour 20 km west to see **Schaffhausen** and the impressive *Rheinfall* (Rhine waterfall). To do so, simply follow the **north bank** of the Rhine **west**.

Otherwise, head on for Radolfzell with the official route, crossing back into Germany and passing little **Wangen**. Again, the route follows sections of road, sidetracking a quiet path around the tip of **Horn** later. Bypass uninteresting **Radolfzell**, pedaling along to reach the last important Bodensee sight, **Reichenau**. Monastic centers on this quiet island date back to the seventh century. Eleventh-century wall paintings are still visible in Oberzell's St. George Church, the island's principal attraction. You may also venture farther to see Mittelzell's old abbey and more of Reichenau's extensive fields and gardens. Finally, retrace your route to the mainland and return to **Konstanz** along 5 km of main road.

Back in Konstanz, you can look out over distant lakeshores, knowing that you have toured the entire circuit. Check at the *Bahnhof* for train connections to your next destination. If heading east toward München, remember that a ferry to Lindau may help avoid multiple connections. Besides riding on to other tours described in this book, cyclists may also choose to head south into Switzerland, bringing those distant mountains into closer range. To connect into the Black Forest and Rhine Valley tour (Tour No. 7) at Freiburg, simply follow the Rhine River west and then north via Basel.

TOUR NO. 7

RHINE BORDERLANDS
The Black Forest to Baden-Baden

Distance: 271 kilometers (168 miles)·
Estimated time: 6 to 7 days (6 biking days,
including two day trips)
Terrain: Gentle terrain but strong winds
along the valley floor
Map: ADFC #24
Connecting tours: Tour Nos. 8 and 9

Beginning high in the Black Forest, this tour glides down into the
Rhine Valley to visit the university city of Freiburg, vineyards and
medieval towns of the Kaiserstuhl, and the spa town of Baden-
Baden. One of the most appealing aspects of this ride is the great
cultural mix easily within bicycle range. The tour includes day-trip
rides into France to visit two beautiful Alsatian towns; experience
for yourself the contrasts—and similarities—of life on either side of
the Rhine.

Titisee-Neustadt

Titisee-Neustadt, a pleasant lakeside resort, is one of the most
popular retreats in the Schwarzwald (Black Forest). Although the
Black Forest is best appreciated by hiking remote trails, the short
and easy bicycle ride from Titisee to Freiburg offers a quick, enjoyable glimpse of the region—and perhaps will tempt you with future
explorations on foot. The lake at Titisee is ringed by campgrounds,
and there is a hostel along the road to Bärental. In summer it is
wise to check ahead on vacancies in the hostel or rooms in town.

Unless you are cycling into Titisee, you will probably arrive by
train, which will most likely connect through Freiburg. If this is the
case, consider establishing a base in Freiburg (see below) and making this ride into a day trip, thereby eliminating the need to schlep
panniers and gear over hill, dale, and the *Bundesbahn.*

Titisee to Freiburg: 31 kilometers

If challenging mountain touring is not a high priority for you at
this point, choose the direct downhill ride to Freiburg. You will not

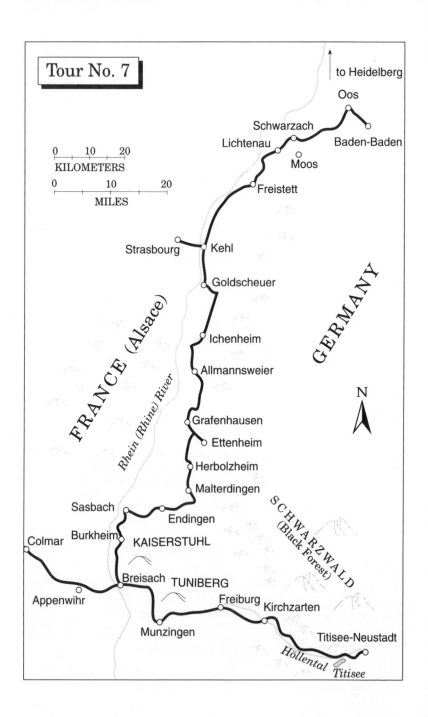

find Road 31 too narrow or traffic too heavy and will probably enjoy the twisting, effortless ride down the Höllental (Hell Valley). On the other hand, if you are excited about hills, crooked valleys, and quiet corners of the Schwarzwald, it is also possible to follow a quieter, more circuitous route along any of the area's numerous side roads, following the suggestions of the ADFC cycling map.

Otherwise, cruise down **Road 31** and turn into **Kirchzarten**. Ride to the town center following signs for **Oberried**, but then continue on for Freiburg to access bicycle trails for the remaining distance. There are two campgrounds on the eastern outskirts of Freiburg, as well as a hostel on the city limits near Ebnet. Look for rooms in the surrounding towns or check at the tourist office near Schwabentor for help.

Freiburg im Breisgau has a character all its own, a wonderful stopping point between the Black Forest and Rhine Valley. Although the city was bombed in World War II, many buildings of the old town center survived, and reconstruction was undertaken with a careful eye to original detail. The *Münster* at Freiburg's heart dominates a cobblestone square where morning markets create a lively scene. For an eagle-eye view of the city and hills beyond, climb the cathedral's Gothic tower. Better yet, hike up the Schlossberg or Roßkopf for hilltop views. Wander old town streets to find the *Rathaus* and city gates, or trace the running waters of the *Bächle* (small water channels) around town.

Freiburg is also a handy place for errand running. Most bookshops carry cycling maps, and bicycle shops are located on Salzstrasse near Schwabentor and on Josephstrasse near Martinstor.

Freiburg to Breisach: 32 kilometers

Arm yourself with a city map to leave Freiburg, or you may discover how quickly this charming city can become a perplexing labyrinth. From the **south bank** of the river, pedal Kronenstrasse past **two large intersections**, following signs **right** and then **left** for Opfingen. This road becomes Opfinger Strasse, with a **bicycle lane**. Continue **straight** across a large intersection and take the **left-side** bicycle path. Enjoy a quiet 5 km ride through the woods to **Opfingen**, taking a lakeside break if you wish (watch for *Zum See* signs).

In Opfingen turn **left** to skirt the Tuniberg. If you don't mind the hill, **climb** directly over it by following signs to **Merdingen**. Two bumps on the otherwise flat Rhine plain, **Tuniberg** and **Kaiserstuhl** are small enclaves of vineyards and wine-producing towns observing a traditional way of life. If Kaiserstuhl is the Emperor's

Vineyards stretch around the Kaiserstuhl.

Throne, little Tuniberg must be the prince's highchair, a miniature version of the large hill.

On the ride from Opfingen to Munzingen you will gain excellent views of Schwarzwald peaks rising to the east. At a **stop light** in **Tiengen** turn **right** onto Freiburger Landstrasse and ride the **left-side** bicycle path to **Munzingen**, with its pretty church and small *Schloss*. There you will join the Breisgau Radwanderweg all the way to Breisach. The trail alternates between bicycle lanes and quiet road shoulders.

Look for square white signs with green letters leading to **Ober-rimsingen** and **Niederrimsingen**. A **right** turn on Tuniberg-strasse takes you on a short detour to the half-timbered houses and *Rathaus* of this pious town (just count the crucifixes). Turn left 3 km later, with Breisgau Radwanderweg signs to **Gündlingen** and **Hochstetten**. The trail meanders a bit but remains clearly marked. If ever in doubt as to which turn the arrows indicate, look at how signs would look to cyclists coming from the opposite direction.

The campground in Hochstetten is clearly signposted left. This is the nearest campground to Breisach. Continuing on to Breisach, the trail crosses a quiet road—go **straight** to the **bicycle trail** paralleling the second, busy road (**B31**) more directly into **Breisach**. This route conveniently passes a grocery store on the outskirts of town. For the hostel or rooms, follow *Sportanlangen* signs. In a large square in the center of town, an information board lists many rooms and displays a helpful map. To reach the comfortable hostel, follow *Jugendherberge* signs to the Rhine, pass under the first bridge, bear left, and the hostel will be on your right.

In Breisach, explore the pedestrian zone or sample local wines at a *Weinstube*. For terrific views of the Rhine Valley, climb up to the old town and *Münsterplatz* to see the Kaiserstuhl and Schwarzwald hills in the distance and France on the opposite bank of the river. Except for a bizarre sculpture recently added, the church and square have gone relatively unchanged for centuries. The varied history of this strategic border town is recorded on the *Rathaus* with a display of each ruling power's crest, from Austrian princes to French kings and German states.

Day Trip to Colmar: 40 kilometers round trip

Take a good look across the Rhine from your vantage point in the old town. Tempted? Yes, this is a book on biking in Germany, but it is time to take a modern, one-Europe approach and discuss a day trip to Colmar in France. Colmar is in Alsace, a long-disputed border region with a curious mix of both French and German influences evident in its culture, language, and food. Colmar itself is a beautiful town, picture-perfect timbered houses reflecting in flower-lined canals. For an unbeatable picnic, stock up on bread, cheese, meats, wine, and some goodies for dessert, stake out a canalside spot, and *Voilà! Bon appetit!*

To reach Colmar, **cross** the Rhine bridge in Breisach (don't forget your passport) and cycle the **shoulder of a busy road** through **Neuf-Brisach**. In **Wolfgantzen**, leave N415 behind and head to **Appenwihr**, **Sundhoffen**, and finally **Colmar** via quieter roads. To stay the night, check for rooms in town or head for camping in nearby Horbourg. The round trip to Colmar covers flat terrain (though strong winds are a possibility) and is easily covered in one day. For money exchange, try a bank in either Colmar or Breisach (on weekends head for the *Bahnhof*).

Breisach to Ettenheim: 54 kilometers

Follow the Rhine along a **bicycle path** that parallels a busy main road circling Breisach. Once **north** of town, watch for Kaiserstuhl Radwanderweg signs pointing **left**, leading to a quiet ride through cornfields with nice views of the hill. Church aficionados can turn off the bicycle path 7 km later to see **Niederrotweil's** historic church. **Burkheim**, farther down the road, is a unique place to be discovered, enjoyed, and remembered long after you move on. Head toward the church to enter the old town, full of antique shops and *Weinstuben*. Burkheim truly conveys the character of a traditional wine-making Kaiserstuhl town: overflowing with grapes and not a tourist in sight.

Pedal out of the opposite **town gate** in Burkheim. At the bottom of the hill, turn **right** onto a **dirt bicycle path** to cycle along a stream through the **woods**. Sponeck, a partly ruined, partly inhabited *Schloss*, dominates a large clearing. Here, you can **choose** to pedal straight ahead to Sasbach, or turn left to cycle a secluded section of the woods and the Rhine. (If you chose to go left, double back to Sasbach when the path ends and follow the main road to Endingen.) Don't be alarmed if the apparition of a bizarre cyclist crystallizes before you. Radio suspended between Texas longhorn handlebars, feathers, hood ornaments, and clown horn adorning his three-speed bike, this eccentric native of Burkheim has pedaled to Portugal and back and may join you for a few kilometers of cycling and storytelling.

Once in **Königschaffhausen** turn **left** for Wyhl, **cross** the train tracks, and bear **right** at *Sportplatz* and Kaiserstuhl Radwanderweg signs. Hang a **right** at the crucifix to swing into **Endingen**, another pretty town full of old houses and *Weinstuben*. Turn one block up (**south**) from the *Marktplatz* to see the eye-catching St. George memorial, its dragon covered with just enough green moss to make him come alive.

Exit town, keeping an eye out for *Radwanderweg* signs pointing away from the main road. In **Riegel** the *Radwanderweg* winds through a residential section. Just before rejoining the main road,

Tiny wine towns dot the Rhine Valley.

look for a **gray gate** on the right to see small ruins of a first-century Roman Mithros Temple.

At the main road, turn **right**, then take the **first left**, passing through a schoolyard. Bear **left** in front of the *Apotheke* to head to Malterdingen and Radwanderweg Baden-Württemberg (green signs with white writing). Leaving Riegel, **cross** a bridge **on the left-hand sidewalk** and go **under** a mini-underpass, then ride **straight** along a small road. Pass under the *Autobahn* and turn **right** at the tracks to cut **beneath** another underpass. At the **T**, turn **left** and then **right** for **Malterdingen**. **Cross** another overpass and go **left** on Hecklingerstrasse to access the bicycle path.

In **Hecklingen** you will find an appealing town center and a ruined castle above. A hiking path leads to the castle and good views over the Rhine Valley and sleepy towns below—watch for it as you leave town. Biking to **Kenzingen**, you will **cross over** two busy roads. At a **bicycle-crossing light** after the second road, go straight ahead and then turn **right** on a small path which emerges at a **T**. Turn **left** and follow bicycle signs to the **right**. Use the **green dome** of Herbolzheim's church as a guide through twisting trails **north**.

You will ride through a residential section of **Herbolzheim**. At a busy intersection turn **left** on Rheinhausenstrasse, riding the sidewalk by an overpass. Go **straight** past two supermarkets and swing **right** at a soccer field to return to **bicycle paths** through cornfields. This trail **parallels** the *Autobahn*, then **jogs right**. Turn **left** at the next intersection and follow the **path opposite** to continue paralleling the *Autobahn*. At the end of the trail turn **right** for the last 5 km into **Ettenheim**. Ettenheim is nestled in a pretty valley behind the hills, with an old town center and nearby campground. Check for rooms in Ettenheim or smaller towns in the valley. For an evening walk in town, see the old Kirchberg residential quarter, including *Rathaus* and former bishop's palace.

Ettenheim to Kehl: 47 kilometers

Retrace your route **west** from Ettenheim and follow bicycle signs to **Lahr** over the *Autobahn*. Pedal through and past **Grafenhausen**, back **over** the *Autobahn* and **north**. From **Kippenheim** follow only green Baden-Württemberg Radwanderweg signs through a confusing stretch. Though the route does not correspond exactly to that on the map, signs do eventually lead **under** the *Autobahn* on a **dirt path** through the woods. Bear **right** after this underpass and head **straight** for the dome of Allmannsweier's church. **Allmannsweier**, another half-timbered farm town similar to many others along both sides of the Rhine, reminds one that geographic boundaries are in many cases more influential than political ones.

Continue following Baden-Württemberg Radwanderweg signs to **Meißenheim**. The direct road to Ottenheim and Meißenheim makes for a faster ride but at times traffic can be uncomfortably fast along this road (particularly so after a day of quiet countryside cycling). For a more pleasant ride, try the main bicycle trail. Pass in front of the **church** in Meißenheim, keeping **right** along the wall. Follow this road **past one turnoff** and swing **right with the second twist** to Ichenheim. The path is sometimes dirt but suitable for cycling. Turn **left** on **Road 36** through **Ichenheim**, then bear **right** near the end of town on Trudenweg to ride a quieter road **north**. In **Dundenheim** bear **right** toward **Shutterwald**, then **left** to **Müllen**. Ride **straight** through this town to pick up *Radwanderweg* signs again. Head past the church and *Rathaus*, **cross** a stream, and go **left** at the **T**. Continue **straight** past a *Vorsicht* (caution) sign, but be careful: This road also serves as a model-airplane runway. The path degenerates to dirt but soon emerges onto **Road 33A**. Turn **left** and follow the **bicycle lane** there.

Ignore the tempting Kehl bicycle sign in **Kittersburg** as it takes an extremely circuitous route to Goldscheuer. For a more direct ride follow **Road 33** into **Goldscheuer** and **Marlen**. At a **fountain** in Marlen, turn **left** on Narzissenweg and head for the church via a **footpath**. Turn **right** in front of the church, then **left** on Schlossergasse. **Cross** over a stream, ignoring the first two bicycle paths leading right. Look **straight ahead and then right** for a Kehl bicycle sign. This path is sometimes rough but always peaceful and pleasant to cycle. If in doubt, stay along the river. As you approach the city, this path passes Kehl's campground and hostel, both clearly marked to the right. To reach Kehl city center continue straight along the trail.

Day Trip to Strasbourg: 16 kilometers round trip

Kehl's postcards will clue you in to the city's cultural highlights—they all show the bridge and the French border. The best thing about Kehl is Strasbourg, so make your way over the Rhine to Alsace. Stop at money-exchange points on either side of the border for French *francs*. You can day trip from Kehl by bicycle or stay in Strasbourg's campground, hostel, or rooms. To reach Strasbourg center, simply follow an **excellent network of bicycle trails to the cathedral spire**. There are also frequent **train connections** across the border.

An enlarged version of Colmar, Strasbourg is nevertheless an easily managed city with its own special character. Highlights include the city center and cathedral, as well as meandering, canal-lined side streets—all demonstrating the unusual Alsatian mix of both French and German elements. Watch the clock figures on the cathedral at midday (or watch tourists watching the clock figures, sometimes more entertaining), and see the Gothic Doomsday column. Cyclists who have toured or are planning to tour Thuringia (Tour No. 12) will be delighted to know that yes, Goethe was here in Strasbourg, too, ascending the cathedral tower daily to cure his fear of heights.

Kehl to Baden-Baden: 51 kilometers

From Europabrücke (bridge) in Kehl, **cross** the main road and head to the *Bahnhof* to begin the final day of this tour. **Cross under** train tracks from the right side of the main station building and go **straight** for **Hafen Nord**. Eventually you will come to a road paralleling a **canal**. The bicycle path follows the canal's high bank. Signs for Rheinau lead **across** the canal and **north**, once again paralleling the Rhine. Though the trail is rough, you will soon join a quiet side road along the woods.

After 10 km, turn **left** for **Badensee Honau** to continue paralleling the Rhine (but do not follow more signs directly to the lake). After passing a **yacht harbor** 5 km farther north, watch closely for signs to **Freistett** and Lichtenau. Keep alert as the bicycle route often takes **sharp turns**. Ride through **Helmlingen**, watching for a **right** turn on Hindenburg Gasse (sign for *Post*). Follow this street out of town and **straight** into **Lichtenau**. At the **T** intersection with a busy road turn **left**, and at the next **T** look for **bicycle signs** to Schwarzach straight ahead. Once in **Schwarzach**, follow road signs to **Bühl** over train tracks and toward the woods. Eventually turn **left** at a marked turnoff for Sinzheim. In **Sinzheim** go **left** for Baden-Baden, pedaling the bicycle path that **parallels** the busy road.

For the most direct ride into Baden-Baden, it is possible to follow signs for *Zentrum*, but that road is quite busy. For quiet roads but an indirect route, turn **right** for **Kartung** and **circle over** an overpass. Turn **right** to head **north** on Buchtungerstrasse along train tracks. Eventually you will emerge in **Oos**. **Recross** the tracks and **return** to the main road. Turn **left** onto **Road B3** and then **right** for *Stadtmitte*. The train station is located on the left at this intersection. A final 4-km ride along a **bicycle trail** will bring you into the center of town at last.

Baden-Baden lost its "well-kept secret" resort status about 2,000 years ago when the Romans came to town and established the first large baths. Since then, Emperors, royalty, and elite have taken the waters, trod the promenade, and gambled nights away at Baden-Baden's elegant casino. But not to worry. Centuries of popularity have not spoiled this interesting town, and even modern-day cyclists can find their niche in Baden-Baden.

If a limited budget—or wardrobe—denies you admittance to the casino, take solace in the beauty of the surrounding park or defiantly stroll Lichtentaler Allee clad in Lycra. Ruins of the Roman Baths remain visible beneath the modern bathhouse at Römerplatz. For excellent views and a strenuous side trip from Baden-Baden, head to either Yburg or Hohenbaden castle ruins. Accommodations options in the resort town include a hostel (west of town on the road to Oos, family rooms also available) and some reasonably priced rooms (Oos being your best bet). In the summer, make reservations ahead of time. Unfortunately, there are no campgrounds conveniently nearby. Campers must pedal on to Rastatt (10 km north) or stop at a lakeside site near Moos (east of Lichtenau) before visiting Baden-Baden.

If your legs are still itching to pedal, trace the hills north along the Rhine Valley to Heidelberg to connect with Tour Nos. 8 or 9 (see below). Another appealing option includes circling back to Freiburg via the High Black Forest Road (Hochstrasse), a strenuous but rewarding ride. Finally, consider looping south through France for a more thorough tour of Alsace. For quick connections with other tours or cities, head for Oos *Bahnhof*, a stopping point for many long-distance trains on the main Rhine line (including *Inter-Regio* trains on the north-south run from Konstanz to Heidelberg, Frankfurt, and other points).

Connection to Tour Nos. 8 and 9

Baden-Baden to Heidelberg: 97 kilometers. To ride from Baden-Baden to Heidelberg, trace the hilly edge of the Rhine plain north. The recommended route highlighted on ADFC Map #20 combines bicycle lanes and quiet side roads for a pleasant valley ride. Follow bicycle trails along Road 3 until Bruchsal, where the route jogs west through farmlands for the remaining distance to Heidelberg. Valley cycling means easy terrain throughout, though potentially strong Rhine winds may turn against you at times.

To break the journey into shorter segments, stop in Weingarten, a wonderful wine town, or Bruchsal, with its large central square and old castle. There are campgrounds in Bruchsal and Reilingen.

It is also possible to connect directly into Tour No. 8 by cycling west from Reilingen to Speyer and tracing that tour in either direction.

TOUR NO. 8

RHINELAND VINEYARDS AND SPIRES
A Loop around Heidelberg

Distance:	150 kilometers (93 miles)
Estimated time:	4 days (3 riding days)
Terrain:	Flat vineyard country on Rhine Valley floor, often strong shifting winds
Map:	ADFC #20
Connecting tours:	Tour Nos. 7 and 9

This pleasant three-day loop offers a varied sampler of the central Rhine Valley, visiting medieval towns, vineyards, pilgrimage centers, and castles along two German tourist routes, the Bergstrasse (Mountain Road) and Weinstrasse (German Wine Road). The Rhine Valley has long been an important highway of Europe, and this tour circles three of its most significant cities—Heidelberg, Worms, and Speyer. In between, explore less known, non-touristy sights

Heidelberg's ruined Schloss *dominates the old town.*

and enjoy pleasant valley scenery. Every mile covered (and every wine bottle emptied) along this history-rich tour rewards cyclists with more insight into the region's long traditions.

Heidelberg

Heidelberg, home to Germany's oldest university, lies tucked within the narrow, steep walls of the Neckar Valley on the edge of the Rhine plain. Though a popular tourist destination ("the nicest Japanese city in Germany"), the old town streets, ruined *Schloss*, and lively atmosphere make Heidelberg an excellent stop. The city

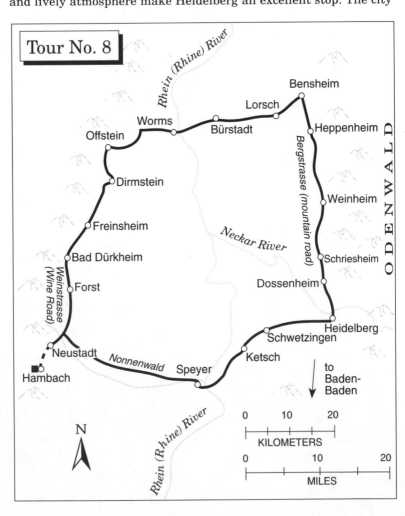

is full of students on the go; thanks to their influence, cyclists enjoy an excellent network of bicycle paths and the respect of motorized traffic.

Heidelberg lies on the main Rhine train line, easily reached from all points in Germany. The helpful tourist office, located directly outside the train station, will direct you to the hostel (near Tiergarten), the nearest campground (6 km east in Schlierbach), or help find rooms.

Heidelberg to Worms: 53 kilometers

This tour begins with a ride along the Bergstrasse, a centuries-old route along the ridge of hills bordering the Rhine Valley plain. The Bergstrasse was already an established route when the Romans came to town and occupied strategic outposts along the broad valley. The official Bergstrasse is today's Road 3, paralleled by bicycle lanes in most stretches between towns. Though many bicycle trails also crisscross the surrounding area, these are often not clearly marked. Therefore it is best to adopt the following strategy: Arm yourself with a good, detailed cycling map and use quiet trails when possible. When these aids are not enough, remember to keep the mountains on your right and the plain to the left, resorting to Road 3 if necessary. Some trails have dirt surfaces but are usually fine for cycling.

To begin the tour, pedal the **bicycle lane** of busy **Road 3** north toward Weinheim and Darmstadt. After the tram stop beyond **Handschuhsheim**, turn **right** over train tracks, then **left** to follow a small, pleasant road through garden plots to **Dossenheim**. Keep **left** of Dossenheim's church to continue along side roads to **Schriesheim** and **Leutershausen**. Follow Obere Bergstrasse, Brunnenstrasse, and then Sachsenstrasse through the Sachsens. As you enter **Weinheim**, **bear right** to ride to the town center.

Weinheim is a real highlight of the Bergstrasse, its crooked streets winding from the hilltop *Schloss* to the medieval old town on the slopes below. Head for the wonderful *Marktplatz*, complete with requisite fountain, fancy *Rathaus*, and decorated *Apotheke*. To shorten this biking day, stop in Weinheim's hostel or check for room vacancies in town.

To continue along the Bergstrasse, try following the bicycle route (a sometimes tricky proposition). Cross **west** of the train tracks, turn **right** on a small road, then **guess** your way around winding paths to **Heppenheim**. (If your tolerance for meandering has already been exceeded, you can also resort to Road 3.) Heppenheim is another wonderful Bergstrasse town that draws many visitors. Old town walls and towers stand guard over twisting cobblestone streets, the *Marktplatz*, and a cathedral. There are many opportunities for wine tasting in this town, as well as rooms for rent and a hostel in nearby Schlossberg.

Heppenheim and Bensheim are connected by a labyrinth of bicycle trails. Outside **Bensheim**, note signs for Lorsch, but first head for the **town center**. Though similar to other Bergstrasse towns, Bensheim has its own unique character and a particularly appealing market square.

Leaving the Bergstrasse behind, pedal the **marked trail west** to **Lorsch**. Turn **left** into the town center to find Königshalle, the entry gate of an eighth-century Carolingian abbey. Though other abbey buildings have not survived, their foundations are visible in the pleasant park. For an appreciation of the complex's vast scale, look for the reconstruction drawing on an information board there.

None of the confusing bicycle signs in Lorsch lead where you need to go, so stay on the **main road** for Worms. When **Worms B47** turns off to the right, pedal **straight** on for **Einhausen**. As soon as the **road bends**, enters the **woods**, and **crosses** train tracks, you should turn **left** onto a dirt path paralleling the tracks. In **Riedrode** turn **left over the tracks** and immediately **right** for a bicycle lane to Bürstadt. **Enter, cross, and exit Bürstadt** on Nibelungenstrasse to keep along a quiet side road. Eventually the road merges with **B47** where a **bicycle lane** to Worms begins. Crossing the Rhine **bridge** into **Worms**, you will leave Hessen behind and enter the state of Rheinland-Pfälz, known for its fruity wines.

The riverside campground across from Worms (still in Hessen) offers good views of city spires and barges gliding down the Rhine. The hostel directly in the center of Worms faces the *Dom* and offers family rooms. Signs lead to the helpful tourist office in town, where you can find information on *Zimmer*.

Worms is well known for its important role in German history, particularly in regard to Luther and the Reformation. The Lutherdenkmal (monument) commemorates Luther's appearance before Worms's Imperial Diet in 1521. The Diet exiled the reformer from the Empire, but he went on to continue his work in Thuringia's Wartburg Castle (see Tour No. 12). Of the many churches in Worms, the impressive Romanesque *Dom* reigns as the city's centerpiece. Other interesting sights include the secluded Jewish cemetery and nearby remains of the original city walls.

Worms to Speyer: 67 kilometers

You will likely meet with little success if you try following the bicycle path west from here. A better strategy may be to suffer busy roads for a stretch and head directly to **WO-Horchheim** and **WO-Weinsheim** (direction Grünstadt). Otherwise you may get tangled in another "gardenplotland" maze as I did. (If you are a fan of mazes, on the other hand, head out of Worms on Gibichstrasse, cross an overpass, and turn right for Seeber. Cut down into the garden plots and head straight to cross a park and two highway underpasses. Hopefully you will emerge in Weinsheim.)

Speyer's historic cathedral

Jakobspilger sets out from Speyer's Dom.

In either case, once you are in Weinsheim, follow signs to **WO-Wiesoppenheim**. Turn **north** as if to Pfeddersheim, then **west** to **Heppenheim** and **Offstein**. A **bicycle path** parallels the quiet road west. In Offstein watch for Dirmstein bicycle signs. From **Dirmstein** *Ortsmitte* pedal to **Laumersheim** and **Freinsheim**, gaining quiet country roads and pleasant vineyard views. Freinsheim is a wonderful, genuine, walled wine town, not a postcard or tourist in sight. The small central square in town makes a great place for a break.

Follow signs along quiet roads to **Bad Dürkheim**. Unless you are in Bad Dürkheim during the annual wine fest in early September, however, there isn't much of an old (or new) town to make you linger. At this point the tour swings **south** to follow the Weinstrasse (German Wine Road), a tourist route linking towns of the Rhineland wine-producing area. Ride **west** from busy **Road 271** (the official Weinstrasse) to reach vineyard tractor trails and follow the edge of the hills south. Though these side roads and the elusive bicycle route are often difficult to follow, you can resort to less peaceful tracks paralleling 271 if necessary. Many towns along this route offer wine tasting and selling. If you would like to stretch out your tour, there are also many rooms for rent, as well as hostels in Bad Dürkheim and Neustadt, and campgrounds near Bad Dürkheim and Wachenheim.

Forst and **Deidesheim** are both nice towns that preserve their traditional character as wine centers. After Deidesheim, head for **Königsbach** and **Gimmeldingen** on the way to **Neustadt**, entering that town on a bicycle path along the main road. In Neustadt center you will discover another well-preserved wine town at the foot of the mountain ridge. The ruins of Hambach Castle, just south of Neustadt, also make an interesting detour as the site where the modern German flag was first raised in 1832.

A smooth, well-marked bicycle trail through the **Nonnenwald** rewards cyclists with a pleasant and peaceful final leg of this day. Pick up the trail on the corner of Martin Luther Strasse and Robert Stoltz Strasse in Neustadt. Reach Martin Luther Strasse (running north-south) by pedaling **east** from Neustadt center, then turn north to reach the intersection with Robert Stoltz Strasse. Turn right here. (Alternatively, head for **Haßloch** along the main road.)

The bicycle trail passes through a residential area. At the T go over a **bridge** and immediately turn **left** on a small **dirt path**. When the **trail emerges** from the woods look for the continuing bicycle path to the **right of a barn**. Most intersections are well marked but if in doubt, always parallel streams through the woods. After 20 km, the trail emerges right at the spires of Speyer.

Upon entering **Speyer**, **pass** two churches, **continue** along, and watch for the *Altportel*. This gate opens onto the heart of Speyer, Maximilianstrasse, an avenue dominated by the *Dom* at its opposite end. The eleventh-century cathedral is an architectural wonder, its simple decoration allowing undisturbed appreciation of the vast interior space. Don't miss the crypt with its tombs of the Holy Roman Emperors. Back on the street, see the Jakobspilger statue, a monument to those whose faith took them on the long pilgrimage from Speyer's *Dom* to Santiago de Compostela in Spain.

To reach Speyer's campground, follow Bahnhofstrasse and Worms Landstrasse north to the lakeside site. For rooms check the tourist office on Maximilianstrasse, or head for the hostel in the direction of the Rhine bridge.

Speyer to Heidelberg: 30 kilometers

Bicycle signs to Heidelberg begin directly in front of the *Dom* on Maximilianstrasse. Cross **over** the Rhine **bridge** and back to the state of Baden-Württemberg to finish this tour. Signs 2 km down the road lead cyclists into the countryside to the **left**. Though only occasional signs mark the first part of the day, by **Ketsch** every turn is well signed. Pedal **under** a red suspension **bridge** and take the first **right** onto tractor roads. Use the green bishop's-hat tower of Ketsch's church as a beacon through the fields. **Green bicycle signs** will take over near town to guide you for the rest of the day.

The bicycle trail offers a direct vista of Schwetzingen Palace and its French gardens, curving around the park's edge to arrive at the entrance. A miniature Versailles, the eighteenth-century palace served as a retreat for the Heidelberg Electors. A nominal admittance fee brings you to a fantasy world of constant surprises—pagodas, statues, and fountains around every hedge or wooded alley. Come prepared with a lunch for this perfect picnic area.

Afterward, **rejoin the bicycle trail** to Heidelberg. Pass by Schwetzingen *Bahnhof*, use the **pedestrian underpass** to cross the tracks, then pick up **signs** to Heidelberg. As you near the city, follow **signs** for *Zentrum* or *Hauptbahnhof*.

Close the circle by cycling back into **Heidelberg**, enjoying another chance to explore this lively city. After touring three different German states and two of its famous tourist roads by pedal power, you will enjoy the feeling of cycling back to a familiar place.

If this varied tour leaves you excited for more, ride Tour No.9 over the pastoral Odenwald. For a quick start of the Mosel Valley tour (Tour No. 10), catch a train to Trier. Heidelberg's excellent rail connections will bring you to any point in the country quickly and easily (Konstanz and Tour No. 6 on a direct *Inter-Regio* line three hours away, Frankfurt only one hour by train, München four).

THROUGH ODIN'S WOOD
Heidelberg to Darmstadt

Distance: 124 kilometers (77 miles)
Estimated time: 2 to 3 days (2 riding days)
Terrain: Long, rolling hills with several long climbs
Map: ADFC #20
Connecting tours: Tour Nos. 7, 8, and 10

The Odenwald is one of Germany's quiet oases from the modern world, its rolling hills protecting farm communities, medieval market squares, and peaceful woods from the hubbub of nearby industrial centers. Often overlooked by travelers making a beeline from Heidelberg to the airport in Frankfurt or to better-known retreats, this region offers quiet sanctuary to cyclists ready to earn their passage over challenging terrain. Named for the mythic king of gods, the Odenwald (Odin's Wood) is steeped in legends of Siegfried and the Nibelungen, figures of German folklore recalled in Wagner's

A quiet oasis from the modern world: The Odenwald ridgeline near Rothenburg

operatic cycle, *Der Ring des Nibelungen*. The compact nature of the Odenwald allows for a short and thorough tour, ideal for cyclists seeking to escape well-beaten tourist paths.

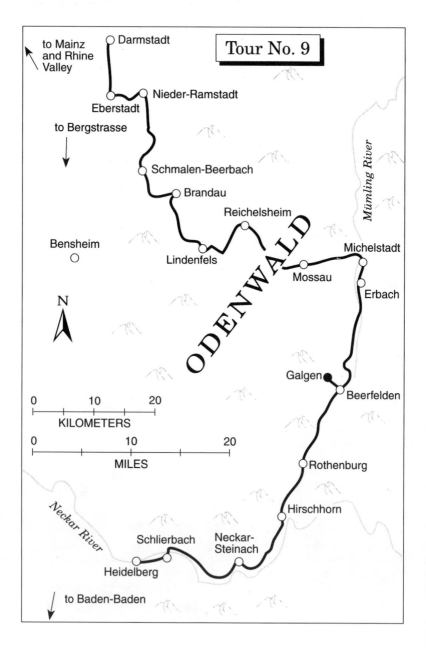

Heidelberg

The Odenwald route runs between Heidelberg and Darmstadt in Germany's Rhine Valley. A beautiful university city with easy train and biking connections, Heidelberg makes a convenient starting point for this short tour. Soon, however, you will leave Heidelberg's packed streets for the solitude of hilly woodlands, the focus of this ride. For more Heidelberg city information, see Tour No. 8.

Heidelberg to Michelstadt: 59 kilometers

This tour begins with a short ride along the beautiful Neckar Valley east of Heidelberg, turning north into Odenwald hills at Hirschhorn. Pedal along the **south shore** of the Neckar, following a **bicycle lane** on the left sidewalk of the road (**B37**). In **Schlierbach cross** to the river's north bank. Though the bicycle lane ends for a short stretch, signs for **Neckar-Steinach** soon lead cyclists to a wonderful **riverside path**. The trail offers excellent views of Neckar-Steinach's four castles, each guarding a point of the river's sharp bend. When the path ends, rejoin the **main road** to Hirschhorn.

Take a last break along the Neckar in **Hirschhorn**, a picture-perfect walled town topped by a high, dramatic castle. On quiet mornings you will have the cobblestone streets to yourself, enjoying a rest before climbing high into the Odenwald. Cyclists coming through the region in early fall will find small towns like Hirschhorn enlivened by wine festivals. Try Federweisser, wine made from the first grapes picked, available only at this time. The Hirschhorn wine festival is also enlivened by song and dance led by monks of the town's historic monastery.

From Hirschhorn, follow signs along quiet roads to Rothenburg. Ready to tackle the Odenwald? Test yourself on the long, steep climb into **Kortelshütte**. Beyond this small town the ride continues **uphill, but more gradually**. At **Rothenburg** your efforts will finally be rewarded as you reach and follow a **ridgeline** for 10 winding kilometers through farmlands and deep woods to **Beerfelden**.

In Beerfelden's central square turn **left** and pedal a short distance in the direction of **Airlenbach** to see sixteenth-century gallows (*Galgen*), a solemn sight on an open hillside outside of town. Yes, this is a morbid detour, but it's not every day that one can visit Germany's oldest gallows (or would want to, for that matter). Return to town and follow **Road B45** to Erbach and Michelstadt. A short **bicycle trail** offers only brief respite from the moderate traffic of this road (mostly residential, no heavy traffic).

Head for *Stadtmitte* in **Erbach**. The day's short cycling distance allows you plenty of afternoon exploration time in this and another of the Odenwald's best medieval towns. Twisting streams gurgle

past half-timbered houses in Erbach, its large market square dominated by a castle. Only 2 km down the main road lies **Michelstadt**,
another wonderful Odenwald town. Pedal through a gate in the old
town wall, aiming for the pinnacled roof and arched foundations of
Michelstadt's unique fifteenth-century *Rathaus*. No self-respecting
medieval town would be complete without an immaculate market
square and pedestrian zone, and Michelstadt is certainly no exception, town fountain and all.

There are two campgrounds in the area, both on the eastern
fringe of Michelstadt, as well as a hostel in Erbach (*Sportpark*
area). Private rooms are available in both towns and in surrounding villages. For more tips, ask at the tourist offices in either
Erbach or Michelstadt.

Michelstadt to Darmstadt: 65 kilometers

The second day of the tour brings you across the compact Odenwald to Lindenfels Castle and finally Darmstadt, back in the bustle
of the lower valley. Cyclists should plan ahead as this end point
presents several choices. Darmstadt is a point of convenience
rather than an interesting tourist destination; bypass the city if
convenient to your plans for further travel (see below).

From Michelstadt, ride **B47** in the direction of Worms. Soon after, **exit for Mossautal**, a hilly but quiet road with several steep
sections. Road B47 is also quite hilly and much more busy, making
the side road your better choice for the ride west to Lindenfels.

Climb from **Mossau** to **Rohrbach**, then descend to **Unter
Ostern**. Turn **left** to ride the shoulder of busy **Road B38** into
Reichelsheim and on to Lindenfels. (For a brief respite, turn right
for Klein Gumpen, returning to B38 after this town.) This stretch of
road has been dubbed the Nibelungenstrasse after the medieval
legend. The twelfth-century epic (*Nibelungenlied*) was handed
down by minstrels and early written records, and provided the legends on which Wagner based his *Ring*. The story's poetic ideal of
Treue (faithfulness) may provide some inspiration as you pedal
faithfully on, sweating up a gradual 3-km hill to **Lindenfels**.

The highlight of this day, Lindenfels's old town and castle offer
expansive views across rolling fields and woods of the Odenwald to
the Rhine plain below. Walk through a pedestrian zone to the old
Marktplatz to see the *Rathaus* and two historic churches before
climbing up to the castle. The *Marktplatz* fountain is guarded by a
lion statue, trying his best to look ferocious. With excellent views
and in a good state of preservation, the castle is sure to inspire
dreams of medieval quests and adventure in imaginative minds.

Leave Lindenfels on **B47**, the main road down to the Rhine Val-

A ferocious lion guards Lindenfels castle.

ley. (With the best of the Odenwald tour now behind you, consider cruising straight down this road to Bensheim, linking into Tour No. 8 there.) Complete this tour by turning off for **Schlierbach** to gain quiet roads through peaceful farm towns. Unfortunately, this initially exhilarating downhill ride is followed by a **long haul back up** to **Winkel** and **Kolmbach**, where you will briefly rejoin B47.

In **Gadernheim**, turn **off** B47 for **Ober-Ramstadt**, gradually nearing the lower slopes of the Odenwald. In **Brandau** keep **left** for Beedenkirchen. On the way, consider a short, steep detour to the war cemetery (*Kriegsgräberstatte*). A reminder that the surrounding hillsides were not always so peaceful, the small site makes a strong and personal impression.

Once in **Beedenkirchen**, turn **left past** the turnoff for Allertshofen and take the **next right** through **Schmalen-Beerbach** (direction Ober Beerbach). Turn **right** 2 km later on a small road marked with a blue dot and Hof Gruenau signs. This tiny road gives cyclists a wonderful ridgetop ride with wide open views. Continue **straight** along the main track until the **T** in **Frankenhausen**. There, turn **right**, then **left** at the next **T** for the last part of the ride, descending from the Odenwald through **Waschenbach** and **Nieder Ramstadt**. In Nieder Ramstadt, turn **left** for **Eberstadt** where a **bicycle path** parallels the *Bergstrasse* (mountain road) right into **Darmstadt**. (If you don't mind traffic and another hill, take a shortcut into the city via B449, which has a separate bicycle lane once inside city limits).

Although its university draws many aspiring young engineers, Darmstadt is not exactly a tourist mecca since most of the city was destroyed in World War II. The *Schloss*, Russian church, and Luisenplatz are all interesting, but your cycling experience of Germany will not be seriously lacking if you decide to forego these sights. Therefore you should tailor the end of this tour to suit your plans.

Darmstadt's two tourist offices are located outside the *Hauptbahnhof* (to the west, down Rheinstrasse) and in Luisencenter on Luisenplatz in the city center. Accommodations in Darmstadt are limited. To reach the hostel near *Ost-Bahnhof*, take Landgraf Georg Strasse from the southeast corner of the *Schloss*. The nearest campgrounds are not too near: 6 km away in Gräfenhausen (northwest), or 15 km away in Stockstadt an Rhein (southwest; a good option for cyclists planning to skip Darmstadt and follow the Rhine in either direction).

To head back south, follow the Bergstrasse from Eberstadt to Bensheim and connect with Tour No. 8 there. Another day's ride brings you north to Mainz and Bingen, connecting with Tour No. 10 of the Mosel and Rhine valleys in reverse. However, the Mosel Valley ride is more ideally completed in the described direction, and busy stretches of the Rhine between Darmstadt and Mainz make train connections to Trier the most ideal option. Darmstadt *Hauptbahnhof* also offers quick train connections to Frankfurt and other points in Germany or abroad.

Connection to Tour No. 10

Darmstadt to Mainz and Bingen: 70 kilometers. The Mosel Valley tour (Tour No. 10) runs downriver from Trier to Koblenz, then upriver along the Rhine to Bingen, an ideal approach for bicycle touring. Cyclists intent on continuing north from Darmstadt can reverse that route, taking advantage of downriver Rhine Valley cycling from Darmstadt to Mainz and Koblenz. From Koblenz to Trier you must ride upstream along the Mosel, but the valley's gentle slope will barely affect your progress. On the other hand, a busy urban tangle between Darmstadt and Mainz discourages cyclists from traversing the area.

Not discouraged? Off you go. On the busy Rhine Valley floor between Darmstadt and Mainz you must cycle along large roads for a time. Take **B42** for 13 km from **Darmstadt** to **Groß Gerau**. Once **across** the train tracks and **on** the ring road in Groß Gerau, turn **left** and watch for the **turnoff** to **Wallerstädten**. Back on quiet side roads, pedal **west** toward the Rhine, bearing **right** instead of left for Geinsheim. Intersect and turn **right** on a **bigger road** to **Trebur** and **Ginsheim-Gustavsburg**.

Cross the Rhine in **Gustavsburg** and follow a **riverside trail** into **Mainz**. Take the time to visit the old cathedral quarter in Mainz, exploring city squares and side streets. To end the day there (42 km), head for Mainz camping across the river, or the hostel or rooms in town.

From Mainz, an **unpaved trail** continues along the Rhine's south bank to Bingen. Set off along the riverfront in Mainz center and keep a careful **eye on your map** to find the trail. Do not curve too far inland with the road. Pedal quiet trails to **Ingelheim-Nord** and then **Bingen** (28 km). For Bingen information, see Tour No. 10.

TOUR NO. 10

MEANDERING THE MOSEL
AND RHINE VALLEYS
Trier to Bingen

Distance: 263 kilometers (163 miles)
Estimated time: 5 days (4 biking days)
Terrain: Flat riverside cycling throughout
Map: ADFC #15 or BVA's *Moselland Radwanderführer*
Connecting tour: Tour No. 9

This ride along the meandering Mosel Valley is one of the best bicycle tours in Germany—and in all Europe. Nowhere are the advantages of bicycle travel better combined with a beautiful natural setting, interesting historic sights, and an array of convenient traveler services. Cycling allows a relaxed pace and closeup view of medieval towns, Roman ruins, and sloping vineyards. The valley route takes advantage of easy downstream cycling on riverside trails.

The Mosel tour is organized into four days, ending with a ride along the most scenic stretch of the Rhine Valley. Follow these guidelines loosely; it's unlikely you will manage to break up this tour in exactly the way described. The great advantage of touring in this region is the number of sights and facilities that allow the ride to be tailored to your own style or mood. Never more than 10 km away from the nearest room, hostel, or campground, you can call it a day—or ride on past the next river bend—at any point you wish. Some establishments conveniently combine accommodations and wine tasting under the same roof. Not only do travelers gain consumptive advantages from the labors of vineyard workers, they also benefit indirectly—benches and tables line vineyard slopes, making convenient picnic points for merry little bands of wandering cyclists.

Be warned—the secret is out. Thousands of tourists flock to the Mosel and Rhine valleys annually. While some towns swell with camera-wielding tour groups, however, many others go about their traditional way of life undisturbed. As a cyclist, you are well equipped to discover these pockets of genuine Mosel charm. Even in high season, road traffic is not a problem thanks to a good network of bicycle trails and marked routes along quiet side roads. The best time to cycle this tour is in early fall, when most of the tourists have departed and the grape harvest has just begun.

As an extremely popular bicycle-touring destination, much documentation is available about the Mosel Valley. The most exhaustive cyclist's guide to the area is the BVA's *Moselland Radwanderführer*, a booklet of 1:50,000-scale maps indicating bicycle routes, sights, repair shops, campsites, and inns.

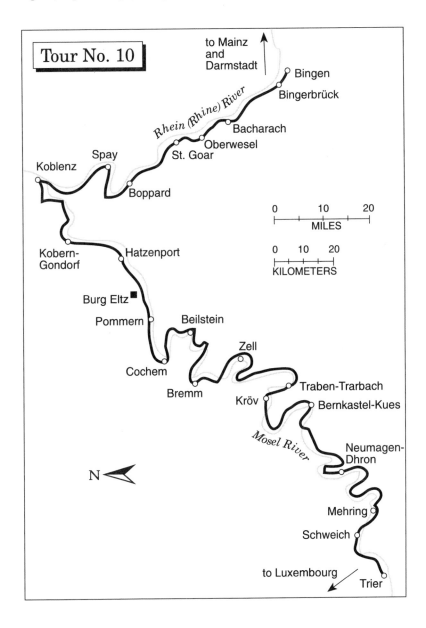

Trier

Trier, the starting point of this trip, can be reached by train via Koblenz from any point in Germany. Other options include cycling in from Luxembourg or combining this tour with a ride of the less touristy Saar Valley southwest of Trier. Ferries (*Rundfähre* or *Fähre*) offer a more expensive but exciting alternative, linking towns of both the Mosel and Rhine valleys (see tourist offices for time-tables and fares).

If arriving in Trier by train, stop by the station's information booth for a city map. Navigating Trier from the *Bahnhof* is a snap—just head straight out of the station and down the main street (Theodor-Heuss Allee). The road passes several supermarkets and the Porta Nigra, a monumental Roman gateway around which the city still centers. The main tourist office sits tucked behind the Porta Nigra, across from Marx's birthplace (Karl's, not Groucho's). Keep straight past Porta Nigra for signs to the large riverside hostel (east bank of the Mosel) or the campground 1 km away on the opposite shore.

Trier is an appropriate jumping-off point for a Mosel Valley tour, with many reminders of the region's long history and wine-making tradition. The city deserves a full day before heading out for the delights of Mosel cycling. The Roman amphitheater and baths are excellent sights, as are the medieval market square and impressive *Dom*. Keep an eye out for modern-day Romans who occasionally hold camps in Trier, fully decked out in robes and armor.

Trier to Bernkastel-Kues: 64 kilometers

Well-marked bicycle paths and beautiful valley scenery mean idyllic cycling on the first day of this tour. To leave Trier, **cross** Kaiser-Wilhelm Bridge to the west bank. Follow **bicycle signs** for Pfalzel and Ehrang, circling **left** and then **north**. After a short distance along this road, turn off **under train tracks** to access the **riverside bicycle trail** on the right. This excellent path leads northeast past **Pfalzel**, **Ehrang**, and **Schweich**. Like the Mosel itself, the trail takes some wild detours. Follow signs to successive towns instead of pedaling directly into any town center. At some clearly marked points the bicycle trail joins quiet roads and tractor trails.

In Ehrang stay on the main trail—**do not cross the river until Schweich**, then follow signs to **Longuich** and **Mehring**. Once past the **bridge** in Mehring, look for the **Zur Romischer Villa sign** to the right. The short, worthwhile **detour** to this partially reconstructed Roman villa rewards visitors with a glimpse of life on the Mosel sixteen centuries ago. **Return** to the same riverside bicycle trail and 2 km later watch for more Roman remains—an inscribed stone distance marker beside a short stretch of original Roman road.

Meander on through **Detzem**, **Thörnich**, and **Köwerich** along **paved and dirt roads**. When the bicycle path ends in **Leiwen** take a sharp **right** up to town and watch for bike signs to the **left**. The trail to Neumagen-Dhron leads along tractor trails through vineyards, offering spectacular views of the river bend. Views? Yes, this does involve a long uphill climb, one of the very few of the tour. But don't curse the climb; photo opportunities from this angle are unbeatable.

Neumagen, with its Roman *Weinschiff* (wine ship) sculpture and shady churchyard, is one of my favorite stops in the Mosel Valley. The sculpture (a copy of the third-century A.D. original now in Trier) depicts a heavily loaded galley, unenthusiastic (or hung-over) rowers peeping out between barrels of wine. The *Weinschiff* is a good reminder that the Mosel Valley's wine-producing tradition

Viniculture, past and present: Roman Weinschiff *and bottles of Mosel wine*

Partially reconstructed Roman villa in the Mosel Valley

stretches back over 2,000 years. Neumagen makes a nice picnic spot, and there are a few small stores in the town.

Ride on past **Piesport** on the opposite bank, then by **Minheim**, **Wintrich**, and **Brauneberg**. In **Mülheim cross** toward Maring and turn **right** for **Lieser**. The last few kilometers into **Bernkastel-Kues** follow a road with moderate traffic and a good wide shoulder on the opposite side, leading past the riverside campground near Kues. (Many towns in the Mosel Valley are partner towns, identified either together, with a hyphen, or divided into their separate halves, just as the river divides them.)

Bernkastel, on the east bank of the Mosel, is a town that has it all—a castle, beautiful surroundings, charming old market square with half-timbered houses, wine tasting on every corner, and many rooms for rent. Unfortunately, having it all also includes tourists—hoards and hoards of tourists. Nevertheless, Bernkastel remains a worthwhile if somewhat crowded Mosel highlight.

You can bike or hike up to the castle (3 km one way) by heading straight through the old town and following signs to **Burg Landshut**. Walking takes 20 minutes, biking about 15. Consider the journey up for outstanding views of the Mosel bend. Planning to stay at Bernkastel's hostel? Naturally, the hostel is also located atop this hill. Unfortunately, the pricey restaurant in the ruins discourages sweaty cyclists from playing knight in the castle. If you are saving yourself for only one high castle viewpoint, wait for the shorter climb up to Beilstein Castle near Cochem, where the castle is as nice and the setting more original.

Bernkastel-Kues to Cochem: 84 kilometers

To begin the ride to Traben-Trarbach, **follow the river downstream** from Bernkastel center on the wide shoulder of a moderately **busy road**. Bike through **Graach** and **Zeltingen**, where the bicycle trail to **Rachtig**, **Erden**, and **Lösnich** resumes. Continue in the **downstream direction** at any unmarked intersection along these vineyard roads. Keep alert for arrows occasionally painted on road surfaces that also point out the correct route.

In **Kindel** cross the **bridge** to **Kinheim**, then go **right** for the **bicycle trail** to **Kröv** and Traben-Trarbach. **Cross** the river again to **Wolf** and cycle the last 3 km to **Traben-Trarbach** along the road's shoulder. Though a convenient shopping stop, the town is otherwise not of great interest. Both the pleasant riverside campground and the hilltop hostel are clearly marked from Traben center, and there are many *Zimmer* in the area. A bicycle shop lies just north of the bridge's gate in Trarbach.

From Traben (on the river's north bank), ride **uphill** in the direction of the hostel (passing two large supermarkets) and rejoin the main **bicycle trail** after descending. Ride toward **Kövenig**, then Reil. Watch for the dramatically situated town of Starkenburg, perched high above the river on the opposite shore. As one progresses from Trier toward Koblenz, the bicycle trail gradually peters out, leaving cyclists on quiet roads or shoulders. However, the main route remains well marked throughout.

Cross the Mosel in **Reil** and ride on to **Pünderich**. For a closer look at this wonderful town, take a short **detour** right, opposite the ferry landing. You will be the only tourist wandering between Pünderich's medieval houses, where grapevines are decoratively laced over doorways and cobblestone streets. Continue riding the **marked trail** (some unpaved stretches) to **Zell**, a lively market town with a pleasant riverside promenade. Gazebos, picnic tables, and pretty views make Zell an ideal lunch spot.

Cycle along the river to **Bullay**, where the official Moseltal bicycle route crosses to **Alf** by ferry landing point 1 km past the main bridge in Bullay). You can also follow bicycle paths and road shoulders on the east bank, crossing a bridge in Neef and continuing to Bremm and Eller on the opposite shore. The ruins of Stuben Convent (twelfth to eighteenth century) occupy a bend opposite **Bremm**.

Though the official trail continues along the west bank all the way to Cochem, this route bypasses Beilstein. To visit the lovely town, pass **under** and then **circle back** to the bridge in Nehren. **Cross** the river to Senheim and **follow** a quiet road to **Beilstein**. The tiny town is one of the nicest stops in the Mosel Valley, yet receives relatively few tourists. A little huddle of medieval buildings sits snugly under the protection of Beilstein's Castle, only a five-minute hike away. This is by far the easiest place to get a high-castle-plus-river-and-vineyard view on the whole tour, so get the camera and munchies ready and enjoy a wonderful break.

To finish the day off, continue cycling along the east bank to **Bruttig**, **Valwig**, and **Cond**, eliminating a ride through the camper/tour bus gauntlet on the opposite shore. There are rooms for rent in and around Cochem, a campground in Valwig, and a hostel in Cond.

Cochem is another fantastically preserved medieval town complete with the requisite town square, fountain, and castle. However, the town is the main Mosel destination for day-tourists detouring from Rhine cruises, and therefore Cochem's streets are literally choked with crowds. For this reason, consider gaining quieter ground and a head start on the next day by riding on to a room in Klotten or camping near Pommern.

Cochem to Koblenz: 52 kilometers

Continue following the Mosel Radweg northeast to Koblenz from Cochem. The ride to Koblenz is entirely along shoulders of moderately busy roads, though most traffic is diverted to the *Autobahn*. Along the way, there are campgrounds in Burgen and Treis and a hostel in Brodenbach. Roads along both shores are suitable for cycling, though the north/west bank is the officially recommended route, offering unobstructed river views.

For a 10-km (one way) **detour** to highly touted Burg Eltz Castle, grind up the road to Wierschem from Moselkern. Or, for a quieter ride, ride from Hatzenport to Metternich and then double back to the castle. Those who don't mind the climb will be rewarded with excellent views, a visit to one of the nicest castles in the valley, and a terrific downhill run back to the river.

To **briefly escape** the main road, turn **left over** the train tracks in Lehmen, then **right** to parallel the rails. **Follow** small tractor roads through vineyards all the way to **Kobern-Gondorf**. When the road turns inland in Gondorf be sure to **continue in the downstream direction** by turning **right on any side street**. Both are nice towns, with a *Schloss* and tower in Gondorf and a ruined castle above Kobern.

Leave town by pedaling just **inland of train tracks** to reach **Winningen**, another pleasant, vine-laced wine town. As the tractor trails soon come to a dead end, you must turn **right** on Bachstrasse and **left** at the T. Pass **under** train tracks and return to the shoulder of **Road B416**. Do not be tempted by side roads to the right 2 km later; they both end in muddy impasses.

As you near Koblenz, keep directly along B416. Follow **bike**

signs to **Metternich** until the **bridge** where these signs turn left (inland). There, continue **straight** ahead on a **sidewalk bicycle lane**. Soon after, B416 dips below an overpass, while the bicycle lane rides **up** and faces **House No. 159**. Turn **right** at this house and follow **bicycle signs** that begin at the end of the block, leading to the **river's edge**. When the path ends, **rejoin the street** up on the left and continue riding **downstream**.

Follow signs to *Stadtmitte* or *City*. Signs for the pleasant riverside campground point straight ahead. To reach the city center, ride this road, circling up and across the bridge in the bicycle lane. The old town center of Koblenz lies directly across the river. The tourist office is located next to the main train station to the south, and there is a hostel within the walls of the fortress across the Rhine. Located at the confluence of two important rivers, Koblenz offers a great vantage point for barge-watching. Bid the lovely Mosel goodbye as you prepare for cycling the most dramatic stretch of the Rhine Valley on the final day of this tour.

Koblenz to Bingen: 63 kilometers

Like the river traffic that has flowed through the valley for centuries, you will pass through the territory of one precariously perched castle to the next during this ride along the Rhine. A steady stream of barges attests to the continuing importance of the Rhine as a vital artery of commerce in central Europe.

From the center of Koblenz, head **upriver (south)** on the **west bank** and eventually join the **bicycle path** to **Rhens** and **Spay** (part dirt and cobblestone). Pause in a small riverside park to see the old town walls and towers of Spay, its gateway marked with record highwater marks from centuries past.

Soon the **trail ends**, forcing cyclists to join the wide shoulder of busy **Road B9**. The remainder of the ride to Bingen follows wide shoulders, though some short stretches degenerate to narrow paths or simply very rough edges (particularly two sections between Boppard and St. Goar, and into Bingen at the end of the ride). Hopefully improvements will be made soon, but until then the ride has unpleasant sections and is definitely not recommended for the kiddies. Do not hesitate to walk your bike over the worst parts or hop on a train to Bacharach if you feel uncomfortable cycling on busy roads.

Wander **Boppard**'s lively waterfront and pleasant old town streets. **St. Goar** and **Oberwesel** are also nice towns, though St. Goar in particular suffers with over-tourism. But who knows, maybe you will unwittingly star in somebody's home video and be described as a typical German cyclist to the folks back home. The famed Loreley Cliff makes a very nice picnic view if you can find a quiet spot away from the tour buses. Take a break from biking and let Loreley legends trickle into your mind.

Uncontested jewel of the Rhine, **Bacharach**'s narrow streets keep tour buses at bay and cyclists in a state of smug delight. Duck under the old town gates to enter a world of tidy timbered houses listing drunkenly along twisting streets. Time-warped beams are decorated with the words of rhyming verses or Biblical quotes. Bacharach's oldest buildings date back to the fourteenth century.

After a day of biking on narrow shoulders, the peaceful riverside bicycle trail from Bacharach to Bingen is especially nice and offers open views of the last several castles along this ride. The trail begins off the **left side of the main road** (B9) just upriver from Bacharach—note signs pointing **under the train tracks**. The trail ends in **Bingerbrück**, where cyclists must ride a **terrible shoulder** and then the **main road** into the town center.

Private *Zimmer* are advertised in every town along this stretch of the Rhine, and many stores (and bakeries) make shopping convenient. There are hostels in St. Goar, Oberwesel, Bacharach, and Bingerbrück, and campgrounds in St. Goar (Camping Loreleyblick), Bacharach (upriver from the town), or near Bingen.

Bingen itself has little to offer besides an unimpressive pedestrian zone, rooms for rent, and convenient train connections (Bingerbrück station). The hostel is clearly signed from the main road, and there is a waterside campground 2 km upriver. For quick connections, hop on a train in Bingerbrück or a ferry in Bingen (near the train station). Mainz, 30 km upriver, merits a day's exploration, with many interesting sights and a pretty town center. Ride a rough path along the Rhine via Ingelheim-Nord to Mainz or take a short train ride (DM 5). There is a hostel on the eastern hill in Mainz and a campground across the river. Trains will also bring you to the starting points of other tours such as the Water Castles of Münsterland Tour (Tour No. 14) or the Vogelsberg tour (Tour No. 11) to the east.

TOUR NO. 11

VOGELSBERG EXPLORER
Marburg to Fulda

Distance: 194 kilometers (120 miles)
Estimated time: 4 to 5 days (4 biking days)
Terrain: Easy valley cycling mixed with challenging, hilly stretches
Maps: ADFC #16 and #17
Connecting tour: Tour No. 12

For a scenic and interesting ride away from standard tourist routes, a short tour of the Vogelsberg area provides a perfect option for cyclists eager to head off the beaten path. While offering many convenient traveler services, this region is no slave to tourism, perfect for peaceful cycling and appreciation of a pleasant, genuine atmosphere. Wooded valleys and sloping fields lead from one half-timbered farm town to the next, with stops at old market towns such as Marburg, Alsfeld, and Bad Hersfeld.

Marburg

Marburg and the Vogelsberg area are easily accessible by train, lying on a line between Kassel and Frankfurt. If arriving by rail, go straight and left from Marburg *Bahnhof*, following signs for Giessen. Soon you will see signs for the riverside hostel and nearby camping (south of town on the east bank of the Lahn River).

Ready for a lesson in "Important Elements of a German Old Town?" Marburg makes an excellent starting point for this tour, introducing many features that will soon form a familiar pattern as you pedal the region. Immaculate half-timbered houses line twisting old town streets while church spires and a hilltop castle tower above. In the *Marktplatz*, the *Rathaus* and Fountain of St. George round out the scene. For good views over the region you will soon tour, head to the terrace of Marienkirche.

Marburg to Alsfeld: 62 kilometers

This first day of cycling keeps entirely to bicycle paths or quiet roads. Be careful to keep an eye open for bicycle signs along the ride, as some turns may be tricky. By pedaling a **riverside bicycle**

path north, leave Marburg along the **east bank** of the Lahn. First follow **bicycle signs** for **Wehrda**, then head on for **Cölbe** and Kirchhain instead.

After **crossing train tracks** and a **bridge** past Cölbe, turn **left**

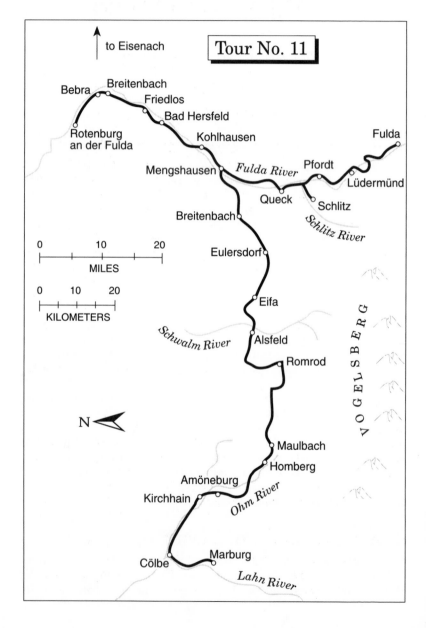

Far off the beaten path in the Vogelsberg area

for **Kirchhain** and circle around to the **bicycle path**, heading for Kirchhain *Stadtmitte*. For orientation, check the information map in the old town center. Although historic buildings and squares suggest traces of the town's original character, Kirchhain's traditional aspect has not been well preserved. To see the real highlight of the area, turn **right** on Amöneburger Tor Strasse for the **bicycle path up** to **Amöneburg**.

This wonderful hilltop town may be similar to other medieval towns in general form, but it guards a truly unique character, a sense of isolation and timelessness on its perch high above the modern world. For the cyclist, unfortunately, the operative word is hill—the climb up grates tired knees but rewards with tremendous views. In town, winding side streets, the open *Marktplatz*, and castle ruins tempt cyclists to tarry. Peek inside Johanneskirche for a hint of how slowly change has come to this tiny hill town. For a longer break, walk the panorama trail outside the town walls.

When you are ready to leave Amöneburg, cruise **back down** the hill. Bear **left**, following signs for **Mardorf**, another neat town of half-timbered houses and farmyards. Signs to **Homberg (Ohm)** draw you farther down the valley. Turn **right** for Gemünden and HO-Büßfeld at the light in Homberg. A short walk through the streets above today's main road presents a good perspective on Homberg's old town center with its fountain and *Rathaus*.

Pedal out of Homberg in the **direction of Gemünden**, turning **left** to Maulbach 2 km later for a long climb up out of the valley. In **Maulbach** turn **right** for **Ehringshausen**. As you near the

Quiet farmlands typify the Vogelsberg region.

Autobahn 3 km later, look for a **path branching to the left** after merging with an incoming road. This trail runs parallel to the *Autobahn* toward Heimertshausen. When the path emerges on a **small road**, turn **right** to cross **under** the highway, then **left** toward **Romrod**. Turn **north** 2 km later on side roads to **Zell**, **Billertshausen**, and **Angenrod** for a pleasant ride through hilly farmlands. In Angenrod turn **right** again on busy, hilly **Road 62** to **Alsfeld**, the lanes wide enough for safe if not peaceful cycling.

For camping, head west from Zell to Heimertshausen, the site nearest Alsfeld (nice site with pool, laundry facilities, and kiosk). Consider stopping here and visiting Alsfeld on the way to Bad Hersfeld the next day. Speedy cyclists may even cycle from Marburg to Alsfeld and Bad Hersfeld in a single day, a total distance of 110 km (68 mi).

Follow **signs** to *Historisches Altstadt* to enter the old town. Tourist information lies just off the *Marktplatz* (no nearby hostel but rooms for rent in town). Alsfeld's old town centers around its compact *Marktplatz*, clustered with many fine buildings dating to the Middle Ages. With an arcaded ground floor and twin towers, Alsfeld's unusual *Rathaus* is the city's trademark. Walk Rittergasse to see the most impressive historic houses in town, or explore smaller alleys nearby with the help of the tourist map's suggested walking tour.

Alsfeld to Bad Hersfeld: 44 kilometers

Ride **east** out of Alsfeld on **Road 62** toward the *Autobahn*. Reach this road from the town center by pedaling past the **left side** of the

Rathaus and turning **right** at the light once back in the modern world. After **crossing** Road 254, take the first **left** on a small road marked only **"GBV"** on small white signs.

Once on this side road, bear **right** on the road with the red circle (indicating limited access), **left** at the next **Y** intersection, and then ride **straight**, paralleling the *Autobahn*. Eventually the road turns to **dirt** but is suitable for cycling. Pass **under** the highway and turn **left** to continue paralleling it until you come to a large overpass. Cross **under** and head **straight down** to **Eifa**.

After the soccer field, keep **right**. Once you rejoin the main road, turn **left** in the direction of Grebenau. Pedal **up** several long hills, finally reaching the crest for a **downhill** ride to **Eulersdorf**. Follow the **valley road** to **Grebenau**, **Wallersdorf**, and **Breitenbach**, climbing occasionally between towns.

In Breitenbach join **Road 62** toward Niederaula (**right** turn). The busy road has sections of bicycle lane and some traffic funnels off to the nearby *Autobahn*. In **Niederaula** turn **right** to **cross** the Fulda River to **Mengshausen**. There, turn **left** on a quiet country road to Bad Hersfeld. To keep to quiet lanes, **cross the bridge** from **Kohlhausen** toward Asbach. On the **opposite bank**, take the first **right** to access a series of **dirt and paved paths** right into the city center. Don't be tempted by Road 62, by now too busy

Medieval houses in Alsfeld's market square

for safe pedaling. Information signs lead a circuitous route to the tourist office in the town *Marktplatz*.

Bad Hersfeld's hostel sits on a hill 1 km from the center of town. To reach it, ride Frauenstrasse from the *Marktplatz* and pedal straight up a steep hill on Wehnebergerstrasse. The hostel lies to the right near the top. For camping, leave *Marktplatz* in the same direction, but turn left at the base of the hill to ride flat Homberg-erstrasse to the nearby campground.

Bad Hersfeld's principal sights test your knowledge of "Important German Old Town Elements." See the *Marktplatz*, *Rathaus*, *Ratskeller*, and surrounding pedestrian zone. In July and August a drama festival is held in the Stiftsruine, the cathedral ruins forming an appropriate backdrop for performances. For information and tickets, stop by the *Festspiele* booth in the *Marktplatz,* where you will also find a map index to *Zimmer* complete with vacancy notices.

Bad Hersfeld to Rotenburg Day Trip: 38 kilometers

This tour turns south from Bad Hersfeld to end in Fulda, but first takes a detour north to Rotenburg an der Fulda. The pretty little town may not boast the attractions of the other Rothenburg (the Romantic Road's Rothenburg ob der Tauber; see Tour No. 1), but merits a visit all the same. Another way to divide the tour involves pedaling this route and continuing on to Schlitz in one day, then finishing from Schlitz to Fulda the next. Cyclists planning to turn east to join the Thuringia tour (Tour No. 12) should consult the Connection route described below, linking Bebra (near Rotenburg) to Eisenach.

To ride north, **parallel Road 27** toward Bebra and Kassel on a separate **bicycle lane** (on the left side) until **Friedlos**. Enter Friedlos and continue riding **straight** ahead, paralleling the main road. As you leave town, **bear left** onto an **overpass** to cross Road 27. Follow signs and bicycle paths to Mecklar, Breitenbach, and Bebra. All the way, enjoy quiet cycling and nice scenery.

Near Mecklar turn **left** for an **overpass** back to the other side of Road 27 and a stretch of **bicycle lane** along the main road. When the path ends near Blankenheim, go straight **under** the overpass, pedal into **Blankenheim**, and **bear right** at *Sportplatz* to regain peaceful trails. Eventually **cross back** toward Breitenbach via an **overpass**. Go **straight**, then take the first well-paved road into **Breitenbach** (right). Bike **down the lane** to the **left** of the church to access the best bicycle trail of the day, pedaling directly **along the banks** of the Fulda. Simply follow signs and the riverbank down the valley to **Rotenburg**.

Like its better-known cousin on the Tauber, Rotenburg preserves an appealing old town center. Unlike the other town, however,

Rotenburg's small size and relative obscurity keep its streets free of tourist mobs. A fountain fills the *Marktplatz* with the sound of running water, while neat half-timbered buildings lean into each other on side streets. For a good overall view of the pleasant town, cross the river. **Retrace** your route **south** to **return** to Bad Hersfeld. This area is sometimes windy. For Bebra and the Connection tour to Thuringia, turn east at Breitenbach (see below).

Bad Hersfeld to Fulda: 50 kilometers

Retrace your route **south** along the Fulda Valley from Bad Hersfeld. Access the same side trails by heading for *Kurpark* in town. At the tennis courts, turn **right** to ride a trail occasionally marked *Rad und Fußgängerweg nach Kohlhausen*. Cross to Kohlhausen, then pedal to **Kerspenhausen** and through **Mengshausen**. Mengshausen serves as a comforting reminder that not everyone in the world is speeding ahead full steam. Don't be surprised if you see a herd of cows blocking the main road, ushered along by a cycling farmer, a husband and wife walking a huge pig on a rope, or a farmer jingling slowly along in a horse-drawn wagon.

Pedal on to **Solms** and **Unterschwarz**. There, bear **right** on a bicycle lane marked *Rad und Wanderweg nach Schlitz* to **parallel** the river for another perfect ride. Follow bicycle *frei* lanes and white-and-green bicycle signs. **Cross** the river into **Queck**, riding the bicycle path to Hutzdorf. Nearing **Hutzdorf, cross** a road and continue on the bike trail. **Cross** over a small bridge and turn **right** for a quick 2-km ride to **Schlitz** (**unmarked**). (Remember this **T** since you will return later for the left branch to Fulda.)

Schlitz is a wonderful town with few tourists, four castles, a nice *Marktplatz*, and an excellent bakery/cafe. Enough said, no? Shop for lunch supplies at a store in the modern town at the foot of the hill. Lock your bicycle to wander cobbled side streets free of extra load and walk to the highest point in Schlitz for good views of the valley. Those tempted to linger in this wonderful town can look for *Zimmer* or head for camping (direction Pfordt).

To continue the ride, **backtrack** to the main valley, **pass by the small bridge** you crossed earlier, and again **follow** the Fulda River south on peaceful bicycle trails. In **Pfordt** turn **left** and **cross** the bridge, pedaling **straight** past a parking area. As the road bends left, turn **right** to keep along quiet country lanes. Use the river for orientation when in doubt, always heading upstream. Wait for the **second bridge** before **crossing** to **Hartershausen**, the next town. There, turn **left** for roads to **Hemmen** and **Lüdermünd**.

The bicycle path indicated on some cycling maps is difficult to find, so continue directly along the **main road** to Fulda after a quick look around little Lüdermünd. Traffic increases near the city but remains only occasional. Follow signs to *Stadtmitte* in Fulda. The helpful tourist office lies tucked away under the main gate to *Stadtschloss*. The office provides maps, room information, and suggestions for walking tours.

An eighth-century monastery first established Fulda as an important center of religion and scholarship. Even today, the city retains its significant role, hosting an annual conference of German Catholicism. Many architectural styles mark Fulda. Most impressive is the Baroque Quarter: See the *Dom*, containing many artworks as well as the tomb of patron St. Boniface, and visit the *Schloss* with its *Orangerie* and gardens. The *Schloss* also contains a museum of porcelain, a local specialty. Explore Michaelskirche and the pedestrian zone in the city center or, for an appropriate end to this tour of medieval towns, find *Hexenturm* (guard tower), part of Fulda's original town walls.

Concerts are frequently held in the *Schloss* theater; for information and tickets, check the office on the right side of the castle. Campers must head 7 km south of Fulda to pitch their tents in Eichenzell. A hostel across the Fulda (near the sports stadium) provides accommodations closer to the center. Ask at Fulda's *Bahnhof* for speedy connections to your next destination. The city's central location in Germany brings many touring areas within close reach (Frankfurt hub station, one and a half hours; Gotha, two hours).

Connection to Tour No. 12

Bebra to Eisenach: 50 kilometers. For contrast, consider pedaling eastward to begin Tour No. 12 of Thuringia in Eisenach, only 50 km away. Bebra, near Rotenburg, lies only 12 km from the former East–West border. A fascinating ride cuts across the serpentine line of the former border several times, repeatedly contrasting East with West. In many places guard towers and even sections of wall remain, reminders of the surreal situation that divided these lands until only a few years ago. Riverside terrain allows for quick and easy cycling.

From Rotenburg, ride south along the Fulda River to Breitenbach and cross to Bebra there. Instead of cycling into Bebra center, keep due east to Weiterode, Ronshausen, and Wildeck along a moderately busy road. Cross over and turn left to parallel the *Autobahn* east toward Eisenach.

Past Wildeck you will near a corner of the border but will not actually cross the line until after Obersuhl. The stark, obvious scar of the former border may dampen your enthusiasm—time to shift mental gears and get ready to meet the East.

Cross the train tracks in Neustädt to access an unpaved trail along the rails, crossing back to the West and Wommen. There, you will rejoin better roads to Herleshausen—last chance to beat a quick retreat to the West. No? Good for you.

Make the final crossing to the East. The road turns sharply north to cross under the *Autobahn*. Take the first right turn toward Spichra and loop back south on another unpaved track, crossing the *Autobahn* again and intersecting a quieter road in Hörschel. Turn southeast along the Hörsel River to Stedtfeld and Eisenach. To reach the tourist office there, ride directly through town toward the *Bahnhof*. The office will be to your left once past the old town (see Tour No. 12).

TOUR NO. 12

A WINDOW EAST
Eisenach to Naumburg

Distance: 180 kilometers (112 miles)
Estimated time: 3 days (3 biking days)
Terrain: Gradually rolling hills
Map: ADFC #13 and #17
Connecting tour: Tour No. 11

Although Thuringia is best known for its role in German history, you will be happily surprised to find far-reaching wooded hills, scenic river valleys, and appealing towns to complement the historic monuments on this tour. Still, biking Thuringia is like pedaling the biographies of Germany's great artists and thinkers, from Liszt and Bach to Luther, Goethe, and Schiller. Even non-history buffs, however, will appreciate Wartburg Castle, regardless of the fact that Luther worked on his translation of the Bible there. Goethe and Schiller aside, Weimar's shady avenues are pleasant in their own right. With moderate to easy cycling, and short stretches between

Thuringian forests surround Wartburg castle.

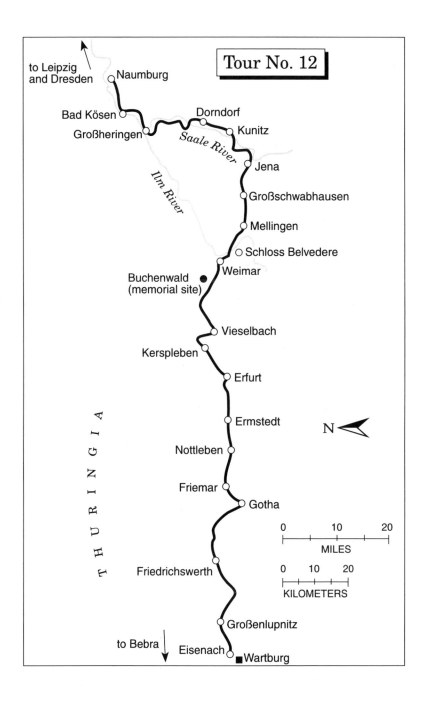

to Leipzig and Dresden

Naumburg

Tour No. 12

Bad Kösen

Dorndorf

Großheringen

Kunitz

Saale River

Ilm River

Jena

Großschwabhausen

Mellingen

Schloss Belvedere

Buchenwald (memorial site)

Weimar

Vieselbach

Kerspleben

Erfurt

Ermstedt

Nottleben

N

Friemar

Gotha

0   10   20
MILES

Friedrichswerth

0   10   20
KILOMETERS

Großenlupnitz

to Bebra

Eisenach

Wartburg

THURINGIA

points of interest, this tour presents a varied menu of sights and activities to cyclists of all types.

Unlike some other regions of the East, Thuringia has many services, stores, and tourist offices in addition to good quality roads, even in the countryside. Only campers will be disappointed at the scarcity of conveniently located sites. Outside Eisenach and Naumburg, travelers must opt for hostels or private rooms, though accommodations services at tourist offices facilitate the search. To avoid a frustrating surprise, be sure to obtain updated information before setting off on any lengthy detours. Many of the campgrounds marked on my map, for example, were no longer open.

If you know little about Thuringian names and places before you set out, you will need a little help getting oriented. The following names are dropped casually throughout Thuringia:

Martin Luther is an important figure in German history, the father of the Reformation. Luther began his translation of the New Testament into vernacular German in Wartburg Castle, a work that had profound impact on both religion and the development of literature. Goethe earns his fame as Germany's greatest poet, an important figure in world literature as well as a statesman and scientist. His best known work is *Faust*. Schiller, Goethe's contemporary, was another great dramatist and poet who lived in Weimar in the eighteenth century. Herder and Wieland round out Weimar's list of four great literary figures. Composers Liszt and Bach, the artist Lucas Cranach the Elder, and philosopher Nietzsche all seemed to move about Thuringia semi-constantly. Today visitors find their houses, birthplaces, workplaces, or deathplaces scattered throughout the cities of this tour.

Eisenach

Eisenach, the tour's starting point, lies on the main rail line between Bebra in the West and Erfurt in the East. Train connections are relatively easy—and interesting as well. Although no longer a border point, Bebra remains a transfer station where electric locomotives are switched for diesel engines (the boys at the *Reichsbahn* are still catching up to Western standards). Follow your map during the trip east as the train crosses the former border several times en route—in places watchtowers and even sections of wall remain. Only 50 km from Bebra, Eisenach is also easily reached by bike from the Vogelsberg tour (see Connection in Tour No. 11).

Eisenach's tourist office lies between the *Bahnhof* and town gate, at a traffic light just outside the *Tor* (on the right if coming from the station). The office helps find rooms and provides town maps. Check there before setting out to the campground 8 km south on

Where Luther worked and Tannhäuser sang: Wartburg castle

Giving Erfurt a fresh face

Road 19. As you pedal to the campsite, turn right for Etterwinden for the last 3 km. The hostel is also on Road 19 south (Mariental 24, 2 km from Eisenach). Room advertisements dot Eisenach's streets.

In Eisenach, hike or bike up to eleventh-century Wartburg Castle (grounds free, admission fee for exhibits). The walk up through undisturbed woods is as worthwhile as the impressive castle, creating a timeless, pilgrimage feeling. Ask for Wartburg *Fußweg* to reach the trailhead. Luther hid in the mighty castle while working on his translation of the Bible. Better yet for the imagination, the legendary minstrel Tannhäuser sang in Wartburg centuries ago (at least according to Wagner, who set his opera *Tannhäuser* here). Eisenach town also merits a visit, with an old town gate and a lively market in the main square. Shops and supermarkets line the small pedestrian zone.

Eisenach to Erfurt: 75 kilometers

Pass the *Bahnhof* to leave Eisenach on **Road 84** toward Behringen. Most traffic on the road exits onto the *Autobahn*, leaving you with a quieter ride. In **Großenlupnitz** turn **right** for **Sättelstädt** for peaceful biking on secondary roads. Several **long, gradual climbs and descents** mark the ride to Gotha (40 km). On the second half of the day the hills ease out to slightly longer but **more gradual** slopes.

Ride through **Hastrungsfeld** and turn **left** for **Burla**. The climb to **Ebenheim** gains excellent views far across the neighboring woods and valleys of Thuringia. In Ebenheim go **left** for **Haina**, a picturesque farm town. There, go **right** for **Friedrichswerth** and pick up signs right into **Gotha**. As the main road approaches Gotha center, it opens onto the city ring. Cut **straight** across the ring road and find your way to the *Marktplatz*. For orientation, check the town map posted on Neumarket.

With two large market squares and many well-kept houses, Gotha makes an easy place to pass an extended lunch hour. Like other Thuringian towns that comprise this tour, Gotha is an important cultural center, its influence reaching far beyond the immediate sphere of the small city. Under its Saxon Dukes and later Charlemagne, Gotha flourished with libraries, scientific institutes, and religious foundations.

From the center ride **northeast** up Kindelbenstrasse for **Gotha Ost**. Entering **Friemar**, go **right** where the main traffic goes left, then turn **left** up Goethestrasse. Ride on and through **Pferdingsleben**. **Cross** the bridge and turn **left** on an **unsigned dirt road** for a bumpy ride past garden plots to **Nottleben**. Back on pavement in Nottleben, ride **straight** through town, on to **Erm-**

stedt, and follow signs to **Erfurt**. Over-optimistic distance markers indicate Erfurt's extreme outer edge, not the center, so don't get too excited yet!

Navigation into Erfurt can prove difficult. Ask for *Zentrum* and head for the *Dom*'s multiple spires. Once in the center, any of three tourist offices will deluge you with information. The offices are helpful, well informed, free, and even open during lunch.

From *Domplatz* walk the pedestrian area to *Fischermarkt* to see the *Rathaus* and beautifully restored houses. Continue straight ahead to reach the Kramerbrücke, Erfurt's top sight and location of one tourist office. Like the Ponte Vecchio in Florence, this picturesque bridge is crowded with narrow houses and shops. The river may not be as romantic or impressive as the Arno (after all, romance is more an Italian specialty) but makes for nice picnic views all the same.

The Augustinian monastery a few blocks north of Kramerbrücke is another noteworthy sight. After a close call with a bolt of lightning, Martin Luther vowed to become a monk and subsequently entered this *Kloster*. Today the pleasant cloister garden is open to the public.

For help with rooms, check at a tourist office (listings price doubles from DM 70). Erfurt's hostel is in the town center (Hochheimer Straße 12). The nearest campground lies 20 km south on Stausee Hohenfelden, an inexpensive but inconvenient option.

Erfurt to Weimar: 30 kilometers

Another short day of gradual rolls brings you to Weimar, one of Thuringia's most important towns. Leave Erfurt **via Krämpferstrasse**, a busy road that becomes **Leipzigerstrasse**. To gain quieter roads, ride **through Kerspleben** and turn **right** in **Kleinmölsen** to **Vieselbach**.

In Vieselbach turn **left** for **Niederzimmern** and **Ottstedt**, a picture-perfect, red-roofed town nestled at the foot of wooded hills. From Ottstedt follow signs directly to **Weimar**, enduring a few more hills on the way. **Alternatively**, turn left (no sign) to Hottelstedt, then south again to reach the Buchenwald concentration camp memorial before riding into Weimar center. Certainly, nobody enjoys visiting such wrenching sites, but they should be seen at least once. Consider the detour if you have never visited one of these memorials.

Most roads lead to Goetheplatz in Weimar. From there ask for the *Marktplatz*, which is nearby but difficult to find through twisting streets. Head for the tourist office at Marktstrasse 4 for a town map or help with rooms. Buchfart campground is now closed, with the nearest site being Hohenfelden. Three hostels round out your options. Maxim Gorky Hostel offers private and double rooms, and proves that not everything in the region is named after its native sons. To reach the hostel, bike Road 85 south, pass a parking lot, and look for the left turn on Zum Wilden Graben.

Chances are good that you'll be nicely surprised by this small city. Bold flags color Weimar's *Rathaus* and *Marktplatz*, both under restoration. The Bauhaus and Weimar Republic were established in the city early this century, both important influences in modern German history.

Walk pedestrian Schillerstrasse, lined with shops and historic houses, including Schiller's house, now a museum. Proceed around the corner to the theater square, where statues of the two Johanns (Goethe and Schiller) stand before the building where many of their works were first performed. Included in Weimar's impressive list of residents is the composer Liszt. Pass the conservatory he founded on the way to Ilm Park, a wonderful place to walk, bike, or sit in the grass and philosophize. Visit Goethe's summer residence in the park or put history aside in the cool riverside shade. For a side trip, pedal 5 km south to Belvedere Palace, residence of the royal family that patronized the city's artists, writers, and composers.

Weimar to Naumburg: 75 kilometers

The last day of the tour continues over rolling hills to Jena, then level river valleys to Naumburg. Leave Weimar on **Belvedere Allee**. Turn **left** for Oberweimar and Jena, then **right** once across the river.

In **Mellingen**, turn **left** for **Apolda**. For peaceful roads with wide views, take the **first right** for **Lehnstedt** (clearly marked). In **Großschwabhausen** cross **train tracks** and follow the **high road** toward Münchenroda, turning **left** for **Remderoda** just outside town.

From Remderoda you will have wonderful, high views over Jena, a city tucked into a steep, wooded valley. Cruise **downhill**, turn **right** and join the **main road** into the city center. Follow signs to *Volkshaus* and ask your way into the *Zentrum*. Once you arrive, stop by the helpful tourist office (on Teichgraben near *Marktplatz*) for a map of principal sights.

Explore the compact *Marktplatz*, where local ceramics are sold beside the usual produce stands. Sections of ancient walls and gates still ring the inner town. Eichplatz, the large square at the foot of a university tower, also offers an interesting market scene. Nearby, walk Kollegiengasse to peek into the archway of Jena's university, one of the oldest in Germany. Back in the good old days

High castle over the river Ilm

of the East German sports machine (when men were men and women were a lot like men, too), the university chemistry department dabbled (rather extensively) in doping research.

Leave Jena north on **Road 88**. Gain quieter roads 4 km later by **turning off for Kunitz**, where a ruined castle perches high above town. Bear **left** for **Golmsdorf**, enjoying level terrain along the valley floor.

Exit Golmsdorf as if riding to Bürgel but make a **sharp left** at the **green bicycle sign** for Dorndorf. This horrendous cobble/dirt road may rattle your fillings loose, but you will soon regain pavement in Dorndorf. Dornburg Fortress looms high on a cliff across the Saale, open to view from your riverside vantage point.

In **Dorndorf**, keep on the **east bank**. Pedal Road 88 until the **hilltop turnoff** to **Wichmar**. There, **descend** through the pretty town, bump over cobblestones past the **church**, curve **left**, and **cross** the river to **Würchhausen**. **Cross** train tracks and **bear right (north)** to Camburg. Cross **under** the tracks only once. Do not cross under the second underpass—rather, go **right** on a marked **pedestrian/bicycle path** along the tracks for a wonderful riverside ride, one of the nicest, quietest parts of this day.

In Camburg, **cross** the tracks and immediately turn **right** for **Großheringen**. At the point where the Ilm and Saale rivers merge, turn **east** for **Bad Kösen**. Bike the **main road**, passing two ruined castles along the way. Bad Kösen is a therapy center with impressive spa buildings and lake gardens. For the last 7 km of the day, make a quick dash on **Road 87** or cross to the river's north bank to follow quiet, partly unpaved riverside roads.

Head for the four green towers of **Naumburg**'s *Dom* and stop by the tourist office nearby (on Steinweg). Ask for help with rooms or directions to the riverside *Campingplatz* 2 km away. To reach the campsite bike down to the *Bahnhof*, cross the tracks with the overpass of Road 180, and follow camping signs to the quiet, inexpensive site with new facilities. There is no hostel in Naumburg.

Naumburg, a thirteenth-century cathedral town, makes an appropriate end to this tour of historic cities. See the *Dom*, then walk a pedestrian area across town to the *Marktplatz* and *Rathaus*, with its colorful doorway. On the edge of town, visit Marientor, part of the original town wall, and Marienkirche. The center neatly divides itself between cathedral and *Rathaus* areas, each half tempting weary riders with small bench-lined squares.

To keep the tour limited to areas most accessible by bicycle in the East, I recommend train transportation to Tour No. 13 (Saxon Treasures: Dresden and the Elbe Valley). Determined cyclists may pedal a few days east to reach Tour No. 13 but should expect traffic snares around larger centers such as Leipzig. Since the area between the two tours is not a major tourist destination, travel services and conveniences may be more difficult to come by. With the experience of this tour behind you, however, you should now be a pro at dealing with the East.

Naumburg train connections run via Leipzig to the east or Erfurt to the west. If continuing to Dresden, consider visiting historic Leipzig on the way. You may ship your bike ahead to Dresden and visit Leipzig *Altstadt* on foot if more convenient.

TOUR NO. 13

SAXON TREASURES
Dresden and the Elbe Valley

Distance: 122 to 150 kilometers (76 to 93 miles)
Estimated time: 3 to 4 days (2 biking day trips)
Terrain: Flat but windy valley
Map: ADFC #14

Consisting of two day trips based from Dresden, this tour explores the scenery and history of the Elbe Valley. Saxon Kings made Dresden their showcase city and guarded their treasury in Königstein Castle, high on a cliff over the Elbe. Despite wartime destruction and years of decay, their legacy remains evident. Now opened and revitalized by reunification, Dresden and the Elbe Valley make a unique touring destination with many possibilities for more cycling along the borderlands between Germany and the Czech Republic. This infrequently traveled area allows cyclists to enjoy quiet roads and unspoiled scenery, as well as to observe the differences that still remain between East and West.

Is it really worth schlepping yourself and your bike to a distant corner of Germany for only two little day trips? Absolutely. The beauty of the Elbe Valley and fascinating Dresden alone make the detour worthwhile. This is perhaps less a hard-core bicycle tour than an eye-opening eastern foray, combining a conventional tourist approach to the city with pleasant bicycle trips in the environs. Casual travelers can rent bicycles in Dresden to eliminate the inconvenience of shipping their own bicycles from afar (see below).

Dresden

Throughout Germany you will be impressed by beautiful historic towns spared from or painstakingly rebuilt after wartime destruction. In this category, Dresden will impress you more than any other. Practically leveled by Allied forces in the last days of the war, Dresden today shows two faces of the results with both untouched ruins and carefully rebuilt buildings. Destruction also left many open spaces around the principal buildings, leaving the impression of an open-air historical museum of baroque architecture—of awesome scale.

Dresden is one of the few places where wartime ruins remain un-

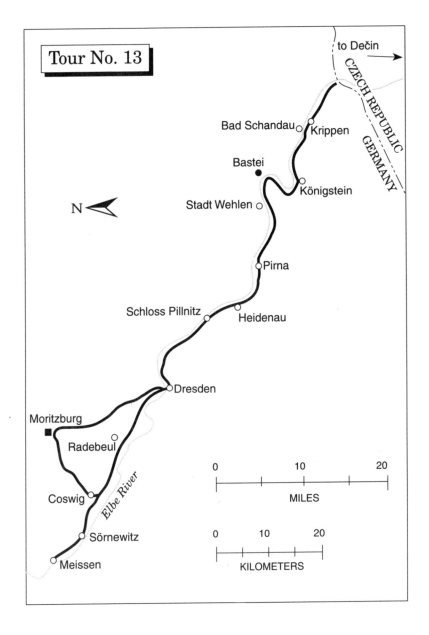

touched, but you will have to move fast to see them as reunification speeds restoration projects along. Dresden's most famous building, the Frauenkirche, remained a huge rubble heap until recently. Now cranes and excavators crowd the scene, restoration cleverly fi-

Zwinger palace and park grounds in Dresden

nanced by the Frauenkirche *Lotto* (look for the booths around town) and other sources. For a sobering look at post-war photographs of Dresden's major buildings and before/after contrasts, stop by a street vendor's table.

You are likely to be accompanied on your explorations by street music appropriate to each sight: a string trio playing at the beautiful Zwinger Palace, now Dresden's largest museum, or a brass duet performing along the King's Procession, a wall of painted porcelain tiles portraying each of the Saxon kings from the twelfth century onward. For music on a grander scale, attend a performance at the elegant *Semperoper* (opera house).

After a morning of sightseeing, take in views of the Elbe from the shaded terrace beside the Katholische Hofkirche. Take in an ice cream, too. Of course, appropriate Dresden reading includes Kurt Vonnegut's *Slaughterhouse Five*. The title building still stands on the outskirts of the city (Schlachthofringe).

From Dresden *Hauptbahnhof* look for signs to tourist information on Pragerstrasse, a fountain-lined pedestrian avenue that leads toward the city center. The well-stocked office will provide city maps, arrange room rental, and sell tickets to performances. Reservations are a must for any of Dresden's three youth hostels, often fully booked.

A detailed city map will prove a great help to campers in locating their choice of several campsites in the Dresden area. The two best options include, first, Campsite R40 in the Kaitz area, the site closest to the city center (6 km). Yuri Gagarin Strasse behind the *Bahnhof* leads to Road 172 and signs to the site. Signs say 3 km but don't believe it. Ride straight on 172 but do not turn left on Sudhöhe (the sign is misleading). Instead, take the next left (Bannewitzerstrasse). At the fifth intersection go left on Boderitzerstrasse and the campsite will be on your left, opposite the third bus shelter.

Camping R36 (Meusslitz area) is farther from the city center (15 km) but a much nicer, quieter site near the Elbe and Pillnitzer Insel (island indicated on the biking map). This site also gives you a head start on the longer day trip east. Starting from one of the bridges in the city center, follow bicycle paths and small roads close to the Elbe's south shore. The first 10 km of the way are paved, but the last 5 km wind along a narrow dirt footpath along the shore. Pass a ferry landing, Schloss Pillnitz across the Elbe, and a small marina. When you pull even with the end of the island, turn away

Dresden's Semperoper, *raised from the ashes*

from the river (right) at a building marked *Kindergarten*. The campground entrance is 300 meters farther, to the right.

Wherever you choose to stay, stock up on supplies in the city center, as stores are difficult to find in Dresden's outskirts. For Camping Gaz, stop at Karstadt on Pragerstrasse. Rent bicycles from Paperer on Körnerplatz or on Wallstrasse, two blocks west of the *Altmarkt*.

Königstein Day Trip: 62 to 90 kilometers

Riding upriver toward the Czech border brings you through the most beautiful Elbe Valley scenery, where rocky cliffs jut high over the river. Since the dramatic valley is so clearly defined, navigation is easy—just keep along the Elbe's **southern shore**. Dresden's suburban tangle may put up some resistance, but once past Pirna you will have little problem finding the way. This route may be ridden as a single day trip, or it may be broken up by stopping at the pleasant Königstein campground or one of the *Zimmer* advertised along the way. As the route parallels the main Elbe rail line, you may also take a train to make a one-way ride.

Strong easterly winds may accompany you throughout the Elbe Valley, putting up resistance on the outward leg but speeding you along on the return trip. Keep alert for landmarks since you will be returning along the same route. Though few stores line the route, there are several cafes and small shops along the way. Shop ahead at a larger store in Dresden or be prepared to spend extra time searching out supplies along the way.

The Elbeufer Radweg is only sporadically marked. If in doubt just remember to keep as close to the water's edge as possible. Many sections of this bicycle path may still be unsigned and unpaved, although road crews have been working on helpful improvements. Due to the changing situation, these directions are somewhat vague, but route finding should be straightforward thanks to the clearly defined valley and few confusing road choices.

From wherever you are staying (either the city center or the recommended Meusslitz campground) begin by heading for the **Elbe's south bank** and following it **upriver** (east). Keeping along the water in **Heidenau** is tricky, but the general direction regardless of specific route is clear and you will soon arrive in **Pirna**. Take the time to walk Pirna's pedestrian area, tiptoeing around the inevitable construction zones. In the *Marktplatz* see the house where Napoleon once stayed (House No. 20) and the *Rathaus*, unusually placed like an island in the center of the square. Both buildings are shadowed by the hulk of Sonnenstein Castle on a hill high above the market square.

Pick up the **official bicycle route** near the **Elbe bridge** in

Pirna. The first 6 km from Pirna to Stadt Wehlen should be the best of the day in terms of surfaces. Nicely paved, quiet roads will allow your eyes to wander to the scenery instead of scrutinizing perilous roads ahead. For the last 3 km into **Stadt Wehlen**, however, switch back into defensive biking mode on a terrible dirt track. Whatever the road conditions, the beautiful Elbe landscape remains a constant, with green, forest-lined hills interrupted only by outcroppings of stone.

Beyond Stadt Wehlen you will be treated to views of the magnificent Bastei, most impressive of the Elbe's towering cliffs. From the open, grassy spot near the ferry landing between **Weißig** and Rathen you may sit in sun or shade, watch the ferries cross, and take in views of the cliff. Another perfect spot for my favorite biking activity—picnicking.

From Weißig the trail is again smooth, crossing **inland of the train tracks** and emerging on busy **Road 172** in **Königstein**. The fortress high above town (operative word here being high) once guarded the treasury of the Saxon kings. Today it offers outstanding views of the valley and houses museum exhibits. To reach the fortress, bike 2 km west on 172, then turn left for the long uphill. (On the other hand, you may be content with your riverside vantage point when you consider the hill.) For lunch or a snack, try one of the several cafes, bakeries, or *Imbiss* stands in Königstein. Over-

Picnic views across the Elbe valley near Stadt Wehlen

night visitors will find the riverside campground indicated off Road 172 1 km east from the center.

The round trip to Königstein is 62 km from Meusslitz Campground, 92 km from Dresden center. Another 7 km east and across the river lies Bad Schandau, a tourist center by virtue of its border location rather than the town's character. However, the ride east from Königstein toward the Czech border is worthwhile for views of more valley cliffs and forests. Follow **Road 172 east** until the **bridge** to **Bad Schandau**, then stay on the **south bank** for **Krippen**. In Krippen turn **right** at *Zur Börnfähre* to access the **bicycle trail** toward the border (which may still be under construction). Unless you are aiming for a point farther inside the Czech Republic, the small city of Dečin is not worth biking to—there is little of particular note there. The round trip to the border is 90 km from Meusslitz camping, 120 km from Dresden center.

Retrace your steps for the return—a sometimes tricky proposition in reverse perspective. Again, the narrow valley serves as a guide back to Dresden, where you can look back on a full day of exploration—and ahead to the next.

Meissen and Moritzburg Day Trip: 60 kilometers

Meissen, 30 km downriver from Dresden, is famous for its fine porcelain and castle/cathedral high above the Elbe. Unfortunately, the ride along this section of the Elbe is not scenic, the roads poorly paved and often crowded. After the lovely scenery and quiet roads of the previous day, you may be somewhat disappointed in the ride. Nevertheless, historic Meissen is worth seeing and the ride rounds out your tour of this corner of the Elbe. The round trip to Meissen is 60 km from Dresden center, 90 km from Meusslitz Campground.

From the center of Dresden **cross** toward Dresden-Neustadt and the Elbe's **north bank**. Turn **west** to **parallel** the river along the main road (clearly marked for Meissen). Although some sections of this road have been repaved, you will bounce along cobblestones and cracked pavement for most of the way.

Bear **left** for the *Autobahn* and **cross under** it, then head **straight** on. This vague "head straight on" is unfortunately the best advice I can offer for this stretch of the ride, as landmarks and signs are few. However, route finding is not as vague as it may sound, since the road continues to parallel the Elbe and head for Meissen. The river is out of sight but the valley's contours are easy to trace. Stay on the **river side of the main rail line**. When the road bends or merges with other roads, **always keep along the main way**.

Traffic remains light as you pass through the outskirts of **Radebeul** and **Coswig**. Near Kötitz you will emerge on the larger, busy **Road 170**, with only a **narrow shoulder** for the last 8 km into Meissen. A short, perfect stretch of bicycle trail near **Sörnewitz** provides temporary relief, but soon comes to an end. Finally you will round a corner of the valley and arrive in **Meissen**. Unless you plan to stop at a cafe or restaurant in the center of town, stop at a grocery store before crossing the bridge to the old town.

Signs lead to the tourist office in the old *Brauhaus* (behind the *Marktplatz* and church). A town map will facilitate your trek up to the Albrechtsburg, the castle and cathedral complex dominating the old town. The *Schloss* now houses a museum with changing exhibits, and the *Dom* is open for viewing. For good views and shade, head for the terrace *Biergarten*. The tourist office can also direct you to porcelain workshops and vendors.

There are hotels and rooms for rent in Meissen and its surroundings, but camping only in Scharfenberg, 5 km away on the south bank of the Elbe. Unless you plan to stay here, **retrace your route back to Dresden** along the quieter north bank.

Another interesting sight west of Dresden is Moritzburg, a baroque water castle (a moated castle that incorporates lakes in its landscaping) surrounded by forests. The castle lies 10 km north of Radebeul and the Elbe. To visit the *Schloss*, **detour from the Elbe in Coswig and follow signs** to **Moritzburg**, or make the castle part of a separate day trip (30-km round trip from Dresden).

More Cycling Options from Dresden

From Dresden you will have many exciting travel options (time permitting a little excitement). Prague, only two to three riverside biking days away, is often compared to Dresden in its splendor—a splendor unblemished by wartime damage. In my admittedly biased opinion, Prague is the most beautiful city in Europe, absolutely not to be missed. Conditions in the Czech Republic are gradually improving, making bicycle travel easier. New supermarkets and rooms for rent are welcome improvements, though road conditions in many places remain poor. Direct trains to Prague, Bratislava, and Budapest allow a quicker foray east, with or without your bicycle.

Train connections to western Germany may require a few changes, but you will quickly reach a major train line. You can take a train south to begin the Romantic Road Tour (Tour No. 1), going on to Franken (Tour No. 2), the Altmühltal (Tour No. 3), and Oberbayern (Tour Nos. 4 and 5). Many westbound trains connect over Nürnberg, making the Franken loop (Tour No. 2) easy to connect into, with the option to next ride either Tour No. 1 in reverse or head south to the Altmühltal.

TOUR NO. 14

THE WATER CASTLES OF MÜNSTERLAND
A Loop of the Münster Area

Distance: 214 kilometers (133 miles)
Estimated time: 4 days (3 biking days)
Terrain: Gentle hills or flat
Maps: ADFC #10 or BVA's *100 Schlösser Route* booklet

Wasserschlösser. Pättkes. Though these words may sound foreign at first, they will soon become two familiar elements of a delightful tour. These ingredients—water castles and countryside bicycle trails—provide not only an endless supply of interesting sights, but also an enjoyable and safe means of exploring Münsterland. Add in a well-developed map/guide, and you are ready for a relaxing, unique tour in a true cycling paradise.

Each moat or lake in Münsterland reflects a unique structure—be it fortress, medieval manor, or stately palace. The region's countless water castles have been connected by the exceptional *100 Schlösser Route* (Hundred Castle Route) for cyclists, a meandering route hundreds of kilometers long. The tour described here connects sections of the official route for a more compact, introductory trip.

This tour is only one of countless cycling possibilities in Münsterland. Over time I have learned the value of detailed cycling maps that clearly indicate all options, allowing bikers to choose and follow their own routes with confidence. Begin with the *100 Schlösser Route* booklet, a complete guide that includes sight descriptions (in German) as well as maps marked with cycling routes, campgrounds, castles, bicycle repair shops, and other points of interest. With the *100 Schlösser Route* booklet and this tour as guidelines, tailor a Münsterland tour to your own cycling style.

Many Germans load up for weekend outings to Münsterland, an excellent family touring destination due to quiet roads and separate bicycle trails. Note, however, that the rough surfaces of some *Pättkes* can be very bumpy for kiddie trailers. Give route planning extra attention with this in mind if touring with children.

Green castle symbols (referred to as "*Wasserschlösser* route signs" in this text) painted along trails indicate the official *Wasserschlösser* Route. The same symbol in black represents alternative routes. Keep alert for these signs while cycling Münsterland—they are usually well marked, but a moment's inattention may lead you astray!

Münster

Few feelings are quite as satisfying as having a sparkling Mercedes interrupt its airy commute to yield to your two slender wheels—

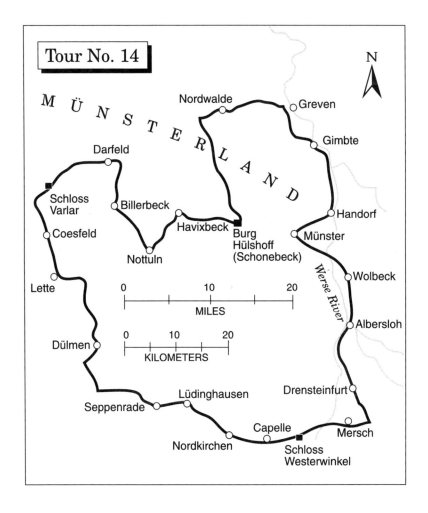

even when the car has the right-of-way. In Münster, the cyclist truly reigns supreme. Broad bicycle lanes around the small city accommodate a steady stream of cyclists. Suited commuters, grandmothers, students, children, and tourists enjoy an extensive network of special bicycle lanes and signals, respected by pedestrians and motorized traffic alike.

Life bustles in Münster's old town center. Wander from one spire to the next and compare ornate burghers' houses on Prinzipalmarkt. For quiet walks or a picnic, head to the shores of the nearby Aasee. Münster's bicycle-friendly character is most evident on the wonderful *Promenade*, a tree-lined avenue encircling the old town in place of medieval walls.

Münster is easily reached from all points in Germany by train (specify Münster in Westphalia; 4 hours, DM 45, from Frankfurt). Make the tourist office across from the *Bahnhof* your first stop. You can pick up a city map, regional maps (including both recommended touring maps) and the indispensable *Münsterland Gastgeberverzeichnis*, listing campgrounds, rooms, and activities in Münsterland. If you are moving on to another tour after Münsterland, check for other city maps at the tourist office as well. The nearest campground is 4 km away (direction Wolbeck), and Münster's modern hostel is on the south shore of the Aasee.

Münster to Lüdinghausen: 60 kilometers

There is no need to despair upon leaving bicycle-friendly Münster—the surrounding countryside is just as much a cyclist's paradise as the city. Follow **bicycle lanes east** along Wolbeckerstrasse to reach signs for a winding bicycle trail to Wolbeck. If you are heading for the campground first, stay beside the main road to reach the site. To resume the ride, simply continue into **Wolbeck** and **Albersloh** (direction Drensteinfurt). Pick up the *Wasserschlösser* route by passing Albersloh's **church** and turning **right** at the stop sign. **Cross** a bridge and turn **left** for **R40 bicycle path**. As you pedal this meandering riverside trail to Drensteinfurt, rabbits and wild pheasants may dart from nearby hedges, a common sight throughout this tour.

Turn **left** down a **shady lane** in **Drensteinfurt** to see your first water castle. Although the *Schloss* is privately occupied (the proof is in the laundry lines), no one seems to mind tourists peeking in the gateway. The *Schloss* gardens are open to the public, and the small town also makes an interesting stop before resuming the ride. Head out of town **toward Walstedde**, then keep along **R40 bike path** to **Mersch**. Turn **right** on a busier road for Herbern, passing two private castle/mansions on the way. In **Herbern** follow

Rest stop near a reflecting water castle

signs **right** for *Parking Schloss* to reach Schloss Westerwinkel, one of the nicest water castles of the route.

Did you ever wonder about who posts all those biking signs? On the way to this castle I met the man whose job it is to maintain the marked routes. He pedals his standard black three-speed around the trails, pausing now and then to paint numbers or symbols. After meeting him I was doubly appreciative whenever I saw another helpful bicycle sign.

Pedal **through forests and meadows** to reach peaceful **Schloss Westerwinkel**. Bump over cobblestones and a drawbridge to see the inner castle courtyard, or enjoy a moatside picnic in the peaceful wooded area. Afterwards, follow **green Wasserschlösser signs** to **Capelle**, where the official route takes a **southerly** meander. For a quiet and more direct road, ride to Nordkirchen via Altendorf, and follow **signs to Nordkirchen's** *Schloss*, the "small Versailles of Westphalia." The decorated palace contrasts greatly with Westerwinkel's more subtle style. Formal gardens and pools surround the palace, making another ideal setting for a rest stop or picnic.

Leave the *Schloss* grounds on any path leading **north** from the main pool. When you **rejoin the road**, look for a **right turn marked F33** before the church. Follow this trail and *Wasserschlösser* route signs for the last 13 km to Lüdinghausen. At an **unmarked intersection** go **right**, and 2 km later turn **left** into **Lüdinghausen** *Stadtmitte*.

Lüdinghausen has a small pedestrian center and two castles. Burg Vischering is *the* classic water castle with painted shutters, the requisite moat, and a wooded setting. If you ever wanted to play fairy-tale princess, this is the place to do it. It helps to have a charming prince on hand, but if you neglected to bring your own, try your luck among the frogs in the moat.

Lüdinghausen's tourist office is located near Burg Lüdinghausen, another large castle. Conveniently, a bicycle path connects the two castles. Campers can choose from one of four campgrounds clustered just west of town. Rooms are advertised in town and in the surrounding countryside. In order to lengthen the day, consider cycling 20 km more to one of two lakeside campgrounds in Hausdülmen.

Lüdinghausen to Nottuln: 80 kilometers

Leave Lüdinghausen behind by cycling **west** to **Seppenrade**, a town inconveniently located at the top of a steep hill. Keep on the **bicycle path straight up** into town and turn **right** on **Road 474** to **Dülmen**. The *Wasserschlösser* route turns **left** on Leversumerstrasse past the Esso station. Eventually it emerges on a **larger road** where you should turn **right** for the **R4** route into **Hausdülmen**. Watch carefully for the *Wasserschlösser* symbol in Hausdülmen because the route takes a **sneaky turn off the main street** behind a statue group. Follow **R29** and **black No. 32** *Wasserschlösser* signs. Not all turns are clearly marked, but the next bicycle sign is usually visible if you look ahead at each fork.

Bear **left at the Y** intersection 5 km **beyond Dülmen**. At the **T** go **left** on a larger road. Rather than pedal meandering trails at this point, you can follow this road to **Lette** and join a **bicycle path** along Road 474 directly to **Coesfeld** from there. Intersect a pleasant **ring road** to pick up *Wasserschlösser* route signs again. Before moving on, however, take a moment to **loop** through Coesfeld's historic old town, still guarded by several medieval towers.

The *Wasserschlösser* route can be frustrating as you leave Coesfeld. The trail is indirect and difficult to follow over terrible dirt roads in the woods. Unless you enjoy orienteering, **leave Coesfeld on the direct road** toward Osterwick instead. Bear **left** for a **side road** to **Varlar** 4 km later, rejoining the official **bicycle route** there. Schloss Varlar hides from the public behind a gate and tree-lined moat, but take a quick **detour** to peek at the pretty castle before moving on. **Backtrack eastward** to find the R1 bicycle route along quiet roads and woods. This route rejoins the *Wasserschlösser* route and leads to beautiful Schloss Darfeld. Only serene black swans disturb the castle's perfect reflection in the surrounding

A black swan glides through Schloss Darfeld's reflection.

lake. Weeping willows round out the scene, providing perfect picnic and photo opportunities.

The *100 Schlösser Route* map optimistically indicates five castles in Horstmar, and you may intend to continue **north from Darfeld**, optimistically expecting five dramatic, perfect castles all vying for picnic rights. However, you will find only two unimpressive castles and a few historic buildings in the town. Admittedly, Schloss Darfeld is a tough act to follow, but nonetheless I recommend riding directly from Darfeld to Billerbeck and circumventing Horstmar, unless you don't mind the extra mileage.

Follow **R29** and **black No. 17** *Wasserschlösser* signs **south** from Darfeld to **Billerbeck**. Billerbeck is another Münsterland delight. Two tall churches dominate their own green squares, and cobblestone pedestrian streets lead to a small shuttered *Schloss* on the outskirts of the compact town.

To complete this day's excursion, ride the **main road east** toward Havixbeck. **Pass** the first marked turnoff for Nottuln and take the **next right** up a hill to rejoin the quieter *Wasserschlösser* route to that town. Unfortunately a campground along the way has been transformed into a cabins-only weekend retreat (no tent sites). Unless you plan to free camp, you will have to opt for a room or the hostel (direction *Sportplatz*) in Nottuln.

When you roll into **Nottuln** you will find a lovely town with a shady churchyard and lively street scene. A pleasant, homey atmosphere prevails in the tidy little town. The ice-cream parlor forms the focal point of much nighttime activity. Lucky cyclists will arrive on Friday—Ladies' Night at the Banana Club. Don't miss it! The tourist office near the church will direct you around town and find rooms for rent.

Nottuln to Münster: 74 kilometers

From Nottuln's church square follow **black No. 31** *Wasserschlösser* signs **or Trail R31** up Burgstrasse. The well-signed route **climbs** rough dirt tracks over a hill, finally leading to **Havixbeck**. You can peek through gates at the private *Schloss* in Havixbeck before riding on to the main water castle of the day in Schonebeck. From Havixbeck follow the **direct road to Schonebeck** instead of the *Wasserschlösser* route, which will eventually leave you stranded in a forest.

Burg Hülshoff is best known as the birthplace of poetess Annette von Droste-Hülshoff, who is world famous in Westphalia. She demonstrated her good taste in country homes by moving to Meersburg Castle on Lake Constance (see Tour No. 6 of the Bodensee). To learn more about her work and her life, visit the castle museum. Outside, swans and peacocks round out the courtly atmosphere of Burg Hülshoff's perfectly manicured grounds (DM 2 admission).

From the *Schloss* parking lot follow **bicycle route R1** and **black No. 30** *Wasserschlösser* signs to the intersection of a small road. Turn **right** toward Hohenholte, then ride **north** past Haus Sieperding to pick up **R31** signs to Altenberge and Nordwalde. You will have farm scenery to yourself on these quiet back roads until joining a larger road near the towns.

In **Nordwalde** head for Haus Bispinghof, located just north of the main road to Greven. Take a quick look at the small *Schloss*, a tall building surrounded by a moat, before rejoining the green *Wasserschlösser* route and **R31** toward Greven. To bypass busy roads, turn **south** along Max-Clemens Kanal for a shaded 2-km ride. At a large intersection, turn **left** on Aldruper Heide. **Cross** the train tracks and **bear right** across rolling farmlands. At the main road turn **left**, pedaling with intermittent traffic for only 200 meters before turning **right**. Pass farmhouses to **crest** a small ridge and turn **right** again on a side road (Mühlenstrasse) to **Gimbte**.

It's easy to spend a few extra minutes in this tidy brick town. A small plaza and churchyard form the town's heart. Gimbte is not in any way superlative, but occasionally it is nice to stop by instead of just whizzing past every tiny town.

From Gimbte head **south** on Dorfstrasse for a quiet road to **Gelmer**. There you can **rejoin** the official *Wasserschlösser* route along the Werse River, which leads conveniently to the campground east of Münster. The route is **difficult to follow** in stretches, so track your position carefully. Most sections of the trail are unpaved. **Leave** the *Wasserschlösser* route when it intersects busy Wolbeckerstrasse. Turn **left** on this road. The campsite will be a quick 200 meters away. Those aiming directly for Münster, on the other hand, should follow diverging bicycle signs for *MS-Zentrum*.

In **Münster** you can take a lap around the *Promenade* and wield your power as a cyclist by stopping luxury automobiles at will. If you plan to connect into another tour for more cycling, however, be careful not to get too self-confident. Soon you will leave the bicycle-friendly environs of Münster for the slightly less sympathetic outside world.

From Münster there are several options for more cycling. One appealing option would be a ride north to the East Frisian Islands (see Additional Suggested Tours). If you enjoy island hopping there, continue on to the North Frisian Islands (Tour No. 17). You can also take a train to Hannover for the start of the Lüneburger Heide tour (Tour No. 16). In this corner of Germany you are also within close bicycle range of Holland, another cycling paradise. For a quicker trip to any destination, head for Münster's *Bahnhof*.

TOUR NO. 15

BEWITCHING!
The Harz Mountains

Distance: 205 kilometers (127 miles)
Estimated time: 4 to 5 days (3 to 4 biking days)
Terrain: Challenging mountains in former border zone
Map: ADFC #12
Connecting tour: Tour No. 16

Centrally located in a reunified Germany, the Harz Mountains nest like an egg in an otherwise flat landscape. Mist-shrouded slopes and dark, deep forests that once intimated sorcery and witchcraft now inspire magic of a different sort, attracting nature and sports enthusiasts throughout the year. The geography of the Harz lends itself perfectly to a compact though challenging bicycle loop that tours historic towns, mountain resorts, unspoiled woods and lakes.

Until recently, visitors were prevented from exploring all of the Harz as the former East–West border cut arbitrarily across the mountains. Today one may travel freely throughout the Harz, observing the sharp differences politics imposed over a single, distinct nature zone. Long slumbering beauties such as Quedlinburg and Wernigerode in the East are quickly regaining their former charm, fascinating examples of all stages of reconstruction—as well as the complex issues of reunification.

Appreciating the beautiful mountain scenery takes hard work—including challenging climbs of 5 km or more. Constant gains and losses in elevation demand good physical condition and reliable equipment. Witches are said to hold their Sabbath atop Brocken, highest peak of the Harz; seeing for yourself requires determination and endurance, not to mention the cooperation of supernatural elements. However, short daily rides over the Harz landscape are punctuated by stops at interesting towns, easing your passage over the challenging terrain.

Goslar

Since the Harz is a popular vacation area, frequent (if slow) trains link Hannover and Goslar, with less frequent and direct connec-

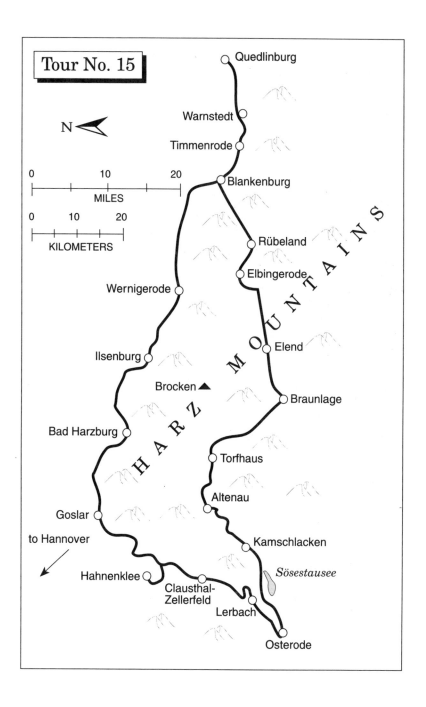

tions from points south or east. This tour can also connect with the
Lüneburger Heide tour (Tour No. 16) via Hannover or more directly
between Goslar and Celle. Strong winds may offer some resistance
across the flat landscape between but seem impossible to predict.

Goslar provides an ideal introduction to this tour of the Harz.
Chock-full of perfect half-timbered houses, the town cozies right up
to the edge of the Harz. Although Germany is dotted with many
pretty half-timbered towns, Goslar stands out with houses intri-
cately painted with a rare attention to detail and individual character. The impressive buildings attest to the city's wealth, primarily
due to silver mined from the Harz.

The *Marktplatz* tourist office in Goslar offers room information,
town maps (including suggested walking tours), and tips on upcoming events such as concerts in churches or other historic buildings.
Exploration of side streets, the Kaiserpfalz, and the old town walls
can easily occupy a full day. Inside the *Rathaus*, visit the decorated
meeting hall; outside, watch the *Glockenspiel* (clock figures). For an
interesting contrast, visit Mönchehaus, a traditional building housing a museum of modern art.

Goslar's large hostel is on Rammelsbergstrasse on the south side
of town. Camping will gain you a head start on the first biking day,
with the site located 3 km south off Road 241 to Clausthal.

Goslar to Osterode: 41 kilometers

Beautiful views of misty woods blanketing the hills compensate
the long, nasty climb high into the Harz that starts here. Side
routes suggested on cycling maps are either terrible, rutted dirt
tracks or impossible to find. Despite the tough initial climb from
Goslar, this day is short, giving you leeway for a late start from
Goslar, a lazy afternoon in Osterode, or a head start on the next
day. It's easiest to follow **Road 241** most of the way. Traffic comes
in moderate spurts, but generally the road is easy to share.

After 10 km on Road 241 turn **right** for a side trip to **Hahnenklee**,
a small mountain town with an appealing location and a wooden,
Scandinavian-style church. You can relax and have a good look
around the nearby woods as this day's ride is short with no other
specific sights until Osterode.

Return to 241 and ride through **Clausthal-Zellerfeld**, where
there is little of note other than nearby skiing and hiking opportunities. Follow signs **through** *Stadtmitte* to avoid a lengthy detour
for through traffic, and then continue for Osterode on **241**. South
now becomes **downhill** as you cruise back out of the Harz.

Leave 241 for an exhilarating **switchback descent** through the
narrow valley of **Lerbach**, ending with a perfect **brick bicycle
trail** right to the edge of **Osterode**. The pedestrian zone of the

Cyclists can be both tourists and tourist attractions.

town center lies straight ahead. Osterode, like Goslar, is a pretty town of carefully tended half-timbered houses on the edge of the Harz. Despite basic similarities, however, Osterode maintains its own character. In the main square you will find a lively scene of shoppers, vacationers, and children playing in the central fountain.

The tourist office on the edge of town will help you find rooms. Head east on Road 498 to Sösestausee to pick up signs to the hostel and two campgrounds, but buy food in Osterode before heading out. One campsite is located in the woods near town. The next site's "lakeside" location turns out to be a muddy puddle at the foot of the Sösestausee Dam, but its situation in a wooded area near a bird preserve is nice all the same.

You may consider riding on to finish at Torfhaus, a high lookout point with views of Brocken (hostel and hotels but no camping).

Osterode to Braunlage: 50 kilometers

From Osterode you will have to work hard to regain high Harz views. Follow **Road 498** to **Sösestausee** and Altenau. Climb up beside the dam to reach lake level and a nearly flat ride. Enjoy it while you can: The 4 km from **Kamschlacken** to Road 242 consist of one long, nasty climb back over 500 meters. Turn **right** on **242**, then **left** for Altenau, the downhill ride both a relief and a curse since you will lose hard-won altitude. Climbing up and coasting down the Harz's endless slopes, the mechanically minded can entertain themselves with designs for a combination cyclometer/altimeter or other handy gadgets for mountain touring.

Altenau looks the part of a small resort town, lined with sports and souvenir shops. Torfhaus is only 8 km away, but you may well set a slowness record over the first 7 km, another **mean climb** to over 800 meters. Click into granny gear, be patient, and take in wide open views of the Harz along the way. Near Torfhaus, crest a last sneaky **uphill** to gain an excellent panorama of Brocken and the eastern Harz.

Torfhaus pretends to be a town but actually consists only of a lookout point, a few souvenir/snack stands, three restaurant/inns, and a hostel. Tourists stop here to gawk at the mountains and at cyclists foolhardy enough to tackle the Harz without a motor, icebox, and video camera.

When you are finished looking (and being looked at), head on for **Braunlage**. The main road there may be quite busy at times, but wide lanes allow safe if not peaceful cycling. A bustling resort town cluttered with tourists and postcards, Braunlage is also a convenient stop, with shops, food stores, rooms, a hostel, and camping (1 km south off Road 27 to Bad Lauterberg).

Quick cyclists can reach Braunlage, drop off their baggage, and head out for a masochistic grind up the summit of Brocken (1,100 meters). You will earn excellent views and the macho honor of topping the highest point in the Harz by pedal power—plus a terrific descent. It is also possible to take a train excursion up the mountain from Wernigerode, if knee problems, limited gears, or sanity keep you from pedaling up.

The next day's ride ends in Quedlinburg, requiring some pre-planning as accommodations options there are limited to rooms. Campers can rearrange the next days around sites in Elbingerode or Bad Harzburg, the only sites convenient to this tour. There are also hostels in Blankenburg and Wernigerode.

Braunlage to Quedlinburg: 50 kilometers

To leave town follow **signs** for Bad Harzburg, then **Road 27** to **Elend**. Stock up on supplies as there are few convenient shops along the day's ride. While the former East–West border 2 km away is difficult to recognize, characteristics of the East will become immediately apparent in Elend, from which point you will bounce through gray towns on bumpy roads. As always, one never knows what to expect in the East. Towns like Quedlinburg and Wernigerode sparkle with freshly painted facades, new roads, and Western-style shops; in contrast, overlooked mining towns without tourist appeal have not seen much improvement since reunification. Even the character of the mountains seems different across the border. You will see the occasional ski jump emerging from the wooded slopes of the West, while in the East the outline of mining equipment against a deforested landscape is a more likely sight.

At times it is difficult to keep a fair and positive attitude when visiting the East in face of stark inequalities. This is particularly true of areas such as the Harz, where artificial divisions are so clearly imposed on a single, distinct region. Remind yourself to shift mental gears and take the East on its own terms.

The ride to Blankenburg along busy Road 27 throws a few last ups and downs at wayward cyclists, but the toughest part of the tour is behind you. Despite uncomfortable road conditions, I took a direct line back out of the mountains in order to get through the worst and on to the best as quickly as possible. After **two long climbs** near **Königshütte** and **Rübeland**, enjoy the **descent** to **Blankenburg**.

Blankenburg has a *Schloss*, a few churches, and the like, but the town is drab overall. Push directly on to Quedlinburg, where your time is better spent. Follow the **main road to Thale**, then signs to Quedlinburg via **Warnstedt**. To enter Quedlinburg's old town, pedal on as if to Halberstadt, then turn **right at the second parking sign**.

With reunification and the opening of the East, a curiosity-inspired rush across the border resulted in the "discovery" of many overlooked towns and resort areas. **Quedlinburg** became an instant attraction,

Marktplatz *in Quedlinburg*

distinctive as the town with the most half-timbered houses in Germany. While post-war rebuilding and growth in the West destroyed many historic sites, the slower pace of the closed East left many architectural landmarks undisturbed, if poorly tended.

Quedlinburg still has a long way to go, but reconstruction progresses rapidly out from the center of town with the renovated *Rathaus* and *Marktplatz*. Head up to the *Schloss* for fine views over the old town, exploring twisting streets along the way. Quedlinburg's unique situation also allows a good appreciation of the before-and-after aspect of reconstruction—you will observe examples of every building stage around town.

Unfortunately Quedlinburg has not yet developed a good accommodations network, offering neither hostel nor campground. Although there is still no central assistance office, *Zimmer* are advertised around town. Several large grocery stores and a number of specialty shops can be found in the center.

Quedlinburg to Goslar: 64 kilometers

After visiting Quedlinburg, don't head north for Halberstadt; you'll likely find it a disappointing detour along busy roads. Instead, try the following route.

Backtrack to Blankenburg and continue **west** to **Wernigerode** along **Road 6**. In sheer numbers, Wernigerode may not boast as many historic buildings as Quedlinburg, but speedy renovation has put the town far ahead of its neighbor. Wernigerode also benefits from a head start: As a showcase town of the former East, it received closer attention than most others. Cafes and shops line the streets around the small central square with its fountain. There are several grocery stores and a well-stocked information office in the old town. You may puff up to the *Schloss* high over town or let a historic train do the puffing on an excursion up to **Brocken**.

When you are ready to move on, **choose** either a hilly side route indicated on the ADFC biking map or continue west on Road 6 to join the suggested bicycle route beyond Ilsenburg. Most tourists whizz by the town en route to Wernigerode, leaving **Ilsenburg** in sleepy peace. Take a break by the lake with views of neat houses and a small *Schloss* in the woods above.

Leave town on **Road 6 west**, turning off on the **first dirt road** to the **left** 1 km later. Take the smooth dirt road through quiet woods, following cute **witch-biker signs right** at the **first T**. After a few kilometers **cross** the former border, an open, obvious scar through the woods. Continue **straight** along **forest trails** and eventually emerge back on **Road 6**, with a bike lane into **Bad Harzburg**.

There is a campground on the east edge of Bad Harzburg, but as the town is of little interest, you should go on to Goslar and enjoy an evening there. Ignore Goslar signs in Bad Harzburg; instead go **toward** *Zentrum*, *Bahnhof*, and then **Harlingerode** for moderately trafficked roads with **sections of bike path** over the final 15 km to Goslar.

Once back in **Goslar** you can visit new sights or return to familiar favorites. Your best option for more cycling is the Lüneburger Heide tour (Tour No. 16). Bike to Hannover or directly to Celle to see the best *Heide* (heath) scenery. For another cycling possibility, circle south of the Harz to connect with the Thuringia tour (Tour No. 12) in Eisenach or the Vogelsberg tour (Tour No. 11) near Bebra.

Train connections from Goslar inevitably involve several transfers and a few slow-paced local shuttles, but once you reach main rail lines at Hannover or Göttingen you will be sped along your way. Unfortunately, East–West rail connections remain inconvenient and roundabout.

Connection to Tour No. 16

Goslar to Hannover: 90 kilometers. To bike directly into the Lüneburger Heide tour at Hannover, pedal northwest toward Hildesheim. Leave Goslar by riding west to Langelsheim on busy Road 82 (bicycle path only in sections). Pass Langelsheim on Road 82 and turn left for a parallel side road 2 km later. Return to Road 82 in Hahausen, turning south on Road 248 to Seesen. After another 2 km leave traffic behind for little Bornhausen.

From Bornhausen, follow signs to Rhüden, crossing under the *Autobahn*. Then turn north on another quiet side road to Bockenem. There, you must join busier Road 243 over a high ridge to Bad Salzdetfurth and on to Hildesheim.

Hildesheim makes the best stopping point along this route. Find the *Dom*'s monumental bronze doors, outstanding examples of Romanesque art. The eleventh-century doors depict Old and New Testament scenes, with bronze figures leaning out from higher levels, the better to be viewed from below.

For the final 35 km to Hannover, wind along side roads near the Innerste and Leine rivers. Pedal north to Giesen, then zigzag west to little Giften. Turn west past the church for unpaved back roads across the Leine to Schliekum and Koldingen. There, rejoin larger roads to Hemmingen and Döhren, riding a riverside trail into Hannover center. If heading for the hostel with campsite, do not go straight to the center. Turn west from the Maschsee to reach the site, 1 km away. See Tour No. 16 for more information on Hannover.

TOUR NO. 16

THROUGH WOODS AND HEATH
The Lüneburger Heide

Distance: 187 kilometers (116 miles)
Estimated time: 3 days (3 biking days)
Terrain: Long rolling hills
Map: ADFC #7
Connecting tour: Tour No. 15

Durch den Wald und auf der Heide: Through Woods and Heath. When I asked German cyclists for touring suggestions, many identified the Lüneburger Heide (heath) as one of their country's premier cycling destinations. Beautiful scenery, quiet country roads, and easy terrain combined with accessibility and interesting sights make this region a favorite. Much of the Lüneburger Heide consists of protected land. Despite quick connections to the outside world, a rural atmosphere and medieval towns preserve a sense of timelessness.

This tour quickly leaves Hannover behind for peaceful country cycling and the charming town of Celle. Continuing through woods and heath, the ride takes in a bird park, thermal baths, a village closed to mechanical transportation, and finally the historic city that gives its name to the region, Lüneburg.

Although the Lüneburger Heide is a popular getaway area for residents of the nearby Ruhrgebiet industrial sprawl, biking will quickly bring you to a peaceful landscape of farmlands and purple heath, where regional traditions carry on. Many farmhouses are freshly thatched, not just relics of the past. You will also note various house decorations, from targetlike medallions to crossed horse heads on barn gables.

Hannover

While Hannover is better known as a center for industrial fairs than tourism, the city makes a convenient starting point for this tour. Besides, any city with life-size dinosaur models lining the main shopping street (Bahnhofstrasse) is okay with me! Hopefully the display is not just temporary. Dinos aside, your time in Hannover is best spent cycling a long tree-lined avenue (no cars allowed) to

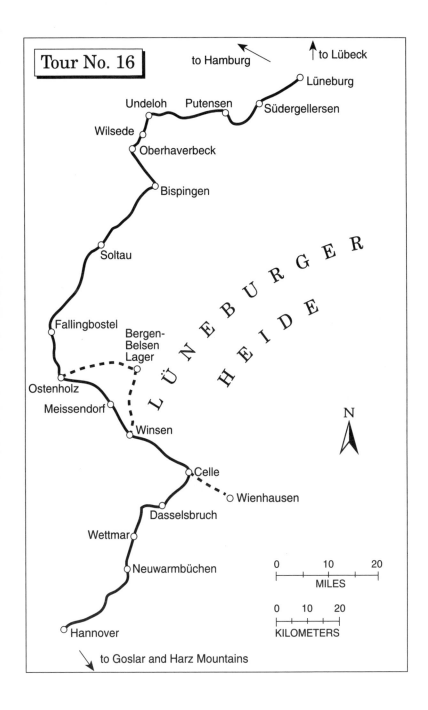

Tour No. 16

to Hamburg
to Lübeck
Lüneburg
Undeloh   Putensen   Südergellersen
Wilsede
Oberhaverbeck
Bispingen
Soltau
LÜNEBURGER
HEIDE
Fallingbostel
Bergen-
Belsen
Lager
Ostenholz
Meissendorf
Winsen
Celle
Wienhausen
Dasselsbruch
Wettmar
N
Neuwarmbüchen
0   10   20
MILES
0   10   20
KILOMETERS
Hannover
to Goslar and Harz Mountains

the gates of Herrenhausen Gardens, the grounds of a former palace where you can attend a summer concert or relax in a quiet spot.

The tourist office is on the right if exiting the *Bahnhof*. Hannover is absolutely aflutter with city maps, making orientation easy. A riverside hostel offers the nearest camping. Ride straight down Bahnhofstrasse, Karlmarschstrasse, and follow *Stadion* (Stadium) signs down Lavee Allee. Turn left onto Bauermannstrasse before crossing a bridge to reach the hostel/campsite. To purchase cycling maps, stop by the large bookstore on Bahnhofstrasse.

Hannover to Celle: 45 kilometers

To begin the ride, head **through Eilenriede** (the city forest) and **follow bicycle signs**. Different animal symbols indicate Hannover's bicycle routes. Lucky Celle-bound cyclists can follow the lovely mosquito-larvae trail (signs like a winged bug). **Parallel** the highway and **circle** a small lake outside the city. Sadly, the mosquito-larvae trail ends here.

Head **left** away from the lake and aim for Altwarmbüchen Church to **emerge** on a larger road. Turn **right** and pedal **bicycle trails** beside the busy road to **Kirchhorst** and **Neuwarmbüchen**. To regain quiet side roads, **follow** signs to Wettmar, catching an early view of farmhouses typical of the area. In **Wettmar** bear **left** for Fuhrberg but then go **right** on Bruchstrasse (which becomes Hauptdamm) for a wonderful solitary ride **past** woods and fields.

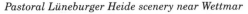

Pastoral Lüneburger Heide scenery near Wettmar

Celle's Schloss *and park*

Pedal 6 km along this road, turning **right on the second paved road after the train tracks** to continue to **Dasselsbruch**.

Once past Dasselsbruch go **left**, not right for Nienhorst. Eventually this quiet road **merges** into the main road with bicycle lanes into **Celle**. Follow signs to *Zentrum*, *Innenstadt*, and information. Celle is a lively town of colorful sixteenth-century houses, carefully reworked to fit modern practicality with medieval character. The upper levels of each house lean successively farther into the streets, exposed timbers decorated with quotes or proverbs. French gardens south of town remind visitors of Celle's one-time Duchess, as the moated *Schloss* reminds them of the former Guelph princes, who made Celle an important regional center.

For camping, take Hehlentorstrasse across the river and follow camping signs 5 km north to Vorwerk. The hostel lies northwest of town. To reach it, take Hehlentorstrasse across the river and then turn left on Bremerweg to follow *Jugendherberge* signs 2 km later.

If you don't mind adding a few more kilometers to this short day, hop back on your wheels for a **quick 20-km round trip** to **Wienhausen**, southeast of Celle. The pretty town's main attraction is its convent, founded in the thirteenth century. The convent's small museum remains open year-round; with luck you may pass by in time for the limited annual exhibit of medieval tapestries.

Celle to Soltau: 67 kilometers

Leave Celle **westward** on Bremerweg (becomes Winsenerstrasse). From the campground join this road via **Groß** and **Klein Hehlen**. In **Winsen** the main road turns **north** for **Bergen**, passing the location of **Bergen-Belsen Lager** (concentration camp) where a monument and exhibit now stand. Though it may be easier to bypass the site, I believe it is important to visit at least one of these camps at some time; consider the side trip. If not detouring to Bergen, follow signs from Winsen to **Meißendorf** and **Ostenholz**.

Wondering about that thunder on a sunny day? The hilly area around Ostenholz is a British-military training ground, so quell any sudden urges to explore off the road and save the picnic for later. Bump over the cobblestones of this typical farm town that had the misfortune to become permanently surrounded by an army. From there ride on to **Örbke** and **Fallingbostel**. Between army outposts you will pass stretches of undisturbed *Heide*.

Although the world's largest bird park (*Vogelspark*) claims to be in Walsrode, it is actually located north of Honerdingen. Pedal **toward** Soltau from Fallingbostel and follow *Vogelspark* **signs left** off this road. Walsrode itself is not worth a detour. If you can't wait until the bird park for a break, stop by the large riverside park in Fallingbostel or see the open-air farmyard exhibit north of town (across from the hostel).

Do not confuse *Vogelspark* with Safaripark, an exotic game zoo farther south. The hefty bird-park entrance fee (DM 10) allows you to view species from around the world wandering freely or in enclosures in a pretty park. To shorten the day, stop at the riverside campground 3 km north of Fallingbostel. Otherwise, return to the road north to Soltau, a moderately trafficked road with parallel bike lanes. **Follow information signs** on a circuitous route through **Soltau**.

You will find a nice park center in Soltau, crowned by an even more pleasant surprise—the Soltau Therme, a bath complex. Just the thing for sore legs and a weary mind! The modern complex offers lap, kiddie, and diving pools, as well as saltwater pools, a sauna, and other curative treatments. Bring a bathing suit and towel (prices DM 4 for basic pools and up; includes locker with key). Soltau Therme is perfect for cooling off after a hot day, warming up after a cool day, and relaxing sore muscles in either case.

The tourist office provides town maps and information on rooms. There is a hostel in town and camping 2 km north off the main road

Thatched houses in Wilsede, a town closed to motorized transport

to Schneverdingen (follow Harburgerstrasse). Soltau is quite the leisure center, with the Heide Amusement Park also nearby.

Soltau to Lüneburg: 75 kilometers

Leave Soltau for Bispingen on Winsenerstrasse **or** ride north from the campground to Ahlften and turn east to join this road. The 16-km ride to Bispingen passes several stretches of picture-perfect heath scenery and thatch-roofed farms. A pleasant, tidy town, **Bispingen** makes a nice stop. Head for **Wintermoor** for a peaceful ride through wooded nature preserves. Motorists heading toward Wilsede (nature preserve) reach the end of the road in tiny **Oberhaverbeck**, but as a cyclist you may pedal on past the end of the road for cars.

The small settlement nestled within the nature preserve is closed to motorized traffic. Take a **right** past restaurants and wagon-ride centers in Oberhaverbeck to reach **Wilsede**'s peaceful corner of the world. Although there may be a Volkswagen or two hidden behind Wilsede's barn doors, the thatched farmhouses and tranquil setting offer a glimpse of slow-paced life long gone elsewhere. For a unique splurge, check one of the village's few restaurants or, better still, hotels.

To continue your ride, bear **left** in Wilsede for **Undeloh**, watching for signs painted on roadside boulders. Back in the modern world, you will find that Undeloh capitalizes on its little neighbor's charm by renting out dozens of bikes to unfortunate, bicycle-poor travelers confined to the modern world. Pedal on to **Sahrendorf** and **Egestorf**, with a long, gradual climb on the way. Egestorf's pretty churchyard merits a quick detour (direction Evendorf), but leave town on the **road to Lüneburg**.

Pedal to **Eyendorf**, **Putensen**, toward Oldendorf, and **turn off** for **Wetzen** on the way. Enjoy wide views from the peaceful **side road** to **Südergellersen**. There, first turn **right** for **Melbeck**, then **left** for **Heiligenthal**, where signs and spires guide you into **Lüneburg**.

Lüneburg's information office is located on the market square in the center of the old town. A campground is located 5 km south off the main road to Melbeck and the hostel is 3 km south on Soltauerstrasse. Am Sande, the main street, presents a busy scene of modern business in an old town setting. Compare the gables of historic buildings; many different styles can be found throughout Lüneburg. At the riverfront, an old crane adds character to a small park. In the middle ages, Lüneburg thrived as an important stop along the Old Salt Road to Lübeck via Lauenburg and Ratzeburg (see Tour No. 18 for possible connections).

Having completed the Lüneburger Heide tour, you now have several options. To round out your tour of the region, cycle back to Celle via Uelzen and Hermannsburg. Killer headwinds from both north and west make train connections your best option to reach coastal tours in Husum or Lübeck (Tour Nos. 17 and 19). Remember, the forces of nature are not worth challenging.

A regional railroad hub, Lüneburg offers frequent departures to points near and far (even *ICE* trains pass through). If you are heading north, stop over in Hamburg to view the busy port scene and city lakes. Ask for the *Stadtbummel Hamburg* booklet in Lüneburg's tourist office as it includes a city plan. Again, roaring northerlies discourage cyclists from pedaling to Hamburg. You are far better off visiting the city by train (ask at Lüneburg's *Bahnhof*).

ISLAND HOPPING
Nordfriesland

Distance: 282 kilometers (175 miles)
Estimated time: 6 days to infinity (5 to 7 biking days)
Terrain: Strong coastal winds roar
over flat islands
Map: ADFC #1
Connecting tour: Tour No. 18

This island-hopping route offers bicycle touring of a different sort, a relaxed ride combining ferry trips with short biking tours of the principal North Frisian Islands. The area is Germany's answer to Cape Cod in many ways, a popular vacation destination with lighthouses, dunes, bird preserves, and yes, beaches. Tourism aside, the region retains many traditions. Thatched cottages and windmills dot the landscape, and Friesian is still spoken here. Many islands even use their own sub-derivatives of this northern dialect. After a series of hops across the islands, the tour finishes in Flensburg, crossing from the North Sea to the Baltic Sea.

The waters and beaches of Nordfriesland form one of Germany's first national parks, the Wattenmeer. *Watt* refers to mud flats exposed by tides, complete ecosystems in themselves. Though most island lands are not part of the sea-focused national park, many

Island pony on Nordstrand

areas are locally protected. Seals (*Seehunde*) bask on the outer sand banks, and the entire area is a birdwatcher's delight.

It is important to appreciate the fragility of this ecological zone and the high impact of tourism. Follow the easy but fundamental rules: No free camping on the beach or any protected area, no biking on the beach or promenades, and keep to bicycle lanes where they exist. Ferry prices, lack of free camping, and park surtaxes make budget touring more challenging than usual, but not impossible. Happily, one of these factors—ferry rates—also keeps the number of motorists vacationing on the islands down, a boon to cyclists.

APPROACHES TO ISLAND TOURING. There are two approaches to touring this area, each with its advantages. First, you can use a base-camp approach in the off-season, settling in one spot on the mainland and visiting the islands on day trips. This permits the luxury of cycling with less baggage, a great plus in view of strong westerly winds guaranteed to turn against you on at least one leg of each island loop. The base-camp strategy also allows you

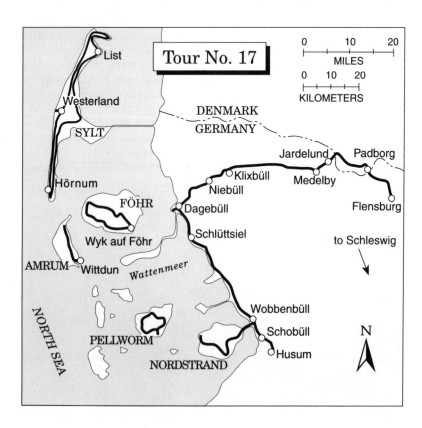

to return to a familiar "home" each evening, getting to know one place well (see Part I, Tips for Touring). In Nordfriesland this approach also lends itself well to families or groups of mixed interests (cyclists, non-biker beach bums, etc.) traveling together. The nomadic-wanderer approach, on the other hand, allows more flexibility and more time to explore each island without fretting over ferry timetables.

Another factor to weigh in this decision is the season. In summer, ferry departures are more frequent and extra connections make direct hops between islands possible. However, in the off-season, you will share the islands with fewer tourists. Decisions, decisions.

This tour is organized loosely, divided into islands rather than strict day-by-day routes. You will find recommended routes and sights on each island. Distances in parentheses refer to the routes suggested. Consider the possibilities and redesign the tour according to your own interests.

Whatever your level of German, you will have to work on some new vocabulary in Nordfriesland. *Koog* means new land, reclaimed from the sea by dikes and landfill. *Kiek*, to look or a view, frequently appears in house or place names. Points of interest commonly indicated on maps include *Hügelgraber*, ancient burial mounds, and *Schutzgebiet*, protected areas. *See* (sea) and *Sand* are easier to translate. These elements make for a great vacation but can play nasty tricks on bicycles. Remember to keep your bicycle clean and well oiled to prevent damage.

Husum

Easy to reach by rail, Husum receives almost hourly connections from Hamburg-Altona train station (2 hours, DM 40). Get started at Husum's tourist office (to find it, refer to the map outside Husum *Bahnhof*). Pick up ferry schedules for all the islands, a *Gastgeberverzeichnis* (rooms-for-rent catalogue), maps, and information on sights, including boat excursions to the seal banks. You can also inquire about boats to Helgoland, where walking is the best way to tour this small island far in the North Sea. Information may also be found on billboards and leaflets around town.

Follow narrow cobbled streets to Husum's pretty *Schloss* and its garden, or head for the harbor (*Hafen*) to watch fishing boats at work. Husum is especially appealing on quiet weekend afternoons, when the only shops open are ice-cream parlors and restaurants, and the only people on the street are those enjoying a leisurely stroll. Pass over the Husum campground for the site in Schobüll, on the beach and nearer the islands. To get there, ride a quick 5 km north, passing the hostel on the way.

Nordstrand and Pellworm (61 kilometers)

The first two islands of the tour are Nordstrand, linked to the mainland by a causeway, and Pellworm, connected by ferry. Unfortunately, you missed the chance to simplify connections by about 350 years—Nordstrand and Pellworm were a single island until a storm blew the center away in the seventeenth century.

If you want to stay on the islands, there are rooms for rent everywhere, though summer reservations are recommended. There are two campgrounds on Nordstrand (Süderhafen's offering the better location) but none on Pellworm. Supermarkets can be found in Tammensiel on Pellworm, and England (a different England) or Herrendeich on Nordstrand.

NORDSTRAND. The island provides a good general introduction to Nordfriesland, though the best scenery comes later, on Amrum and Sylt. Fluffy sheep dot farmlands while fishing activity bustles along the coast. There are few specific sights on Nordstrand other than modern wind turbines whirring like giant pinwheels. **Schobüll** is a windy 18 km from Nordstrand's Strucklandungshörn ferry dock, with bicycle lanes for most of the ride. **Süderhafen**, with its beach and traditional windmill, offers the most worthwhile side trip. From there, bike to the ferry via **Herrendeich**.

PELLWORM. A 45-minute ferry ride to **Pellworm** (DM 20 round trip with bike), population 1,000, brings you directly to **Tammensiel** harbor or to a long causeway 2 km south. Pellworm has three main sights apart from the beaches (which are all part of

A classic sight in Nordfriesland

Wattenmeer National Park). A 25-km loop brings you to each of these sights, though there are also many side roads if you are happy to take a less exact course.

The seventeenth-century windmill at **Waldhusen**, now a restaurant, contrasts with its modern counterparts nearby (central north coast). From there, head for **Klostermitteldeich** on the west end of the island to see Pellworm's oldest church (Alte Kirche). Be sure to find the map inside showing the islands before the big storm. Finally, ride to the red-and-white lighthouse on **Kaydeich Beach** (south coast) for a classic Nordfriesland sight. These tall structures on a flat landscape make navigation easy. "Street" signs indicate village names only, simplifying matters further. On the small island, it is hard to go "wrong"—in the worst case, you'll end up on a beach! Darn!

Schobüll to Dagebüll: 40 kilometers

Get a ferry connection directly to the next islands, or return to the mainland and ride north. An easy ride brings you to Dagebüll, a good base for trips to Föhr and Amrum. The short distance allows plenty of time to settle a base and relax on the beach in Dagebüll or head immediately to the islands if using the wanderer approach.

Ride **north** from Schobüll, turning into **Wobbenbüll**—not back across the causeway to Nordstrand. In the center of Wobbenbüll watch carefully for signs **left** to **Hattstedtermarsch** for a quiet road past fields and marshlands. Since a dike blocks your view of the sea, turn your attention to spotting birds instead. The road is not marked at every turn, but simply **keep left** along the dike.

Follow signs to **Schlüttsiel**, a ferry landing near a bird preserve, and then **Dagebüll**. A separate **bicycle lane** parallels the busy road between Dagebüll and Niebüll. Dagebüll has two campgrounds, a Spar supermarket, a beach, and plenty of ferry-bound traffic. For rooms or a hostel, continue on to Föhr or settle a base camp in Niebüll on the mainland.

Föhr and Amrum (54 kilometers)

Buy tickets at the W.D.R. ferry office by the dock in Dagebüll (one-day return ticket DM 25 with bike). The office also distributes handy guides to the islands, simple colored sheets with maps, index of sights, and general information. Inquire about connections directly to Sylt from Amrum, a handy option when offered in the high season. Each ferry hop takes about an hour.

FÖHR. The ferry lands at **Wyk auf Föhr**, a small town offering just about anything you need: information office, stores, bicycle shops, restaurants, and so forth. The tourist office arranges for rooms or holiday house rentals. There is a hostel in Wyk but no campground on the island.

A number of interesting sights dot Föhr. You can visit most by way of a **34-km loop** through the center of the island to the west coast, returning to Wyk via the southern shoreline. **Follow signs** to **Boldixum** then **Alkersum**, next **Oldsum** and **Dunsum**. Don't pedal past **Süderende** without a side trip to see the little town's thatched cottages and tidy streets. You will also pass two windmills on the way to Dunsum's windy beach.

This western point looks out on the North Sea with good views of nearby Sylt and Amrum. Tired of ferries? A wading trail to Amrum begins here in Dunsum. The walk may only be done at low tide and with a guide (possibly easier to arrange from Amrum). Not only a unique experience, the excursion also provides an up-close view of the unique *Watt* ecosystem.

From Dunsum turn **south** for **Utersum**, then **Witsum**. After the bus shelter on the south edge of Utersum turn **right** on Waaster Jugen street for a quick side trip. When this road comes to a **T** look **straight** ahead to see three Bronze Age burial mounds. Tut's tomb they're not, but worth a quick look all the same.

On the way to Witsum you will see **Borgsum**'s windmill. Another **detour** near Borgsum takes you to a Viking ringwall. Stop by St. Johannis church in cobblestoned **Nieblum** for a quick break before returning to **Wyk** via the **south coast** (turn **right** off the main road directly to Wyk).

To shorten this loop and eliminate a long windward stretch, turn **south** at **Alkersum** to the south coast and then **east** to **Wyk**. The northern half of Föhr has no specific sights or towns—therefore fewer visitors and more opportunities for quiet meandering. You should have plenty of time, however, to cover the longer loop and explore Wyk before catching a ferry to Amrum. Narrow lanes of tidy brick houses—Carl-Häberlin Strasse being the best example—and a pleasant promenade are highlights of the town.

AMRUM. More wild and quiet than the others, Amrum was my favorite island. Dunes cover the entire western half, all a nature preserve. The island is only 10 km from Wittdun in the south to Norddorf in the north. For a complete tour, follow one clearly marked **bicycle trail up** the island and another **down** (both unpaved tracks). Amrum's striped lighthouse is a classic, the tallest on Germany's North Sea coast. Other sights on the island include more burial mounds 2 km southwest of **Norddorf**, and **Nebel**'s two windmills. **Wittdun** has a Spar market, a hostel, and private rooms to rent. Amrum's campground lies among the dunes just south of the lighthouse.

SYLT

A well-known, fashionable resort and the northernmost point in Germany, Sylt is the next island of this tour. If you can't catch a **ferry** directly from Amrum, **bike** 12 km from Dagebüll to Niebüll and take the **train** there (DM 30, arrives in Westerland). Sylt is connected to the mainland by a causeway for trains only (no cars, cyclists, or pedestrians permitted to cross). You can reestablish a base in Niebüll (nearby camping and hostel) or go directly to Sylt and settle in there. Day tripping from Niebüll is advantageous in that you will significantly shorten the final leg of this trip into Flensburg, although you will lose island time.

Town and island maps are available at Westerland's tourist office, beside the *Bahnhof*. Depending on your tastes, Westerland's promenade, shopping area, and casino will either call for extra time or have you running for the dunes. Either way, the nearby campgrounds make the most practical base for those staying on the island. There are hostels near List and Hörnum and a campground at Hörnum as well. Each of these towns has stores and conveniences.

Sylt stretches 40 km north to south; count on side or headwinds on at least one leg of your exploration. The island neatly divides itself into **two loops**, northern (34 to 50 km) and southern (40 km). You can tour the entire island in one long but unhurried day, but a day for each half would be ideal. Vacationers on Sylt are not particularly attentive drivers, so keep alert on the roads.

Follow road **signs from Westerland** to List to pick up the **bicycle trail** north. The **unpaved** track takes you on a scenic ride right through the **dunes**—but beware for the occasional sand patch. For a slight **detour**, turn **east** for a closer look at **Kampen**'s lighthouse and neighboring burial mound. Don't miss the **lookout platform** high on a dune 2 km farther north, near the trail. You will gain excellent sea views and an impression of the island's layout from the high platform. Sylt's dunes stretch far into the distance but barely a kilometer from side to side.

Eventually the dune trail emerges by the road. **Bear left** to loop through a nature preserve. On the way you may also take an extra 8-km **side trip** to **Ostellenbogen**. Two picture-perfect lighthouses and miles of unspoiled dunes highlight this ride to the island's most remote corner, but you will fight headwinds on the return trip.

List has a few shops and a dock. To continue island hopping, catch a **ferry** to **Rømø** in Denmark from List's port. A paved **bicycle trail** parallels the main road south from List but ends after a few kilometers so you are better off back on the **dune trail**. Instead of returning directly to Westerland, however, turn off the trail to ride quiet side roads via **Kampen** and **Braderup** to **Keitum**. Thatched fishermen's cottages and tree-lined lanes make Keitum the island's most appealing town. It occupies the most sheltered spot on Sylt, where the sound of singing birds replaces howling wind in your ears.

Three **bicycle trails** run along the southern half of Sylt, characterized by long stretches of uninterrupted dunes. For a quick but noisy ride to Hörnum, follow the **paved trail** beside the main road. **Unpaved trails** run along either side of the road (*Strandradweg* on the west is better marked) for quieter biking close to nature. Not close enough? Head for the nudist beach at **Sansibar**.

Hörnum's lighthouse and promenade command wide views of the sea. You can view Föhr and Amrum from a new perspective and watch distant wind turbines spinning bright white against a blue sky. Before, during, and after a day of biking you can hit the beach. Eastern beaches are not as picturesque as western but are somewhat more sheltered. Many areas rent out giant transformer picnic baskets—actually wicker beach chairs that double as changing booths, quite the fashion on Sylt.

Niebüll to Flensburg: 57 kilometers

The final day of this tour crosses from the North Sea to the Baltic and Flensburg, pedaling along the Danish border. From **Niebüll** *Bahnhof* follow **signs** to Bundesstrasse 5. Ride the bicycle path **north** along **Road 5** until **Klixbüll**. Ignore bicycle signs there and pedal the road until a **right turn** on a small road for **Tinningstedt**. From this point on you will enjoy quiet, **tree-lined lanes** for most of the day. Follow signs through **Karlum**, then bear **right** for **Boverstedt**. After this town, go **right** on a street marked Boverstedt 12. After 2 km **watch carefully for Abroer Weg** on the **left** to ride directly into **Medelby**.

From here you can turn **north** to ride through a corner of Denmark. To do so, pedal to **Jardelund**, keeping straight on Hauptstrasse and *Zur Fehle*. You may be a bit disappointed to find the border unmanned, only a well-trod foot path curving around the bar across the road. No dreaded *Paß Kontrolle* (passport control) here. Take a **sharp right** at the bar and follow signs to Padborg.

Enjoy peaceful cycling through a **dense forest** before entering **Padborg**. This town is no cultural highlight—even Flensburg is more typically Danish, so enjoy the woods while you can. A **bicycle lane** brings you across the busy **border** (*Groense*) to Germany. Follow this **lane** along the busy road for the last 8 km into **Flensburg** *Zentrum*.

Flensburg's "Danish" harbor

Eventually emerge at Flensburg's picturesque harbor, known for its Danish flavor. Many traditional wooden sailboats line the docks, as do traditional sailor dens. Bypass The Tipsy Sailor and the Tattoo Pit in favor of historic buildings and shops on Norderstrasse, one block up and parallel to the water.

Signs lead to Flensburg's information office and hostel. The nearest campground is 6 km south of town in Jarplund, convenient only as a head start if pedaling the next tour to Schleswig (Tour No. 18). Unless you are in a hurry, bike 10 km east to Glücksburg, location of a picturesque castle and fjord-side campground. For faster travel to more distant points catch a train in Flensburg *Bahnhof*.

TOUR NO. 18

BALTIC HARBORS, HOLSTEIN LAKES
Flensburg to Lübeck

Distance: 256 kilometers (159 miles)
Estimated time: 4 to 6 days (4 biking days)
Terrain: Gentle rolling hills or flat
Maps: ADFC #1 and #2
Connecting tours: Tour Nos. 17 and 19

Continuing west along the Baltic Sea coast, this tour explores historic harbors and tranquil Holstein scenery between the port of Flensburg (more Danish in ambience than German) and the Hanseatic capital of Lübeck. Along the way, the route dips inland to meander through the Holsteinische Schweiz (Holstein Alps), a patchwork of countless lakes. In spite of its lofty name, the region is nearly flat, a biker's delight of uncrowded side roads and beaches.

The Plön to Lübeck stretch of the tour, including a day trip around the lakes, offers the best cycling for those short of time or wishing to explore a smaller area in greater detail. Connecting with the Nordfriesland Island Hopping tour (Tour No. 17) from the west, the ride continues east toward the island of Rügen with Tour No. 19 along East Germany's Baltic Coast. Strong westerly winds ease your way along gentle terrain throughout. Riding the tour in reverse, on the other hand, is not advised.

Flensburg

Gateway to Denmark, Flensburg makes an interesting and convenient starting point for this tour. Rail connections are easy though a trip to this northerly city can take some time from central or southern Germany. See Tour No. 17 for accommodations and city information.

Flensburg to Schleswig: 37 kilometers

The first leg of this tour runs south from Flensburg's picturesque harbor to Schleswig's historic sights. The short distance allows plenty of time for an afternoon of sightseeing or a late start including a side trip to Glücksburg Castle, 10 km east of Flensburg (see Tour No. 17).

Use a city map to avoid confusion when leaving Flensburg. Follow **Road 76** (Schleswigerstrasse) **south** out of the city. A **bicycle**

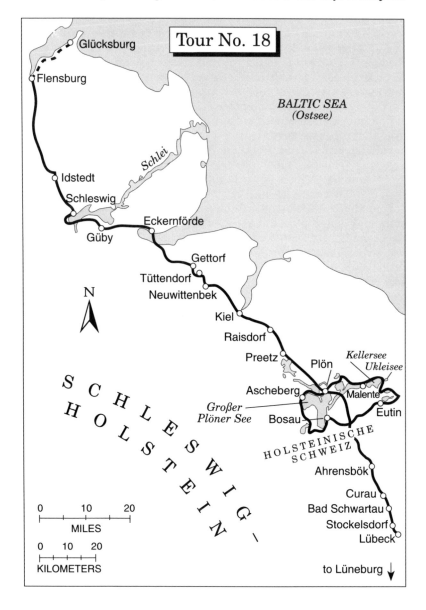

trail parallels this busy road, making for a quick but noisy ride. Just 6 km beyond Flensburg you can pull over to see third millennium B.C. burial mounds beside the trail. Even if you are coming from the Island Hopping tour and have seen enough burial mounds, informative diagrams and history boards help make sense of the lumpy site.

After 20 km the bicycle trail turns **away from the main road** and **yellow bicycle signs** take over, leading you on quiet side roads from **Poppholz** to Idstedt and Schleswig. After **Idstedt** traffic picks up considerably and the road becomes quite hilly, but near **Schleswig** city limits you will regain a **separate bicycle lane**. Follow signs to *Zentrum* and *Dom*.

The information office occupies the large white building across from the cathedral (signs are a bit misleading—do not turn right to parallel train tracks). Ask for a city map and a guide to the Schleswig-Holstein music festival, which features top performers every summer. A work of art in itself, the schedule is worth seeing even if you are not planning to attend any concerts.

Your time in Schleswig will be easily occupied with visits to the main sights and pleasant walks along the waterside promenade. Everyone insists that the *Dom* is a must see, but any attempts at church appreciation may be thwarted by restoration work. The cathedral's most famous treasure is the Bordesholm altarpiece, well worth seeing if open to the public. Hopefully work will be completed soon.

Abandoning the *Dom*, head to **Holm**, the quaint fishermen's quarter where tidy cottages line cobblestone streets. Keeping with the theme, visit Schloss Gottorf Museum to see the Nydam boat, a well-preserved fourth-century wooden ship. The *Schloss* also houses art and history exhibits.

Schleswig's hostel is located on a hill above town west of the *Dom* (follow signs from near Gottorf Museum). Camping, 5 km south across the waters of the Schlei, will give you a head start on the next day.

Schleswig to Plön: 92 kilometers

If you're eager for the best cycling of this tour in Plön's lake area, you can ride straight from Schleswig to Plön. To shorten this long stretch you may also stop in Eckernförde, 23 km from Schleswig, or Kiel, 52 km (both with campgrounds, rooms, and hostels). While Eckernförde makes a pleasant break point, Kiel's city streets can be a hassle, and you may prefer simply pushing on to settle in pleasant Plön.

Leave Schleswig by **following signs** to Eckernförde around the Schlei. Ride a separate **bicycle trail** along busy Road 76 for 5 km before turning **left** into **Fahrdorf**. Pedal quiet **back roads** past **Borgwedel** and into **Güby** and **Ahrensberg** before returning to **Road 76's bicycle path** for the last stretch into **Eckernförde**. (To get away from traffic, you can try the unpaved trail south of the road, but it may be difficult to follow.)

With lively streets and a pedestrian area dotted with benches, Eckernförde makes a good stopping point. Continuing along Road 76 toward Kiel, catch your first sight of the Baltic. After 3 km **turn off** for **Altenhof** for better country cycling over rolling farmlands typical of Holstein. Head toward Harfe, then turn off for **Gettorf**, **Tüttendorf**, and **Neuwittenbek**. There, signs to Kiel bring you high over the Kiel Canal (connecting the Baltic and North seas) and onto bicycle lanes to the city *Zentrum* and *Bahnhof*.

The best thing to do in **Kiel** is visit the tourist office, located across from the north end of the *Bahnhof* (near the pedestrian overpass). Ask for a city map and the *Ostsee Radeln* brochure listing nearby biking destinations. If ending your day here, the office will direct you to accommodations.

Kiel is no Disneyland, but neither is the city completely void of interest. Kiel is best known to travelers as a ferry terminus linked to ports throughout Scandinavia. Claim a harborside bench to watch shipping and fishermen at work. While you are there, try to locate the three masts of the *Gorch Foch* in the harbor—the square-rigged ship provides sail training and represents Germany in tall-ship regattas around the world. Continuing with the nautical theme, Kiel also offers a submarine museum and memorial.

The 30-km ride from Kiel to Plön is not too exciting as it simply follows a **bicycle path beside main Road 202/76**. (You can parallel the road through Kiel or loop through Ellerbek and Klausdorf suburbs to join the trail in Raisdorf.) The bicycle path twists around small communities along Road 76 near Kiel, making it **difficult to follow at first**. Trace your position carefully, keeping an eye (or ear) on the main road to eventually access the primary, direct trail. After **Preetz** the trail is easy to follow, and terrain throughout the ride remains gentle.

Bicycle signs lead into **Plön**'s pedestrian center and the tourist office. Turn west for Ascheberg to reach both the lakeside campground and hostel. Finally, you can settle in comfortably, ready to enjoy easy day trips to the surrounding lakes.

Plön is a nice resort town, the bustling pedestrian zone transformed into a tranquil strolling ground by evening. Head for the high *Schloss*, where outstanding views of the expansive lakelands

Plön's Schloss *watches over a soccer match.*

provide inspiration for upcoming explorations. A lakeside walk leads from Plön to Prinzeninsel, a wooded peninsula lined with trails. The typical farmhouse at the tip now holds a restaurant; for a "cultural" experience order a beer and watch the sun set over the lake.

Lakes Day Trip: 82 kilometers

A lunch, camera, and bathing suit are all you will need for this pleasant tour of the Five Lakes Region (a misnomer; there are countless lakes here). Take advantage of cycling's flexibility and spontaneity on this day. Your time is as well spent enjoying a perfect swimming spot only a few kilometers away as touring every corner of every lake. Take this loop as a guideline, but follow your own whims. This day trip can be subdivided easily for more leisurely cycling over several days.

From Plön head **east** for Lütjenburg (follow bicycle signs), but **turn off** for **Behl**. Past Behl 2 km go **right** for **Timmdorf**, a pretty lakeside town. Typical Holstein scenery compensates for **unpaved**

sections of road along the way. Follow signs to **Malente**, heading for the **church**. The road to Sielbeck/Uklei **loops** around the **Kellersee**, one of the nicest parts of this ride. Stop for perfect views across the silver lake waters from **Sielbeck**'s ferry landing. Watch carefully for the **second left** in town, which leads to a **4-km loop** of the **Ukleisee**. A smooth dirt trail rings the pretty, wooded lakeside.

Return to the main road toward Eutin. For another lake loop, **detour left** in **Fissau** toward Sibbersdorf, passing a dolmen on the way. In 3 km go **straight** on a dirt road for **Schönewald**. Pedal through a tall forest, eventually emerging on a larger road to close the 10-km loop back to **Eutin**.

In Eutin, see the town square with its weekend markets and a moated *Schloss* by the lake. A summertime opera festival takes place in the *Schloss* garden, featuring works of native son Karl Maria von Weber and other composers. Leave Eutin on **bicycle lanes** along **B76** toward Kiel, branching **left** for **Bosau** 2 km later.

Back on quiet roads, head for **Großer Plöner See** and **Bosau**, a sleepy little town with a pretty lakeside church. Then ride to **Bredenbek** and **Dersau**. Finish the ride on a **bicycle lane** alongside busy **Road 430** to **Ascheberg** and **Plön**. Back in Plön you can **return** to the *Schloss* viewpoint with a new perspective of the lake panorama, having pedaled the area yourself.

Plön to Lübeck: 45 kilometers

Although the cycling map recommends the direct road (76) from Plön to Eutin, you will be disappointed when the bicycle lane there comes to an abrupt end, abandoning you on the busy road. Instead, cut diagonally to Lübeck on a different route.

Take **Road 76** only **past Sandkaten**, then turn **right** for **Pfingstberg**. Follow signs southeast via **Hassendorf**, **Sarau**, and **Barghorst** to **Ahrensbök**, and then continue on to **Curau**, **Stockelsdorf**, and **Krempelsdorf** on the outskirts of Lübeck. Terrain consists of long, gentle slopes through farmlands.

Follow signs and city spires straight into **Lübeck** center, passing the main train station on the way. Lübeck's tourist office is inside the *Bahnhof*, providing city maps and accommodations tips (many official and independent hostels in the old town; rooms; nearest camping 15 km northeast in Travemünde).

The old town crowds onto an island in the Trave River. The city's symbol, the bulky *Holstentor*, welcomes you to the city center. Still called **Hansastadt Lübeck**, the city was the capital of the prosperous Hanseatic trading league that linked many Baltic ports from

Lübeck's Holstentor guards the Hanseatic capital.

the twelfth to sixteenth centuries. Huge salt warehouses outside Lübeck's old town recall the city's connection with Lüneburg (Tour No. 16). Inland salt was shipped here for export to other areas near the Baltic (a sea low in salt content).

Put your bicycle aside and explore cobblestone side streets like Engelsgruberstrasse, where impressive houses reflect the Hanseatic city's great wealth. For a behind-the-scenes look, peep into courtyards off Glockengeißenstrasse (particularly Nos. 25 and 41), or see the unusual *Rathaus* of glazed brick on the *Marktplatz*.

Lübeck's *Bahnhof* provides plenty of train connections to points near and far. To continue cycling along the coast, follow Tour No. 19. Another good option loops south to Lüneburg via the picturesque island towns of Ratzeburg and Mölln, tracing the medieval Salt Road (Die Alte Salzstrasse) between Lübeck and Lüneburg. Ferries also depart Lübeck harbor for Scandinavian ports, the perfect means for exploration of more distant Baltic coasts.

TOUR NO. 19

EAST GERMANY'S BALTIC COAST
Lübeck to Rügen Island

Distance: 453 kilometers (281 miles)
Estimated time: 8 to 11 days (7 to 9 biking days)
Terrain: Rolling hills or flat but windy
Maps: ADFC #2, #3, and #4
Connecting tours: Tour Nos. 18 and 20

Peculiarities of the German language will keep you entertained throughout your trip. Obsessively logical on one hand (*Handschuhe* for gloves), wildly unpredictable on the other (*Oberaffengeil*—"Great!"), German is sure to keep you on your toes. In the case of this tour, you will have it easy: German does not differentiate between enclosed bodies of water (lakes) and open ones (seas), leaving you with just one term for the two main elements of this tour—*See*.

Where shall you go? Coast or inland lakes? Coast to lakes? Lakes to coast? This route takes an all-inclusive approach, a sample of the Eastern Baltic coast's best. From Hanseatic Lübeck this tour follows the shores of the western Mecklenburg lake area to seaside resorts and the holiday island of Rügen.

While disparities between East and West become clear the moment you cross the former border near Lübeck, an influx of tourism to the coast has brought more stores, accommodations, and improved services to the region, long a popular vacation area within the Eastern Bloc. You will curse poorly paved, terribly paved, and completely unpaved roads often on your eastern trek, but the dreaded "waffle-iron" surfaces (tank—but not bicycle—friendly) that once terrorized cyclists here have been smoothed over. Relaxing waterside scenery and friendly people compensate for occasional drawbacks like these. Just remember to remain patient and expect a slower pace in order to enjoy exploration of a new, quickly developing land.

Lübeck

Ideally, you will connect into this tour from the west coast tour (Tour No. 18), gaining a thorough basis for East–West comparison along the way. Lübeck, still an important Baltic (Ostsee) port, is also easily reached by train (often via Hamburg). Among other northern ports, Lübeck is also connected to Denmark, Sweden, and Norway by ferry, the perfect means to link up a multicountry tour. For sights and accommodations in Lübeck, see Tour No. 18.

This route is divided into eight sections of modest length to allow for a relaxed pace and plenty of time along shorelines. Depending on your average speed and interest in the beaches, consider combining two sections into a single day for a quicker tour.

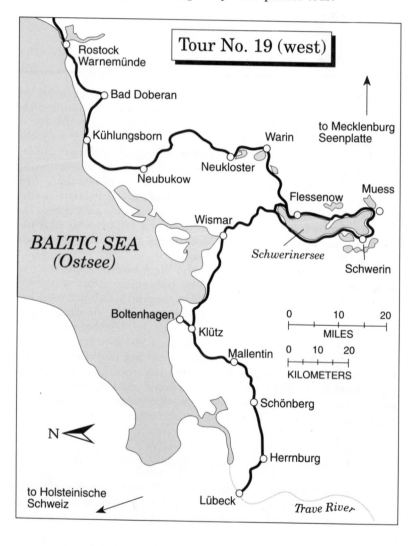

Lübeck to Boltenhagen: 55 kilometers

Ride **east** out of Lübeck on Moltkestrasse, following signs to **Eichholz** and **Herrnburg** to cross the **former border**, 7 km away. Although the walls are now gone, the empty strip of No-Man's Land remains an obvious scar on the landscape. Ready or not, welcome to the East.

Herrnburg provides a capsule introduction to East German cycling. The bicycle path suddenly ends, depositing you on uneven cobblestone streets lined by drab buildings, even more likely to appear so on a drab gray day. Follow signs through several small towns to Schönberg. Once past **Wahrsow**, go **straight** (do not bend to the right for Raddingsdorf). If this road is still under construction, expect detours and delays and inches of sand to slow your progress to a turtle-paced walk. At times the East seems to be one large construction zone. Although bicycle signs are optimistically posted at many intersections, many roads remain rough on your rims.

Schönberg's church and *Marktplatz* are of some interest. Remember to readapt to Eastern standards. Things may be run down, but look beyond peeling paint at the core character of the place. Resources remain scant, but residents do what they can—the thatching may be decrepit, but darn are those windows clean!

From Schönberg **signs** lead through more **small towns** and **bad roads** to **Grevesmühlen** and **Mallentin**. Intersect busy **Road E22**, turning **left** toward Lübeck for less than 1 km. Turn **right** to **Tramm** with signs to **Roggenstorf**. Bicycle past the town and on to **Grevenstein**. There, go **left** for **Rankendorf** and continue pedaling to **Klütz**.

Who could resist a town named Klütz? Nearing town, turn **right** to see Schloss Bothmer, an eighteenth-century moated castle. Then head for the town center to pass thirteenth-century Marienkirche, picking up **signs** to your final destination, **Ostseebad Boltenhagen**. Don't even consider riding the gravel "bicycle path" along this road, however. You can call it quits at the beach or ride on to Flessenow in one long day. A few hotels and private homes rent out rooms in Boltenhagen. The campsite lies 2 km east of town, off the road to Tarnewitz.

An old Baltic resort, Boltenhagen has been popular since the nineteenth century. Town architecture mixes original seashore cottages (quaint), prefabricated concrete-slab buildings of socialist days (horrendous), and post-reunification sprucing-up work (relieving)—none of which affects the long, untouched beach, Boltenhagen's main attraction.

Boltenhagen to Flessenow: 53 kilometers

If you try to shortcut east past Tarnewitz, you will find that the road turns into an overgrown path. Instead of trailblazing, return to Klütz and follow **Road 105** toward **Wismar**. This busy road has **no bicycle lane or shoulder**, but a fair number of cyclists pedal it nonetheless since no alternative roads run east. Beyond Wohlenberg the road stretches directly along the Baltic with views far to the sea's horizon.

Look beyond the ugly block buildings on the outskirts of Wismar and head for the old town's **church tower**. Near the center, a **bicycle lane** appears on the **right side** of the road to offer some relief from traffic. Find your way to the **pedestrian zone** in the center of town for a rest and a look around.

In both style and scale, Wismar's architecture reflects the city's status as another old *Hansastadt* (Hanseatic city). Many historic buildings have been restored, creating a fresh, pleasant atmosphere. Stop for lunch on the *Marktplatz* or bench-lined pedestrian area. Be sure to shop ahead for food as there are no stores in Flessenow, the end point of this day.

After visiting Wismar, follow Schwerin **signs** from the **east edge** of town to join the **ring road**. Near the *Krankenhaus* (hospital) branch **left** for Ventschow to gain quieter roads. After pedaling past a few **bends** and crossing **railroad tracks**, you will be reassured of your course by a **Lübow sign**. Turn **right** to pedal through **Triwalk** to **Dorf Mecklenburg**, its windmill visible from afar. On the way, pass peaceful farmlands where little seems to have changed for years. At the **yield sign** in lower Dorf Mecklenburg take a **sharp left** (not right over the train tracks) to ride some good, some bad roads toward Bad Kleinen. In **Hohen Viecheln**, go **left** for **Ventschow**, then **right** on the marked **bicycle route** to **Flessenow**.

Beware of **sandtraps** on this bumpy dirt track. At a small **intersection** with bicycle signs, look at the arrows from all directions as there are several routes to Flessenow. The shortest path is a bumpy but rideable dirt track. Flessenow is a small one-road (unpaved) town. Its appeal lies in its location, the ideal base for a day trip around the Schwerinersee and convenient return north to the Baltic afterward. Ride through the town center to reach both campground and hostel. The summer-camp-like hostel offers private rooms and family bungalows. Don't be put off by the drab exterior—the interiors are freshly remodeled. The equally drab-looking campground is located between the hostel and the Schwerinersee's shores—the condition of the interiors there depends on your own equipment.

On a lake day trip, visit Schwerin castle.

Schwerinersee Day Trip: 65 kilometers

This day trip tours the Schwerinersee, a lake on the western edge of the Mecklenburg *Seenplatte* (lake basin). With the opening of the East, Schwerinersee has become a popular draw for cyclists and other vacationers.

To begin the ride, return to **Hohen Viecheln** to join the **main road** through **Bad Kleinen** and on to **Gallentin**. In Gallentin fork **left under** the train tracks and pass the last buildings to reach a small **track through the woods**. **Choose** either a pleasant track immediately beside the shore where waves lap practically at your side, or the higher, better dirt road. The shore road becomes unmanageably overgrown, at which point you must push your bike up to join the better dirt road on the ridge. The dirt road does not start immediately; count on dismounting and walking your bike more than once. Remember, it's not just a day trip, it's an adventure.

For orientation, simply follow the lakeshore. Eventually you will reach Schloss Wiligrad, a towered castle overlooking the lake. Perhaps a friendly guard will invite you in to see the small museum (changing art exhibits). The *Schloss* does not get too many foreign visitors, so you can make quite a hit there.

Continue on **dirt then pavement** to **Lübstorf** and on toward Schwerin. After passing the **motorcycle store** in **Wickendorf**, turn **left** on Paulsdammer Weg. Ride 2 km, **cross** a bridge, and turn **right** to join moderately busy **Road 104** to **Schwerin**. Depending on traffic, you may or may not be tempted to bump along the uneven bicycle path alongside.

Zentrum signs lead to Schwerin's impressive *Schloss*, built on an island in the lake. Walk around the *Schloss* and its island park, or see the exhibits inside. Then wander past the grand square opposite the *Schloss* to explore the old town's pedestrian area, another pleasant surprise.

To continue **southeast** around the lake, ride along the **shoreside bicycle/walking trail** (unpaved) to **Muess**. The open-air *Freilichtmuseum* displays farm buildings typical of the region, an interesting stop along the way. Bike **through Muess** and join busy **Road 321** for a short distance, pedaling a lumpy bicycle lane. Don't be tempted by a detour to Basthorst (characterized by terrible roads and a disappointing *Schloss*); spend more time in Schwerin or by the lake instead.

After **crossing** the canal, leave Road 321 by turning **left** for **Godern**. The road to Godern, **Leezen**, and **Rampe** is relatively busy. In Rampe go **left** as if to Schwerin, then take a **quick right** to **Flessenow** via a nice, quiet road. Back at your base, you can cook a lakeside dinner and prepare yourself for a return to the Ostsee the next day.

Flessenow to Kühlungsborn: 74 kilometers

Having toured the Schwerinersee, the route now returns to the Ostsee coast. Ostsee beaches are full of Westerners these days, all curious to see the East (the West being full of Easterners curious to see the West). Although prevailing winds are theoretically southerlies, you are more likely to feel crazy winds from all directions throughout this ride. Except for two long dirt stretches early on, this route covers good roads for most of the day, with forest scenery over the first half of the ride and rolling farmlands up to the coast.

Bicycle signs in Flessenow get you started toward Alt Schlagsdorf and Ventschow, riding **bumpy** dirt roads. Emerge on a **paved** road and go **left** toward Dämelow, then take the first right to **Warin**. Turn **right** on **Road 192** to snake through Warin and find back roads. **Cross** over a bridge, turn **left toward a church** on a street marked *Am Markt*, then go **right** on Friedenstrasse. After **cross-**

ing the train tracks, take the **first left** turn for a **dirt road** to Neukloster. You can expect slower progress over this 8-km dirt stretch—try to think of it as a nature walk and remain patient.

Once back on **pavement**, turn **left** into **Neukloster** and follow signs to **Glasin** and **Poischendorf**. At the **T** with a busy road go **right** for a short distance, then take the **first left** for **Tüzen**. A paved road bends through town and emerges on a bigger road in **Passee**. Go **left** there, led on by signs for **Kamin** and **Neubukow**.

In Neubukow **cross** the tracks and **bend right**, then **left** past the *Bahnhof*. Pedal **straight up** a slight incline on this road, following signs to **Bastorf** and **Kühlungsborn** all the way to the **beach**. Finally, you will crest a hill and enjoy glorious views of the seashore before sailing down the last 4 km into **Kühlungsborn**.

Pass up dumpy Ikarus camping for a second site signposted closer to the beach. The resort offers many new improvements, for example, a sparkling new Spar supermarket. Along the waterfront you can stroll a remodelled promenade complete with benches—the perfect place for an evening walk after time on the beach.

Kühlungsborn to Graal-Müritz: 49 kilometers

From Ost Kühlungsborn ride a **dirt track** that parallels the beach to **Heiligendamm**, where you will return to the road. **Do not cross** the train tracks when you emerge on pavement in Heiligendamm. Instead, go **left** through town and pass the *Kurhaus* (literally, cure house). A genuine steam train (right down to the *Choo Choo!* and *Whoo Whoo!*) runs along the tracks you see, operating tourist excursions from Bad Doberan to the beach.

Leaving Heiligendamm behind, pedal a **moderately busy road straight** to **Bad Doberan**. Ride straight into town and turn **right** for **Wismar** to pick up *Zentrum* signs. (On the way take note of a turnoff to Warnemünde, which you will return to later.)

Typical of today's East, signs point optimistically to city information from all points, but the office is nowhere to be found. By the time you complete your search for the office, however, you will have gained a good impression of Bad Doberan. The pleasant town centers around a green, pavilion-dotted park. **Detour** slightly to see the impressive brick church with its pretty grounds and Gothic *Kloster* (on the edge of town in the direction of Rostock).

Exit Bad Doberan by way of the Warnemünde **turnoff** and ride a **moderately busy road** to **Rostock-Warnemünde**. Pedal **straight** through Warnemünde and **straight** through a pedestrian zone. Walk your bike **under** the *Bahnhof* overpass to reach the docks for the ferry across the narrow strait there.

When you emerge, turn **right** to reach the **ferry** (DM 3, departs

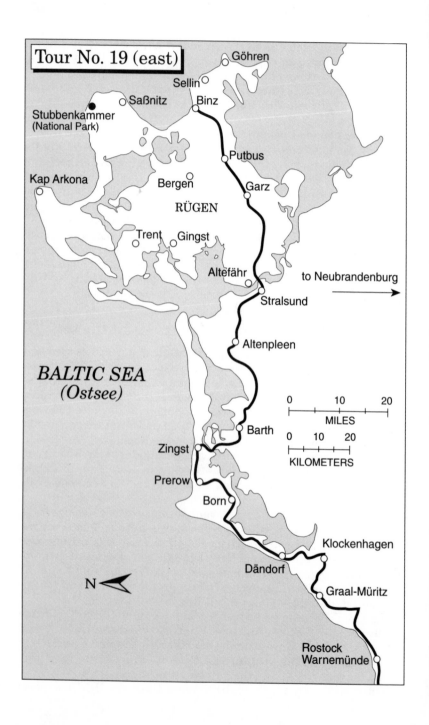

Tour No. 19 (east)

Göhren
Sellin
Saßnitz
Binz
Stubbenkammer
(National Park)
Kap Arkona
Putbus
Bergen
Garz
RÜGEN
Trent
Gingst
Altefähr
to Neubrandenburg
Stralsund
Altenpleen
BALTIC SEA
(Ostsee)
Barth
Zingst
Prerow
Born
Klockenhagen
Dändorf
Graal-Müritz
N
Rostock
Warnemünde

0   10   20
MILES
0   10   20
KILOMETERS

every ten minutes). The short boat ride offers interesting harbor views and a quick break from cycling. Once across the inlet, resume pedaling on a new, perfect **bicycle lane**. The lane ends after a few kilometers, but the road is also new and quiet, a great relief. After passing typical thatched houses in **Hinrichshagen**, turn **left** for **Graal-Müritz**.

Camping lies just east of Graal-Müritz, another *Ostseebad* on the rise. The town is set back from the beach and surrounded by woods, creating a very relaxing setting. Rooms for rent and a hostel in Graal round out accommodations options.

Graal-Müritz to Zingst: 55 kilometers

Continuing your eastward trek, this day extends out to one of the long, thin peninsulas that parallel and protect the mainland, typical of this coastline. Terrain remains flat and winds a constant riddle. While windmills point due south, you may also feel winds from the north or east.

Resume your ride along the **eastward** road toward Ribnitz. In **Klockenhagen**, turn **left** for **Ahrenshoop** to explore the peninsula. The single road **north** along the narrow peninsula to Prerow and Zingst is fairly busy (no bicycle lane). A **detour** through **Dändorf** and later, **Born**, offers respite from traffic and the opportunity to see typical thatched cottages up close. Seemannskirche (Sailors' Church) along the road in **Prerow** makes a good stopping point short of your final stop, **Zingst**.

Traffic lightens considerably by the time you reach the north coast of the peninsula. For nice sea views and quieter cycling, ride the bicycle path atop a dike that protects the road from the sea. Zingst's campground, 1 km west of town, lies across the road from a quiet section of beach. The walk/bikeway continues a few kilometers past town.

Although Zingst is another of many similar *Ostseebad* towns, it proves again that each preserves a distinct character. The dike that separates the long beach from town also protects the natural, remote feeling of the *Strand* (beach). In town you will find supermarkets, restaurants, and *Imbiss* stands, some clustered around a new, brick courtyard near the beach. Indulge in a bag o' sugary doughnut balls and watch the waves roll in.

Zingst to Stralsund: 50 kilometers

From Zingst, **return** to the mainland and Stralsund, another *Hansastadt* and jumping-off point for cliffy Rügen island.

Barth's "fishy" socialist fountain

Use the **dirt bicycle path** beside the road to cross a one-lane **bridge** off the peninsula since lanes are narrow and traffic fast paced. Leaving **Pruchten**, do not continue on the main road at the sign that says BARTH 5 KM. Instead, **bear right** to **cross** unused train tracks within 100 meters and follow the **dirt lane** beside the rails. Emerge on **pavement**, turn **left** and follow **bicycle lanes** right to **Barth**.

Pedal under the old town gate, pass the church, and ride into Barth's *Marktplatz*. Although unrestored, enough elements of the old market remain to convey something of the town's original character. Don't miss the fishy socialist fountain in the market square—a classic DDR relic extolling the joys of seaside socialism.

From Barth, follow **signs** first to Stralsund and then Niepars. The road to Niepars is very quiet and in good condition. After 13 km, turn **left** at signs to **Altenpleen** and then **Stralsund**, pedaling right into the city. Look for the newly constructed red-brick bicycle lane on your way into town, a great improvement for cyclists.

Slowly but surely, Hansastadt Stralsund is being spruced up and rediscovered. Many original city gates and sections of wall remain, the center of town additionally protected by lakes and a narrow sea inlet. Hulking churches tower above the compact town, a testament to prosperous days under the flourishing Hanseatic League. Pedestrians can walk right through the unique *Rathaus* from the old market square. Wander the city streets for smaller discoveries, or sit by the docks for views of Rügen.

Tourist information is located across from The Teddy Bear behind the *Rathaus*. Rooms are advertised around town, and a hostel takes over two historic buildings beside the city walls. Campers will gain good views of Stralsund's impressive skyline and a head start on the next day by pedaling to the nearest campground, 6 km away in Altefähr on Rügen.

Stralsund to Binz: 52 kilometers

Pedal onto Insel Rügen by following **signs** for Bergen and **E22**. A **bicycle lane** across Rügendamm keeps cyclists away from busy traffic, but you will still have to run a gauntlet of fishermen, some blindly readying their hooks for a cast. Rügen is a popular island getaway destination with both seaside resort towns and beautiful stretches of natural coastline.

As you reach **Rügen**, turn **right** onto quiet roads for **Garz** and **Putbus**. This pleasant stretch takes cyclists along good roads with few cars, passing small farm communities of thatched houses. Ride past a large park area surrounding an unimpressive *Schloss* in Putbus. At the top of the hill you will reach the *Circus*, a grand plaza surrounded by impressive houses—a hint of the island's glory days. All over Rügen, buildings like these are being restored as the island reestablishes its reputation as a top Baltic resort.

From the *Circus*, ride in the **direction of Binz** along bad (and soon, worse) roads of horrible cobblestones. After 4 km cyclists can **choose** between a direct and a masochistic route to Binz. For a quick 5-km ride to the resort, turn **left** on a busy, paved road uphill.

Masochists can detour to Jagdschloss Granitz, riding terrible roads to the hilltop castle viewpoint. To begin this detour, go **straight** and briefly join the **main road** until **Lancken-Granitz**. (For a side trip within the detour, follow signs 2 km south to a Neolithic stone monument indicated by signs.) To continue toward the castle, turn **left** at the **bicycle sign** to Jagdschloss Granitz in Lancken-Granitz. This detour qualifies as your basic excursion from hell. The horrible cobblestone road jars bicycle and body parts repeatedly. Adding insult to injury, a short paved section reverts to cobblestones on the steepest part of the hill. Just when you think it couldn't get any worse, the rain may kick in.

However, masochists will be rewarded for their efforts with close-up views of the unspectacular *Schloss*. Assuming for a moment that your knees are still intact, you can trek up the castle tower's many steps for the true reward, wide views over the island and sea. Afterward, bounce down a hill into **Binz**.

Binz preserves an old-fashioned, seaside resort atmosphere in both renovated and unrestored sections of town. Visitors enjoy the new waterside promenade (no cycling) or rest on the beach, taking in terrific views of Rügen's dramatic, cliffy coastline in the distance. There are stores, restaurants, hotels, rooms, and a hostel in town. Check the map posted by the beach to locate the tourist office (slightly south of the center). To camp, pedal 2 km north from Binz toward Saßnitz. Stay east of the train tracks when the main road splits and follow signs to the woodsy site. Another, less appealing site lies 4 km north of town near Prora, signed off the main road to Saßnitz. From Binz cyclists can set off to explore Rügen's extreme corners.

Rügen Island Cycling

Rügen has quickly become an extremely popular biking destination, with many excellent options for touring. Instead of outlining a strict route, I will cover the major points of the island to help you design a tour best suited to your own interests, pace, and schedule.

Ostseebad Binz is one of the nicest holiday towns on Rügen; Sellin and Göhren on a peninsula to the south are two more. Saßnitz, a harbor town to the north of Binz, lost its only object of interest with the downfall of socialism—a statue commemorating Lenin's stop at the *Bahnhof*. Today Saßnitz ferries offer frequent departures to Denmark, Sweden, and Poland.

Naturally, Rügen's star attraction is the seacoast since the center of the island consists only of flat farmlands much like those on the mainland. Follow **signs north** from Saßnitz to the *Stubbenkammer* (cliffs) in **Jasmund National Park** (60 km round trip from Binz). The endlessly hilly ride brings you to Rügen's spectacular chalk cliffs. For great views over nearby cliffs and the sea, walk out on **Königsstuhl**, one of the tallest cliffs on this dramatic coastline. Boat excursions offer the opposite, sea-level perspective on Rügen. Hiking trails also line the national park, where Neolithic graves lie scattered in the woods.

To make a complete tour of the island, pedal **north** to **Kap Arkona**'s lighthouse, connecting **south** via the Wittower **ferry** and eventually **back** to the mainland via **Trent** and **Gingst**. Look for the occasional *Zimmer frei* sign, or camp along the way. Several campsites cluster on the southern peninsula around Göhren, with a few more on Wittow and one in Gingst.

Cyclists looping back to Stralsund can take a train or pedal to Neubrandenburg for the next route, touring the Mecklenburg *Seenplatte* (Tour No. 20). Infrequent trains connect Saßnitz and Binz with the mainland, as well. Travelers gung-ho to continue east may bike along Usedom (another long peninsula) to Swinemünde and Poland. Swinemünde sounds worthwhile if only for the opportunity to send a "Greetings from Swinemünde" postcard to the folks back home.

Connection to Tour No. 20

Stralsund to Neubrandenburg: 120 kilometers. If the Schwerinersee section of this ride has whetted your appetite for Mecklenburg's lakes, pedal south to join Tour No. 20 at Neubrandenburg. The connection may be undertaken in two short days or one long run.

Leave Stralsund heading west, as if to Ribnitz via Road 105/E22. Turn south at the edge of Stralsund for quiet roads to Wittenhagen and Grimmen. The route includes both paved and unpaved roads. From Grimmen, pedal south to Rakow and Loitz, avoiding busy Road 194. Continue on to Demmin via Kletzin.

Sixty km from Stralsund is Demmin, a medium-size town with a hostel but no camping. Several campgrounds ring the Kummerower See, 15 km southwest. From Demmin, head south on 194 to Reuterstadt but turn left for sometimes unpaved side roads to Buschmühl, Beggerow, Altenhagen, Tützpatz, and Altentreptow. Finish the ride into Neubrandenburg by biking to Groß Teetzleben and Woggersin.

TOUR NO. 20

QUIET WATERS ARE DEEP
The Mecklenburg Lakes

Distance: 217 kilometers (135 miles)
Estimated time: 4 days (4 biking days)
Terrain: Flat or rolling hills
Map: ADFC #4
Connecting tour: Tour No. 19

Stille Wasser sind tief. Quiet waters are deep. This German saying, referring to the hidden significance behind superficial impression, appropriately summarizes this tour of the Mecklenburg lakelands. Countless lakes dot vast unbroken forests, one of the most ideal bicycle-touring destinations in the East. Towns along the route will not hold your attention for long—just enough to buy supplies, then head out to confront the greatest challenge of the day: Where to picnic? This tiny, tree-lined lake, or that sail-dotted expanse? It is not just the reflecting waters that make this tour special, but what you find beyond.

Terrain ranges from absolutely flat in the southern *Seenplatte* (lake basin) to somewhat hilly in the north. Strong winds may crop up in open areas but are broken amongst the forests. Westerners are quickly discovering Mecklenburg. As a popular new holiday destination, the region offers an array of conveniences unusual for the East, with numerous campgrounds, hostels, and rooms for rent even in small towns. However, be sure to stock up on food in larger towns to avoid finding yourself empty-handed at a perfect lunch spot or tempting campsite.

Remember that this tour outlines only the beginning. Mecklenburg cycling possibilities are as numerous as the lakes that dot the land. Leave yourself flexibility and venture beyond the limits of this tour for an optimal trip. Camping allows great flexibility due to the large number of organized campsites and open tracts of woods where free camping is possible.

Neubrandenburg

On the map, this tour appears as an isolated loop, but there are several routes that connect into it. For biking connections from Stralsund and the East Baltic Coast tour, see Connections in Tour

No. 19. The Schwerinersee, also part of Tour No. 19, lies on the western edge of the *Seenplatte*. Cyclists may also choose to loop back to Lübeck over that section of Tour No. 19. Before or after touring Mecklenburg, consider visiting Berlin, another two- to three-day journey.

Train connections to points west or afar are circuitous. Frankfurt, for example, requires five transfers and a full day's travel if handling your own bike. Hamburg is three hours and two transfers away. Berlin, on the other hand, is more conveniently accessed by train (direct train, three hours). Plan further travels carefully ahead at the beginning of the tour. The Neubrandenburg train in-

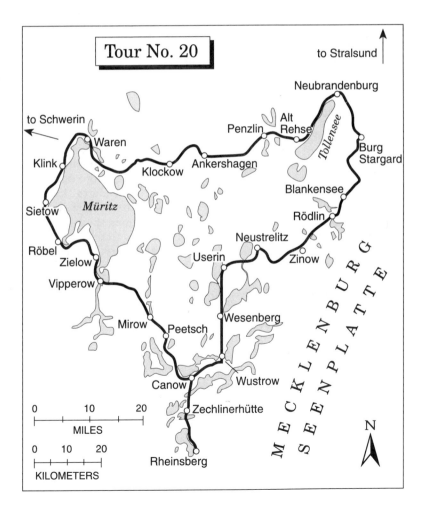

formation office will prove helpful in sorting out complicated connections.

Neubrandenburg, city of four gates, is a strangely preserved old town. While the old town wall remains nearly complete, few original structures survive within or without. The town walls are punctuated by houses built directly into the fortifications—walk or pedal around the perimeter to compare the timbered buildings. Activity focuses on Neubrandenburg's central pedestrian area, where shops and restaurants cluster.

To camp, ride 7 km of the first day's route to Gatscheck on the Tollensesee's west shore (near the ferry landing east of Neu Rhäse). The hostel is 2 km from the city center (direction *Industriegebiet*). The huge, hastily constructed Divi supermarket outside Neubrandenburg's south gate is fully stocked, although it still operates in the old socialist tradition (long lines, slow service). To rent a room do some footwork on your own or ask at tourist information in the city center for help.

Neubrandenburg to Waren: 61 kilometers

The first day of this tour winds between small lakes and small towns, ending in Waren on the edge of the vast Müritz (lake). To begin, leave Neubrandenburg's old town through the **south *Tor*** (gate). **Cross** the street and turn **right** along the **ring road**, then bear off **through a park** to head for the lake. Ride to the **west shore** of the lake and follow TR Tollensesee Rundweg **signs**. The beautiful if bumpy **dirt track** through woods along the lake makes an appropriate introduction to this Mecklenburg tour.

Pass the campground 7 km later and follow signs to **Alt Rehse**. Aim for the **church** there, and turn inland (**right**). Roads are not signed in Alt Rehse but you cannot go wrong by following **any road west away from the lake**—sooner or later you will intersect the main road and see Penzlin's high church tower ahead. Bumpy side roads will soon bring you to **Lübkow** and **Penzlin**.

Penzlin is a decaying old town but also an interesting break point where few tourists venture. Segments of original walls still protect the small town, but many side streets are in terrible condition—forget about a pedaling tour of the walls.

Leave town on Warenerstrasse, then turn **left** for Neustrelitz. Soon after, turn **right** for **Ankershagen** to begin a pleasant ride with wide views over open fields. Heinrich Schliemann, the archaeologist who discovered Troy, once lived in Ankershagen, an otherwise unexceptional town.

Continue cycling in the direction of Möllenhagen, turning **left** in **Wendorf** for Klockow. Just before entering Klockow and passing the **Klockow sign**, turn **sharply right** on a **dirt road** through the woods and turn **left** at the only house. When the track divides, **bear left** to **parallel** and eventually **cross** train tracks. After a short section of jarring cobblestones, bear **left** on a **smooth dirt road** (yes, it's a sad state of affairs when dirt roads provide relief).

Ride **straight** through the woods (national park lands) on this track. Emerge on **pavement** and turn **right**, then take the **first left** at a white bicycle sign (WAREN 6 KM). Ride dirt, then paved roads into **Waren**. Waren stands out for its location rather than town character. Take a quick look at the *Rathaus* and *Marktplatz*, then follow *Hafen* signs to reach Waren's **docks** on **Müritz Lake**. The large lake attracts many visitors, who hike, bike, or take boat excursions. Signs lead from Road 192 to lakeside camping 3 km west of Waren (direction Malchow).

From Waren, try catching a **ferry to Röbel** to shorten the next day's ride. Boats provide easier and more enjoyable connections to Röbel than the bike ride along the Müritz's busy west shore. Camping, a hostel, and rooms are all available in Röbel. Shortcutting to Röbel by ferry also opens the option of biking deeper into the *Seenplatte* the next day—to a campground near Zechlinerhütte, for example. Infrequent ferry departures (and occasional engine trouble) may complicate your plans, however—keep your options open and inquire in Waren.

Waren to Mirow: 50 kilometers

Those not taking a ferry should head **south** along the Müritz's western shore. If you become tired of threatening your rims with every bounce, abandon the uneven shoreside trail for direct **Road 192**. Although the bicycle map does not recommend 192, wide lanes made biking reasonable if no joy ride. For a short break, **detour** past the abandoned *Schloss* at **Klink** for lake views.

Leave Road 192 behind at **Sietow** and follow a quieter, direct road to Röbel, passing an old **windmill** along the way. **Röbel** commands a picturesque location on a quiet inlet of the Müritz. Walk around the church for good views over the inlet and the wider main body of the lake beyond.

Exit Röbel on the **main road** to Mirow but turn **left** on Mühletor. From this street you will pick up **signs to Ludorf** and Zielow, returning to quieter lakeshore roads once again. Pavement ends in **Zielow**. There, head past the hostel and into the **woods** on a narrow **sandy track** to begin the jungle-adventure section of this ride. You will balance along a slim **waffle-grid** block trail with swamp to either side. Eventually, emerge near **Vipperow** and push your bike through a field to reach **dirt** and then **paved roads**. Sections like these inspire a new title for this book: *Germany **with** Bike*.

Back on roads, turn **left** through Vipperow and pedal **Road 198** east to Mirow and Neustrelitz. This road can be surprisingly quiet, but if traffic picks up, turn **right** after **crossing** train tracks 3 km past Vipperow for side roads.

Signs from Road 198 indicate Mirow's campground 2 km before entering town. The neighboring hostel (no sign) offers bungalows, double rooms, and family accommodations. Small stores and rooms can be found in town. If arriving early in the day, consider moving on to one of the campsites sheltered deep in the woods to the south for a more secluded location.

Mirow town, like many along this tour, is secondary to its pleasant lakeside situation. The churchyard on a promontory on the lake offers the best viewpoint. Bike through a gateway onto the promontory, then pass the church and old manor houses to **cross** a bridge. This tiny park, an island in the lake, makes the perfect spot for a sunset walk.

Mirow to Userin: 63 kilometers

Follow **signs** toward Neustrelitz out of Mirow, but then turn **right** for **Diemitz**. Ahead is the best of the *Seenplatte*, where one could spend days wandering forest trails between tiny lakes. This day's trip hooks south and then north, ending near Neustrelitz. Shop at the first convenient point as stores are few and far between in this area.

Luckily, the cobbled road to Diemitz also has a strip of asphalt, allowing for semismooth morning cycling. Just 1 km before Diemitz, follow **bicycle signs** to Canow by riding **straight** on a dirt road. On the way, you will pass **over** a canal—a great break point from which you can watch boats of all types pass through the small lock. Mecklenburg attracts many outdoor enthusiasts, including colorful kayakers and families of cyclists with their pet dogs tucked into bike baskets.

In sections, the road to Canow (3 km) is like a sandtrap. Remember to keep your distance behind other bicycles as the sand can suddenly throw you off balance. Once in **Canow** you will appreciate the **new, smooth road south**. Pedal 6 km more to **Zechliner-hütte**, a pleasant lakeside town with bars, beer gardens, and lakeshore benches. The castle in Rheinsberg (another 6 km south) is another worthwhile destination. Don't agonize over picking the best picnic site, however, when all are excellent choices.

Unless you are off meandering on your own, **backtrack** to Canow. Continue **north** to **Wustrow** and ride **straight** into

Wesenberg. Pedal Bahnhofstrasse, then bear **right** on Linden-strasse for quiet, well-paved side roads toward Neustrelitz via **Klein Quassow** and **Userin**. Take your pick from among the several campgrounds ringing the Userinersee, the site on Großer Labussee, or one east on Woblitzsee. All are located well off this side road, so ask directions carefully and keep patient when striking out for the sites. Hostelers must go as far as Feldberg or Burg Stargard. For rooms, ride toward Neustrelitz and look for *Zimmer frei* signs on the way.

Userin to Neubrandenburg: 43 kilometers

The final day of this tour closes the loop back to Neubrandenburg via Blankensee and Burg Stargard. From Userin, pedal 8 km into **Neustrelitz**, former residence of the Mecklenburg-Strelitz *Herzog* (duke). As you enter the city, ignore twists of the main road and ride **straight**, cutting **shortcuts** through streets of impressive old mansions. The nicest spot in town is a wonderful sculpture garden (*Stadtpark*, former site of a *Schloss*) which opens onto the Zierkersee.

After a look around Neustrelitz, pedal on to Carpin. To do so, follow Berlin **signs** out of the center. Then turn **left** on moderately busy **Road 198** to **Woldegk**. Wide lanes allow you breathing space, although endless rolling hills may take it away again. **Leave** 198 at **Zinow**, turning **north** for **Thurow** and **Rödlin-Thurow** on a quiet road. A thirteenth-century *Kloster* in **Wanzka** may tempt you for a possible detour from Rödlin.

Ride on to **Blankensee** and head **north** to **Holldorf** over 7 km of unpaved road. Back on **pavement**, continue into **Burg Stargard**. Burg Stargard makes a good break point before tackling the last leg of the tour into Neubrandenburg, although the town's *Marktplatz* and churches will not distract you for long.

Leave Burg Stargard by following **signs** to Neubrandenburg. After passing the last fenced warehouse area just outside town, turn **right** on an unsigned road (posted for Neubrandenburg after 200 meters). Part paved, part cobblestone, the road offers high views over the Tollensesee at points. Finally, **descend** a hill and make your triumphant return to **Neubrandenburg**.

Back in town, return to the lodgings of your choice or head for the *Bahnhof* for a train. Cyclists lured by the lakes may circle back to the Schwerinersee and Lübeck (see Tour Nos. 18 and 19). To do so, ride west from Waren to Plau, Lübz (a fourteenth-century town), Parchim, and Schwerin.

For a change of pace, visit Berlin by either biking south or taking

Relaxing by the lakeshore in Waren

a train. The reunified country's capital is an exciting, spirited city as well as an important cultural center and the former focal point of East–West confrontation. Bicycle lanes line the city streets, although traffic and large distances make public transportation a more manageable option when visiting the large city.

ADDITIONAL SUGGESTED TOURS

Why limit yourself to cycling in Germany? Because the possibilities are limitless! The twenty tours in Part II represent only some of the best, most popular, or most unique routes in Germany. Countless other destinations await exploration: well-known cycling routes and untouched backwaters, areas of historic interest or scenic beauty. Challenging terrain, easy cycling. The biggest challenge a cyclist confronts is choosing from the numerous possibilities in Germany.

I began biking with a plan for twenty tours, scheduling plenty of extra days and free time into my trip. But daily input from reference sources or locals soon had me scurrying to fit in more. Soon my days off were exchanged for more cycling days as I added more destinations to my itinerary. I planned to tour Franken in four days, for example, then take a few days off to visit friends and relax before moving on to München. But then a German cyclist tipped me off on the Altmühl Valley, and I began plotting. A day for relaxing could be traded for a day's ride south to the valley. Another day could be gained by cutting extra time from city sightseeing. A third day here, a fourth there. Soon I had managed to add an entire tour ... only to arrive in the Danube Valley.

I began doodling calendar after calendar, toying with the possibilities. My plans called for connections to München and Oberbayern tours. Did I have the time to pedal the Donau downstream a few days, turn south along the Salzach, bike to Salzburg, and then continue to München? Or should I pedal upriver, then turn south, then perhaps fit in another day?

And so on. After a good deal of tinkering I settled on the twenty tours detailed in this book. Other areas with good potential for bicycle touring are suggested below. These hints, together with general touring tips from Part I, will help you design a tour of your own.

The Black Forest

The Black Forest (Schwarzwald) is an extremely hilly region in the southwest corner of Germany. The beautiful area attracts many outdoor enthusiasts, including hardy cyclists eager for a challenge and an uncrowded destination. Visitors concentrate in resort towns like Titisee-Neustadt, leaving most of the Schwarzwald in peace. Cyclists can expect constantly rolling terrain and long climbs.

A popular tourist route runs from Baden-Baden to Freudenstadt, the Hochstrasse (High Road). Cyclists can trace a similar route on parallel side roads or strike off to find their own paths through quiet side valleys. Both Baden-Baden and Freiburg make convenient entry points into the Schwarzwald, as does Basel in Switzerland. Campgrounds and mountain huts dot the Black Forest, and small inns accommodate guests in towns. ADFC Map #24 indicates good touring routes and road suggestions.

Danube Valley Tour

The most obvious omission from this book is the Danube Valley (Donautal) tour, one of the best and most popular tours in Europe. I chose not to include the Donau ride because so much information already exists for the route. Cyclists interested in that tour need only to buy a complete, compact cycling guide to be on their way. In its place I fit in tours of other areas for which less information exists.

One of Europe's major rivers, the Donau runs from its source in Germany's Black Forest to the Black Sea. A long-distance bicycle route linking side roads and bicycle trails runs from the river's source in Donaueschingen to Passau and Vienna in Austria. The route takes advantage of downstream valley cycling as it follows the picturesque, ever-changing valley. In Germany the valley initially cuts a deep gorge near Tuttlingen and Sigmaringen, then widens nearer Passau, passing historic cities like Ulm and Regensburg on the way. Many cyclists cross the border to continue the ride to Vienna (Wien) in Austria and Budapest in Hungary.

Cyclists interested in the valley ride should look for *Donauradweg Radwanderführer* by Esterbauer and Weinfurter (Wien), available in many bookstores in Germany. This compact booklet is a complete guide to the valley ride, with maps (1:100,000), accommodations and sight information, repair-shop locations, and optimal cycling routes. The guides are printed in German, but the key references are easy to translate. Use an English sightseeing guide to read about history and sights. The *Radwanderführer* (bicycle-touring guides) are divided into three booklets, one for each country: *Teil 1: Donaueschingen–Passau*; *Teil 2: Passau–Wien*; and *Teil 3: Wien–Budapest*. Each costs about DM 15, an excellent value (less than the combined price of separate cycling maps for the same area).

The popular Donauradweg (Danube bicycle trail) is lined with campgrounds, hostels, and *Zimmer*. Many establishments cater to cyclists; campgrounds save prime tent sites for late-arriving cyclists and rooms for rent are advertised directly on the trail. The well-established trail itself is clearly marked with square Donauradweg signs at almost every intersection between Donaueschingen and Wien. The tour has something for everyone—gentle terrain, historic sights, beautiful scenery, and plenty of fellow cyclists for company.

Donaueschingen lies on the main Frankfurt–Konstanz *Inter-Regio* train line, a convenient way to reach the tour's starting point. The Donautal may also be intersected later in its course from several of the tours in this book. A tour along the German section of the river takes ten days or more.

East Frisian Islands

The Island Hopping tour (Tour No. 17) uses ferries to link the North Frisian Islands, popular resorts on Germany's North Sea coast. What are the North Frisian islands north of? The East Frisian Islands, which in turn are east of the West Frisian Islands, Dutch territory. Beach bums and sand-castle builders can link a similar tour through these low island chains with the help of ferries. In general, try to plan your tour in a west-to-east direction to avoid countering the strong westerly winds of the North Sea.

Eifel Massif

The Eifel region, like the Schwarzwald, draws nature lovers and active travelers, but the area enjoys relative obscurity unlike the famous forest to the south. All the better for tough cyclists wanting to get away from crowded tourist zones. The Eifel Massif stretches north of the Mosel Valley and west of the Rhine in west-central Germany. Cyclists can design a tour around the region's volcanic lakes and tiny hill towns, riding over the hills or following small river valleys such as the Ahr and Prüm. At the monastery of Maria-Laach, Gregorian Chant still accompanies Sunday mass. The region borders Luxembourg and Belgium, opening the option of a multicountry trip. Hostels, campgrounds, and rooms are available throughout the region, covered by ADFC Map #15.

Neckar Valley

Two tours of this book begin in Heidelberg (Tour Nos. 8 and 9), Germany's famous university city on the Neckar River. Much like the Mosel, the Neckar is a meandering valley of small towns, each bend of the river bringing a new castle or sight into view. Most tourists confine themselves to Heidelberg and its environs at the mouth of the Neckar Valley without venturing upriver, leaving much of the valley to cyclists and others willing to break out of the standard tourist track. Riders can follow the river south to Stuttgart or turn east, crossing to the Romantic Road (Romantische Strasse) in Würzburg or Rothenburg ob der Tauber. ADFC Map #20 covers the Neckar Valley from Heidelberg to Stuttgart.

The author cycling the Danube Valley

These are just a few of the regions that tempted me as I toured Germany by bike. Whatever region strikes your fancy, go ahead and research your own tour by using maps and guidebooks. Write to the German National Tourist Office for a list of local information offices in any specific region for even more detailed information. A German book, *Radfernwege in Deutschland* (BVA: Bielefelder Verlagsanstalt, Bielefeld, Germany), catalogues long-distance bicycle routes throughout the country and includes contact addresses for each region. Remember to factor extra time into your plans. Once in Germany, many new discoveries will no doubt fill your schedule as they did mine.

INDEX

ABOUT THE AUTHOR

Nadine Slavinski is the author of *Cycling Europe*, a guide to budget bicycle travel. She has undertaken five extensive bicycle tours in Europe, cycling solo, with friends, and as leader of a teen travel group.

After Slavinski's first long European bicycle tour introduced her to Germany, she returned for more extensive touring in both West and East. While working on the excavation of a Roman fort in southern Germany, she improved her German language ability and exchanged tips on cycling with German friends.

Since majoring in archaeology at Cornell University, Slavinski has participated in archaeological projects in Germany and Peru. The author's interests in active travel and the outdoors began in 1986 with an international service expedition to northern Australia. Since then she has worked as an orchard hand in New Zealand and has sailed on an oceanographic research vessel across the Sargasso and Caribbean seas. She has volunteered in the national parks of Costa Rica (surviving aerial bombardment by unfriendly parrots and howler monkeys), and has found time to study Russian in St. Petersburg and Spanish in Ecuador.

In 1993 she spent a second season in Germany focused on archaeological excavation, followed by an assignment in Olympic National Park in Washington State. Once she has sufficiently satiated the travel bug, Slavinski plans to become a teacher.